What Should the Left Propose?

What Should the Left Propose?

ROBERTO MANGABEIRA UNGER

VERSO

London • New York

First published by Verso 2005
© Roberto Mangabeira Unger 2005
All rights reserved

1 3 5 7 9 10 8 6 4 2

Verso
UK: 6 Meard Street, London W1F 0EG
USA: 180 Varick Street, New York, NY 10014-4606
www.versobooks.com

Verso is the imprint of New Left Books

ISBN 1-84467-048-1

British Library Cataloguing in Publication Data
A catalogue record for this book is available from the British Library

Library of Congress Cataloging-in-Publication Data
A catalog record for this book is available from the Library of
Congress

Typeset in Bembo by Hewer text UK Ltd, Edinburgh
Printed by CPI Bath

Contents

The dictatorship
of no alternatives

The world suffers under a dictatorship of no alternatives. Although ideas all by themselves are powerless to overthrow this dictatorship we cannot overthrow it without ideas.

All over the world, people complain that their national politics fail to deliver real alternatives: especially alternatives that would give new meaning, new life, and new efficacy to the old progressive idea of a better chance for everyone – a chance to ensure the moral as well as the material necessities of life, a chance to work and to be cared for when one cannot work, a chance to engage in the affairs of one's community and one's society, a chance to do something with one's life that has value in one's own eyes.

Is it possible to suggest a way forward in a short space? And to do so in a manner revealing the similarities as well as the differences between the way forward for richer and for poorer countries? I believe that it is possible, and that it must be possible in brief if it is possible at all.

Many countries are now governed by people who would like to be Franklin Roosevelt, and who do not know how. Many others are ruled by people pandering to the interests of big business and to the desperate and inverted resentments of a working-class majority that feels abandoned and betrayed by the would-be Roosevelts. The self-described progressives appear on the stage of contemporary history as the humanizers of the inevitable: their program has become the program of their conservative adversaries with a falling discount. They disguise surrender as synthesis – for example, of social cohesion with economic flexibility. Their "third ways" are the first way with sugar: the sweetener of compensatory social policy and social insurance making up for a failure to achieve any fundamental broadening of opportunity.

The calamitous ideological adventures of the twentieth century are spent. No global ideology with the worldwide authority of classical liberalism or socialism has yet arisen to take their place and to contest the

2

arrangements now associated with the rich North Atlantic democracies and with the ideas emanating from their universities. With this surprising silence of the intellect and with the consolidation of the American ascendancy, an unquiet order has descended upon the world. Wars are local: punitive expeditions by the remaining superpower against those who defy it, or products of extreme oppression and desperate resistance in disunited countries, under the yoke of despotic governments. No economic collapse seems likely – given the resources of economic management within countries and of economic coordination among them – that could rival in magnitude the economic disaster of the 1930s.

The great European social theorists – Karl Marx first among them – identified the internal dynamics of societies – the revelation of inescapable conflicts and missed opportunities – as the proximate cause of their transformation. These thinkers were mistaken. War and economic collapse have been the chief levers of change; catastrophe – unforeseen and uncontrolled – has served as the midwife of reform.

The task of the imagination is to do the work of crisis without crisis. However, the high academic culture of the rich countries, with its glittering worldwide prestige and influence, has fallen under the control of three tendencies of thought that help prevent this work from being done. Although the votaries of these three tendencies often regard themselves as adversaries and rivals, they are in fact partners. In the social sciences – especially in the most powerful, economics – rationalization rules: the explanation of the workings of contemporary society becomes a vindication of the superiority or the necessity of the arrangements now established in the rich countries. In the normative discourses of political philosophy and legal theory, humanization is in command: the justification of practices, such as compensatory redistribution by the State or the idealization of the law as a repository of impersonal policies and principles, that would make life less harsh for the poorest or the weakest. The most admired theories of justice place a gloss of metaphysical apology on the practices of redistributive tax-and-transfer adopted by the conservative social democracies of today. In this way, the humanizers hope to soften what they no longer know how to change or remake. In the humanities escapism is the order of the day: consciousness takes a ride on a roller coaster of adventure, disconnected from the reshaping of practical life. We are taught to sing in our chains. The silent partnership of these rationalizing, humanizing, and escapist tendencies in university culture leaves the field open for forms of practical political thinking that are as deficient in insight as they are bereft of hope.

In the United States, the Democratic Party, ever the

instrument of American progressives, has failed to produce a practical and attractive sequel to Roosevelt's program, or to make up for the absence of economic ruin and world war as incitements to reform. Much of the white working-class majority of the country holds the policies favored by the Democrats – to the extent these policies differ at all from those advocated by the Republicans – to be products of a conspiracy between some of the rich and many of the poor to promote the moral interests of the former and the material interests of the latter at the cost of their own values and advantages. They see little in the shrunken governmental activism favored by the would-be progressives that addresses their interests and much – especially by way of apostasy from the religion of the family – that offends their ideals. Better to mitigate their losses by cutting the federal government down to size.

The result of the divorce in the preponderant world power between the white working-class majority – a group that thinks of itself as "middle class" – and their would-be champions is fateful for the entire world. Its consequence is to aggravate a circumstance without precedent in modern history. When, during the earlier, nineteenth-century episode of globalization Great Britain and the other European powers exercised a dominance less complete than the one the United States enjoys now, the ideological debates that resounded throughout the world were reflected, indeed anchored, within the most advanced countries. Now the hegemonic power is not in imaginative communion with the rest of humanity. Its leaders, its thinkers, and its population look out and see a world that will continue to be dangerous, poor, and unfree, unless it converges to the same institutional formula by which they believe themselves blessed.

The rest of humanity, full of admiration for the material exuberance and personal space enjoyed by Americans, curses in response, ill concealing the thought that it must ultimately choose war if the requirement of peace is surrender. The commanding beliefs of the American people – that everything is possible, that vast problems can be solved if broken up into pieces and addressed one by one, and that ordinary men and women contain within themselves, individually and collectively, the constructive genius with which to craft such solutions – now find themselves without adequate practical expression.

The richest and freest part of the world has shown two faces to the rest of humanity. European social democracy has seemed to provide an alternative to the harshness of the American model; if the world could vote it might vote to become Sweden rather than the United States – a Sweden of the imagination. In the meantime, however, the heart has been going out of historical social democracy. Under the disguise of an effort to reconcile European-style social protection with American-style economic flexibility, social democracy has given up, one by one, many of its traditional traits, and retreated to the last-ditch defense of a high-level of social entitlements.

This eviscerated version of social democracy can neither address the problems of contemporary European societies nor bear the weight of humanity's hopes. In Europe itself, the erstwhile progressives appear as chastened votaries of the ideas of their neoliberal opponents. In many countries, they find their proposals for reform repudiated by an electorate that is offered no real alternatives and that is told by the political and academic authorities that none exist.

When we now turn to the world outside the North Atlantic haven of relative freedom and prosperity, we see only fragments of feasible and attractive alternatives, unexpressed in any project – or family of projects – that could appeal to the rest of mankind. Among the most successful developing countries in recent decades have been the two most populous – China and India. Each has succeeded by maintaining a measure of resistance to the universal formulas dispensed by the North Atlantic elites, particularly Washington, Wall Street, and the universities of the United States. Each has wanted to join the global economy on terms that would allow it to organize its national life and to orient its economic development in its own way.

However, in the great country that has been most fertile in institutional innovations – China – the scope and development of such innovations have remained subordinate to the defense of one-party rule. The role that might have been played by an alternative set of ideas has been occupied by genuflections to the dead, inherited orthodoxy of Marxism and by fascination with the new, imported orthodoxy of the market economy, as it is understood in the political, financial, and academic capitals of the North Atlantic. In India, with its flawed but vibrant democracy, resistance to this imported orthodoxy has mainly taken the indistinct form of slowness and compromise, as if the point were to take one's time in treading a path from which there is no escape. The region of the world that proved most pliant to the recommendations from the North – Latin America – has suffered a catastrophic decline in its relative position.

In history obedience rarely pays; what pays is defiance. To the question, however, about the directions defiance should take if it is to further the promises of democracy, there is not yet an answer. We see in the world a universal political-economic orthodoxy contested by a series of local heresies. Yet only a universalizing heresy would suffice to counteract a universal orthodoxy. If the heresy is merely local in character and content it is likely to be abandoned at the first sign of trouble and pressure. If the local heresy can resist, its resistance may depend on a religiously sanctioned way of life unsympathetic to the democratic and experimentalist ideals to which progressives adhere.

It is not only for practical reasons that a universalizing heresy seems to be the indispensable antidote to the universal orthodoxy about markets and governments that now provokes such resistance throughout the world – whether in France and Germany or in Russia, Brazil, and South Africa. It is because the causes of discontent – of which the first is failure to anchor economic growth in a great broadening of opportunity – are themselves universal. It is also because the established ways of responding to that discontent are so meager and ineffective. The repertory of institutional and policy alternatives on offer for the organization of economic, social, and political life is now very restricted. If we could progress anywhere in the world – rich or poor – in expanding this institutional repertory and anchoring practical progress in a broadening of opportunity, such an advance might have implications for every country.

The attempt to achieve economic growth with social inclusion fits readily with the search for proposals that are more than local solutions to local problems. It prepares the mind for a universalizing heresy. However, the failure to anchor practical progress in a sustained widening of opportunity is not the sole source of the present unhappiness. There is another powerful source of discontent: the complaint that the orthodoxy prevents countries or regions of the world from developing their different forms of life and ideals of civilization by denying them an opportunity to house them in distinct ways of organizing society. Because it calls for a convergence of all countries to the institutions and practices now established in the North Atlantic, as well as for convergence within that world itself, the orthodoxy seems to be the enemy of deep differences of experience and vision. The demand for pluralism, unlike the search for growth with inclusion, seems incompatible with a political and economic alternative claiming to be general in relevance and reach.

It is not. The semblance of paradox dissolves once two premises are made explicit. The first premise is that an unqualified pluralism – an openness to any form of national life, no matter how despotic and unequal – can form no part of the objective. The aim should be a qualified pluralism: to build a world of democracies in which the individual is empowered both to participate and to dissent. There is no single, uncontroversial interpretation of what a democratic society is or can become. Democratic ideals must be allowed to develop in different, even clashing directions if they are to develop at all. Under democracy the differences that matter most are those that lie in the future rather than those we have inherited from the past. Under democracy prophecy speaks louder than memory.

The second premise is that the small repertory of institutional solutions now available to humanity – the existing forms of political democracy, of the market economy, and of free civil societies – fails to provide the tools we need to develop national difference in a form compatible with democratic ideals. A particular set of innovations in the organization of contemporary polities, economies, and societies can provide them. This set of innovations – a major part of the progressive program that now needs to be advanced throughout the world – defines a narrow gateway through which humanity must pass if it is to strengthen its capacity to produce difference on the basis of democracy. To describe this gateway as it might be approached by both richer and poorer countries is the concern of this hopeful manifesto.

We cannot, however, understand this way forward unless we first grasp the nature of the obstacles with which we must contend, and of the forces and the opportunities on which we can count, in treading it.

The disorientation
of the Left

The Left now finds itself disoriented on four distinct grounds: a missing alternative, a missing idea world, a missing agent, and a missing crisis. To face each of these deficiencies clearly and squarely is to begin to see how they can be addressed. It is to start redefining what the Left should propose.

The Left is missing an alternative. "Dirigisme" is not the way: the idea of the governmental direction of the economy, which was already discredited, has now been made even more irrelevant by the direction of change in a knowledge-based economy. Compensatory redistribution is not enough: not enough to redress the enormous pressures toward inequality, insecurity, and exclusion that result from the increasing hierarchical segmentation of the economy and not enough to address the concerns of social disconnection and personal belittlement that lie far beyond the range of compensatory redistribution.

Today the Left seems unable to say for what, beside the governmental direction of the economy or the redistributive attenuation of inequalities and insecurities, it should stand. If it affirms its critical attitude to the established arrangements, it seems to be hearkening back to "statism." If it contents itself with the rearguard defense of traditional social entitlements, funded by redistributive taxation and public spending, it seems drastically to narrow the scope of its ambitions while making them hostage to constraints of economic growth and public finance it does not know how to loosen.

The Left is missing a supporting set of ideas with which to rethink and to enlarge the narrow stock of institutional conceptions and arrangements to which contemporary societies are now fastened. The dominant tendencies in the whole field of the contemporary social sciences and humanities – rationalization, humanization, and escapism – conspire to disarm the imagination in its struggle to defy and to rethink established arrangements.

In the social sciences rationalization prevails: ways

of explaining the existing arrangements that seem to vindicate their naturalness and necessity. The ideas about structural alternatives we have inherited from classical social theories like Marxism remain entangled in the decaying corpse of necessitarian assumptions. These assumptions have long ceased to be believable: that there is a short list of institutional options for human societies, such as "feudalism" or "capitalism"; that each of these options represents an indivisible system, all of the elements of which stand or fall together; and that the succession of such systems is driven forward by irresistible historical laws.

The rejection of these deterministic beliefs by the contemporary social sciences has not led to a radicalization of the insights that animated classical European social theory: that society is made not given; that the structures of society and culture are a kind of frozen fighting, arising as they do from the containment and interruption of practical or spiritual strife; that our interests and identities remain hostage to the practices and arrangements representing them in fact, and that in changing these practices and arrangements we force ourselves to reinterpret the interests and identities for whose sake we set out to reform society.

To be sure, the positive social sciences delight in exploring the facility with which a society accommodates to "suboptimal solutions" or an economy gets caught in a production-suppressing equilibrium.

Nevertheless, the very instruments with which they probe imperfections deny us the means with which to imagine alternatives. Their central conceit is that experience over time reveals what works better and worse, winnowing out the less effective through a relentless quasi-Darwinian process of selection. The convergence thesis – the idea that contemporary societies and economies converge to the same set of best available practices and institutions, in a narrowing historical funnel of social variation – is simply the extreme variant of this rationalizing bias.

In the normative disciplines of political philosophy and legal thought humanization predominates. The point is to sweeten a world we cannot or will not rebuild. There are two main species of such humanization today. One species is compensatory redistribution through tax and transfer. It forms the central feature of the institutional and ideological settlement defining the historical horizon of social democracy. Many of the most influential contemporary theories of justice seek to lend philosophical prestige to these redistributive practices. The apparent abstraction of these theories – their claim to transcend the historical circumstance in which they apply – conceals their surrender to the limitations of the twentieth-century compromise from which contemporary social democracy arose.

The other species of humanization is the understanding of law as a repository of impersonal principles of right as well as of policies addressed to the public interest. By putting the best face on the law – the face of ideal conceptions – we hope to diminish the influence of privileged interests and to defend those groups least likely to have been represented in the politics of law making. The dominant styles of jurisprudence theorize this idealization of law as principle and policy.

The practical effect of the humanizing tendencies in the normative disciplines is to put these disciplines on the side of accepting the present institutional settlement, corrected by the prescribed improvements, rather than on the side of their reconstruction. It is to deny us the resources with which to develop the practical imagination of alternatives.

In the humanities escapist tendencies hold sway. Their hallmark is the incitement to adventures in consciousness disconnected from the practical reformation of society. The fateful parting of the ways between Modernism and Leftism in modern culture is the immediate antecedent to this divorce. Under the aegis of this disconnection between our projects for society and our projects for the self, we privatize the sublime, relegating to the interior space of consciousness and desire our most ambitious transformative project and seeing politics as the domain of modest decencies and efficiencies.

The secret message is that politics should become little so that individuals can become big. Politics, however, cannot become little without, as a result, belittling people. Desire is by its nature relational; strong impulse seeks expression in forms of common life. If politics becomes cold, consciousness will also, unless it preserves its heat in the self-destructive form of narcissism.

The champions of the rationalizing, humanizing, and escapist tendencies that dominate the social sciences and the humanities think of themselves as adversaries. In fact, they are allies in the work of disarming the transformative imagination.

The Left is missing an agent: a core constituency whose interests and aspirations it can claim to repre-sent. Its traditional constituency was the organized labor force enforced in capital-intensive industry – Marx's "proletariat." This group is increasingly seen by society, and increasingly comes to see itself, as one more interest group with selfish, factional interests rather than as the bearer of universal interests of society. In almost every country in the world it is a shrinking part of the population, its fate tied to the declining fortunes of traditional mass production. In most of the developing countries it remains a relatively privileged part.

To the leaders of the Left there has seemed to be only one alternative to maintaining a special connection with this burdensome constituency: to dispense with any defined social base at all and simply appeal to the whole of the electorate. They have failed to rescue the idea of a special relation to the working class from the narrower loyalty that inherited doctrine sanctioned. In this failure they have been encouraged by disillusionment as well as by calculation: belief in a one-to-one relation between historical projects and group interests belongs to the discredited tradition of necessitarian thinking.

Lacking an alternative, an idea world, and a social base, the Left also lacks a crisis. Contrary to another central tenet of classical social thought, social change in modern history has been driven by the external traumas of war and economic collapse more than by the internal contradictions of contemporary societies. The political and economic institutions of these societies maintain a long distance between our ordinary context-preserving and our extraordinary context-transforming activities; they therefore continue to make transformation depend upon calamity. The institutional and ideological settlement defining social democracy today was itself forged on the anvil of the economic collapse of the 1930s and of the subsequent world war.

Crisis raises the temperature of politics, and helps melt down frozen definitions of interest and identity. Without crisis, politics becomes cold, and calculation

– in the form of reliance on conventional understandings of interests and ideals – reigns supreme.
Denied the help of crisis, the Left seems condemned
to a holding operation: to softening the social consequences of the program of its conservative adversaries.

The reorientation of the Left

Nevertheless, there is an alternative; there is a supporting set of ideas on the basis of which we can imagine this alternative; there are real social forces that can be its constituencies; and there is a way to dispense with crisis as the enabling condition of change while seizing on the transformative opportunities with which our circumstance provides us.

The hallmark of the alternative is to anchor social inclusion and individual empowerment in the institutions of political, economic, and social life. It is not enough to humanize the social world; it is necessary to change it. To change it means to engage, once again, with the effort to reshape production and politics, from which social democracy withdrew when the mid-twentieth-century compromise defining its present horizon was first formed. It means to take the familiar institutional forms of the market economy, representative democracy, and free civil society as a subset of a far broader set of institutional possibilities. It means to reject the contrast between market orientation and governmental direction as the axis organizing our ideological contests, and to replace it with a contrast among ways of organizing economic, political, and social pluralism. It means to root a bias to greater equality and inclusion in the organized logic of economic growth and technological innovation rather than making it rest on retrospective redistribution through tax and transfer. It means to democratize the market economy by innovating in the arrangements that define it, rather than merely to regulate it in its present form or to compensate for its inequalities through after-the-fact transfers. It means to radicalize the experimental logic of the market by radicalizing the economic logic of free recombination of the factors of production within an unchallenged framework of market transactions. The goal is a deeper freedom to renew and recombine the arrangements that compose the institutional setting of production and exchange, allowing alternative regimes of property and contract to coexist experimentally within the same economy. It means to take the overriding aim of social policy to be the enhancement of capability.

Such an enhancement would progress thanks to a form of education addressed to the development of generic conceptual and practical capacities rather than to the mastery of job-specific skills. It would advance as well as through the generalization of a principle of social inheritance, assuring each individual of a basic minimum stake in resources on which he can draw at turning points in his life. It means to advance this democratization of the market economy in the context of a practical organization of social solidarity and a deepening of political democracy. It means never to reduce social solidarity to mere money transfers. Social solidarity must rest instead on the sole secure basis it can have: direct responsibility of people for one another. Such responsibility can be realized through the principle that every able-bodied adult holds a position within the caring economy – the part of the economy in which people care for one another – as well as within the production system. It means to establish the institutions of a high-energy democratic politics: one that permanently raises the level of organized popular participation in politics, engages the electorate as well as the parties in the rapid and decisive resolution of impasse between the political branches of government, equips government to rescue people from entrenched and localized situations of disadvantage from which they are unable to exit by the normal forms of political and economic initiative, allows particular sectors or localities to opt out of the general legal regime and to develop divergent images of the social future, and combines features of direct and representative democracy.

The guiding impulse of this Leftism is not the redistributive attenuation of inequality and inclusion; it is the enhancement of the powers and the broadening of the opportunities enjoyed by ordinary men and women on the basis of the piecemeal but cumulative reorganization of the State and the economy. Its watchword is not the humanization of society; it is the divinization of humanity. Its innermost thought is that the future belongs to the political force that most credibly represents the cause of the constructive imagination: everyone's power to share in the permanent creation of the new.

The Left can be faithful to its aspirations only if it proposes the new in a form that enables everyone to share in its construction rather than leaving this constructive power concentrated in the hands of advantaged elites. And it can succeed in this work only if it learns how to rethink and to reshape the institutional arrangements for production, politics, and social life in the persistence and authority of which conventional social democracy has always acquiesced. Such an alternative is therefore equidistant from a nostalgic State-oriented Leftism and from an eviscerated, all but neoliberal version of social democracy.

This alternative is distinguished by institutional devices applicable across a broad range of richer and poorer contemporary societies. The need to adapt their design to many different national circumstances does not negate the broad reach of their pertinence and appeal. The very general applicability of these devices helps explain both the possibility and the necessity of a universalizing heresy able to counter the universalizing orthodoxy now on offer in the world in the name of markets and of globalization.

Their generality has a three-fold root. The first root is the similarity of experience of contemporary societies after many generations of worldwide rivalry, emulation and imitation, practical and spiritual, among nations and states. The second root is the very restricted character of the ideological and institutional toolbox ready to hand to build alternatives. The third root is the all but irresistible authority a single set of revolutionary beliefs now enjoy throughout the world: beliefs that promise freedom from subjugation as well as from poverty and drudgery, and a larger life for the ordinary man and woman.

Five institutional ideas define the direction the Left should stand for today.

A first institutional idea is that national rebellion against the global political and economic orthodoxy depends for its success on certain practical conditions. These conditions include higher levels of domestic saving than a narrow understanding of the dynamics of economic growth might justify; an insistence on finding arrangements that tighten the relation between saving and production both within and outside the capital markets as they are now organized (an insistence premised on the recognition that this relation is both variable and sensitive to its institutional setting); and a preference for a high tax take and willingness to achieve it even at the cost of the regressive, transactions-oriented taxation of consumption. The larger goal is a fuller mobilization of national resources: a war economy without a war.

A second institutional idea is the view of social policy as being about empowerment and capacity. From this idea arises the commitment to a form of early and lifelong education addressed to the development of a core of generic conceptual and practical capabilities. In very unequal societies it is not enough to guarantee basic levels of educational investment and quality; it is vital to ensure special opportunity to the talented, hard-working, and inheritance-less young. The initial aim of this use of education as an antidote to disempowerment is to broaden the present synthesis of class and meritocracy. The next goal is to dissolve class through the radicalization of meritocracy. The ultimate ambition is to subordinate meritocracy to a larger vision of inclusive solidarity and opportunity, affirmed in the face of intractable disparities of inborn talent.

A third institutional idea is the democratization of the market economy. It is not enough to regulate the market or to compensate retrospectively for its inequalities. It is necessary to reorganize it the better to make it real for more people in more ways. To this end, neither the American model of arm's length regulation of business by government nor the northeast Asian model of centralized formulation of trade and industrial policy by a bureaucratic apparatus are likely to suffice. The task will be to use the power of the State not to suppress or to balance the market but to create the conditions for the organization of more markets organized in more ways – ultimately, with distinct regimes of property and contract – and capable of coexisting experimentally within the same national and global economy.

The democratization of the market requires initiatives broadening access to productive resources and opportunities. It demands an upward tilt in the returns to labor. It is incompatible with any strategy of economic growth predicated on the share of wages in national income declining.

The aim is to produce a series of repeated breakthroughs in the constraints on economic growth. Each such breakthrough produces an imbalance inviting new breakthroughs in another aspect of the supply or the demand sides of the economy. The preference is for those breakthroughs and imbalances that have built into them a bias toward economic inclusion and diffusion of capabilities; they help make people bigger.

The progressive interventions on the supply-side constraints move on a scale between lesser and greater ambition. The lesser ambition is to expand access to credit, technology, expertise, and markets, especially in favor of the multitude of small-scale or would-be entrepreneurs who represent in every contemporary economy a vastly under-utilized source of constructive initiative.

They have as their greater ambition the propagation of the most advanced methods of production beyond the favored terrain on which those methods usually flourish. Government and society must work to democratize the market economy in a way that also faces the dangers and exploits the opportunities presented by a momentous shift in the organization of production. Will the form of production characterized by the weakening of the contrast between supervision and execution, by the attenuation of barriers among specialized roles at work, by the mixture of cooperation and competition in the same domains, and by teamwork as collective learning and permanent innovation be confined to a privileged vanguard in communion with the other such vanguards in the world but only weakly linked to its home society? Or will governments and societies succeed in creating the conditions for the spread of these advanced experimental practices throughout much of the economy and the society, thus vastly enhancing the powers and opportunities of ordinary men and women?

Such progressive interventions on the supply side should be accompanied by initiatives that reverse the long-term decline in the participation of labor in national income and the longstanding increase of inequality within the labor force that has beset a wide range of contemporary rich and developing countries. In so doing they must also reinforce the supply-side interventions in rescuing from the twilight of the informal or illegal economy the hundreds of millions of workers – often the majority of the workforce in some of the most populous countries in the world – who are now deprived of lawful jobs.

These measures will need to take account of what is likely to prove most effective at different levels of the very unequally compensated and equipped national workforces that now exist in the world. For example, profit sharing may begin to be applied to the most advantaged workers and then be extended to larger and larger portions of the economically active population. A labor-law regime strengthening the power of organized workers to represent the interests of unorganized workers in their sectors may prove most effective at the middle range of the wage hierarchy. At the lowest levels of that hierarchy the best solution may be to give outright subsidies to the employment and training of low-wage and low-skill labor, and to abolish all payroll charges and taxes.

None of these initiatives is inherently inflationary. In concert, and in the context of the broader democratizing and empowering project of which they form part, they promise to enhance the rights and powers of labor as well as to produce sustainable rises in the returns to labor, up to and even beyond the frontier of advances in the productivity of work.

A fourth institutional idea is the refusal to treat cash transfers as a sufficient basis for social solidarity. Social solidarity must be grounded as well on a universal responsibility to care for others. In principle everyone who is physically and mentally able must have a caring job that takes him beyond the boundaries of the family in addition to an ordinary job. Civil society must be organized, or organize itself, outside both government and the market so that it can discharge this responsibility. A form of law that is neither private nor public can supply the occasions and the instruments by which it may do so.

A fifth institutional idea is a conception of high-energy democratic politics. The educational and economic empowerment of the individual worker and citizen, the democratization of the market economy, and the foundation of social solidarity in practiced social responsibility require the deepening of democracy if they are to be sustained and taken to heart. A sleepy democracy, woken up from time to time by military or economic crisis, is not good enough.

Such a high-energy democratic politics is both an expression of the greater freedom the program of the Left seeks and a condition for the advancement of the other four themes. It requires a sustained and organized heightening of the level of civic engagement; a preference for constitutional arrangements that break deadlock between the political branches of government quickly (when there is a regime of separation of powers) and that involve the general electorate in this impasse-breaking; innovations that reconcile the possibility for decisive choices in national politics with far-reaching experimental deviations and dissents – appeals to the future – in particular places of the national territory or particular sectors of the national economy; a determination to rescue people – through guarantees of social inheritance or of minimal income, as well as through corrective intervention by a branch of government specially designed and equipped for this purpose – from circumstances of disadvantage or exclusion they are unable to escape by their own devices; and continued advance in the effort to combine traits of representative and direct democracy.

A deepened, high-energy democracy does not seek to replace the real world of interests and of interest-bearing individuals with the selfless citizen and with the all-consuming theater of public life. It is not a flight into republican purism and fantasy. It wants to enhance our ordinary powers, enlarge the scope of our ordinary sympathies and ambitions, and render more intense our ordinary experience. It seeks to do so by diminishing the distance between the ordinary moves we may within institutional and ideological contexts take for granted and the extraordinary initiatives by which we challenge and change pieces of those contexts. Its agent and its beneficiary are one and the same: the real thing – the frail, self-interested, longing individual in the flesh, the victim of circumstance whom no circumstance can ever completely and definitively confine.

The imaginative construction of an alternative informed by these five thematic commitments requires a supporting set of ideas. We may find such ideas in the form of systematic social theory and philosophy. However, we shall far more often and more reliably develop them by revising our practices of explanation and argument. The central point is to rescue the conceptions of structural alternatives and structural discontinuity from the baggage of deterministic assumptions that burdened them in classical social theory while repudiating the alliance of rationalization, humanization, and escapism in contemporary thought.

The history of modern social ideas has misled us into associating piecemeal change with disbelief in institutional reconstruction, and a commitment to such reconstruction with faith in sudden and systemic change. The most important expression of this prejudice is the supposedly all-inclusive contrast between two styles of politics. One style is revolutionary: it seeks the wholesale substitution of one institutional order by another, under the guidance of confrontational leaders supported by energized majorities, in circumstances of national crisis. The other style is reformist: its concerns are marginal redistribution, or concessions to moral and religious anxieties, negotiated by professional politicians among organized interests, in times of business-as-usual.

We must now jumble these categories up, associating fragmentary and gradual but nevertheless cumulative change with transformative ambition. To jumble them up in practice, we must first jumble them up in thought. The foremost expression of this jumbling up is a style of politics defying the contrast between revolution and reform and therefore exemplifying the practice of revolutionary reform. Such a politics practices structural change in the only way such change generally can be practiced: piece by piece and step by step. It combines negotiation among organized minorities with mobilization of disorganized majorities. And it dispenses with calamity as the enabling condition of change. It must be prepared and informed by a way of understanding and using political economy and legal analysis as varieties of institutional imagination.

What real social forces can occupy the space left empty by the organized industrial labor force as the core constituency of the Left? A project like this one requires protagonists, but not the ones that played the starring role in the traditional Left narratives. Not only will the identities of these agents be different but the sense in which they are agents – the relation between project and agency – must also change. Consider the two most important agents – the working class and the nation-state.

The working class can no longer be equated with the industrial proletariat, the unionized labor force with jobs in capital-intensive industry. In every country in the world, the vast majority of those who must work for a wage must do so outside the boundaries of capital-intensive industry – in undercapitalized shops and unequipped services, often in the shadows of illegality, with no rights and little hope. Their eyes, however, are directed upward, to those who throughout the world are developing a new culture of self-help and initiative. Their outlook in the poorer as well as in the richer countries is petty bourgeois more than it is proletarian. Their most stubborn ambition is to combine a measure of prosperity with a modicum of independence, including the desire to develop subjectivity, to have a full life of consciousness, encounter, and striving, like the characters in the movies. By default, given the poverty of alternative arrangements for the organization of economic life, they often identify these aspirations with traditional, isolated, small-scale family business.

The nation-state will not forever be, though it remains today, the preeminent protagonist in world history: the favored ground for the development of collective differences as well as for the conduct of collective rivalries. The nation-state wants to be different, without knowing how. Its people want to see characteristic images of possible and desirable association embodied in distinct national practices and institutions.

The nation is a form of moral specialization within humanity, justified, in a world of democracies, by the belief that humanity can develop its powers and potential only by developing them in divergent directions. If it looks only to the preservation of inherited difference, it soon finds itself torn by conflict between the longing to retain its inherited way of life and the need to imitate: to imitate the successful nations the better to succeed and to survive in the worldwide rivalry of states. In the end the collective ability to make new difference counts for more than the collective capacity to extend the life of old difference.

The forms of political, economic, and social organization available in the world today are too narrow an instrument for the development of collective originality. It is not enough to genuflect to established collective difference; it is necessary to deepen existing collective difference by radicalizing the institutional logic of economic and political experimentation.

Workers wanting to stand on their own and nations wanting to go their own way are the chief forces to be represented by the proposals of the Left. However, the sense of the relation between their interests and these proposals is radically different from the sense Marxist theory assigns to class interests. According to this theory, the broader the scope and the more acute the intensity of class conflicts, the less room there is to doubt or to discuss the objective content of the class interests in contest. The fighting will tear off the masks; and political defeat will provide the salutary correction to any misunderstanding.

The truth about interests and projects is, however, just the opposite of what this picture implies. The interests of nations or class will seem to have a clear content when conflict simmers rather than explodes. As strife widens and intensifies, however, this semblance of naturalness will dissipate. The question – What are my interests as a member of this class or this nation? – will seem inseparable from the question – In what different directions could this world be altered, and how would my identity and my interests shift in each of those changed worlds? The idea that group interests have straightforward, objective content is only an illusion, dependent for its appeal on the containment or interruption of practical and visionary conflict.

As the party of transformation, the Left must turn the ambiguity of the content of group interests into opportunity. It must act on the insight that there are always two sets of ways to define and defend any given group interest. One way is institutionally conservative and socially exclusive: it takes the present niche of the group in the economy and society as fate, and defines the groups closest in social space as rivals. Another way is socially solidaristic and institutionally transformative: it treats the neighboring groups in social space as actual or potential allies, and champions reforms that turn these ephemeral alliances into lasting combinations of interests and of identities. The bias of the Left must always be to prefer the solidaristic and reconstructive approaches, taking them as the reverse side of its programmatic proposals to society at large.

What such a bias implies for the defense of the interests of the working class may be clear enough – negatively and in general, if not affirmatively and in particular. It is incompatible with any insistence on barricading the organized industrial labor force into its shrinking citadel of traditional mass production. It requires the active use of the powers of government to propagate throughout the economy advanced, experimental productive practices.

But what does such a bias toward solidaristic and reconstructive approaches imply for the definition and defense of the interests of a whole nation? It means that a country put high on its list of concerns the mobilization of national resources – savings levels and fiscal surpluses – enabling it to resist and to rebel. That it understand how national heresy ultimately depends for its advancement on global pluralism. That it refuse to accept the view that globalization, like the market economy, is there on a take-it-or-leave-it basis and that all we can do is to have more or less of it on its own terms, rather than having it on different terms. And that it work together with other powers sharing the same vision to reform global economic arrangements and to reshape world political realities. These arrangements and realities now sacrifice experimental pluralism to single dogma and imperial power.

The Left is missing a crisis. Part of its programmatic objective must be to fashion institutions and practices – intellectual as well as social – that diminish the dependence of change on calamity, and make transformation internal to social life. What classical social theory mistook as a feature of historical experience – the existence of an inbuilt dynamic of transformation – is in fact a goal. It is a goal that is valuable in its own right because it expresses the mastery over context of an agent who can participate wholeheartedly in a world without surrendering to it his powers of resistance and transcendence. It is also to be prized because of its causal connection to two sets of stakes that it must always be the aim of a Leftist program to reconcile: the practical progress of society through economic growth and technological innovation and the emancipation of the individual from entrenched social division and hierarchy.

We can no longer assume, as the liberals and socialists of the nineteenth century supposed, under the spell of now unbelievable dogma, that the institutional conditions of material progress naturally and necessarily converge with the institutional requirements for the emancipation of individuals from well-established social division and hierarchy. However, we would be equally mistaken to suppose that these two sets of conditions inevitably conflict. The Left must strive to identify the zone in which the two sets of conditions can be made to intersect, and it must try to move society forward in that zone.

A feature of the zone of intersection is that in it practices have the property of a heightened susceptibility to revision: by laying themselves more fully open to revision they become less like natural objects. They become more like us. They make it easier to engage in the recombinations of people and resources that are vital to practical progress. They subject to heightened scrutiny and pressure the arrangements on which all stable hierarchies of advantage depend.

There is, however, a paradox besetting the effort to establish institutions that loosen the dependence of change upon crisis. How can such innovations arise without the aid of crisis in the first place? How can the Left break the unacknowledged vicious cycle of this reliance on calamity in the real circumstances of the present?

The answer lies in finding crisis under disguise, not in the great collective catastrophes of war and economic ruin but in the hidden tragedies of individual anguish, fear, insecurity, and incapacity, repeated many millions of times over in the life of contemporary society. In even the richest countries of the world today, a majority of working people feel and are in jeopardy. They may be protected against the extremes of poverty and abandonment. They remain, however, locked out of the favored sectors of the economy in which income, wealth, power, and fun are increasingly concentrated.

If they are not jobless, they are afraid of losing the job they have. If they live in a country – for example, a European social democracy – with a well-developed social contract, they have good reason to fear that the contract will be broken – not once, but over and over again in the name of economic necessity, described as competition and globalization. And if they live anywhere else – especially in the large developing countries – they are likely to find no political force that is willing and able to give them both basic economic security and greater economic and educational opportunity.

Almost everyone feels abandoned. Almost everyone believes himself to be an outsider, looking in through the window at the party going on inside. Flexibility – the watchword of the orthodoxy of markets and globalization – is rightly understood to be a code word for the generalization of insecurity. The parties that claim an historical connection with the Left are seen to oscillate between a shamefaced collaboration with this program of insecurity, in the hope that through growth it will generate resources that can be redirected to social spending, and a half-hearted, weakened defense of traditional social contracts.

This fear, justified by plain fact, defeating hope, poisoning attitudes to the outsider, and expressing an immense and unredeemed waste of energy amounts to a crisis. It is lived out, for the most part silently, within the minds of individuals. It finds perverse expression in the occasional support for rightwing populist and nationalist parties. It is the problem. For the Left, however, it is also the chance.

The familiar and unbelievable form of this crisis is the simple refrain: We shall create jobs! People, however, understand or soon discover that governments cannot create jobs directly, other than public-service jobs, except in the anachronistic and limited manner of forced labor mobilization – work teams recruited and paid in a national emergency. Nevertheless, the vain promise to create jobs is the misguided form of an indispensable response to the hidden crisis: a way forward that is productivist and democratizing; that anchors social commitment in economic recovery, innovation, and reconstruction; and that advances the social and the economic projects by designing and building the institutions of a high-energy democratic politics. That we shall humanize only insofar as we energize will be the practical principle of this Left.

An agent: workers wanting to be petty bourgeois

All but the poorest countries in the world today continue to be organized as class societies. Marxism is dead as a doctrine. Socialism, as a program, may have lost its meaning as an alternative to what exists now – something the ex-socialists and the ex-Marxists still insist on calling "capitalism," as if it were an indivisible system, with its distinctive laws of conservation and change. Class, however, survives. It persists as the hierarchical organization of social life into groups of people with very unequal levels of access to economic, political, and cultural power and with characteristic forms of consciousness and of life.

Its special character is now determined by the interaction between the two contrasting principles that shape it: inheritance and meritocracy. The hereditary transmittal of economic and educational advantage through the family continues drastically to restrict mobility among generations in even the most fluid and egalitarian of contemporary societies. As a result, the simple abolition of the right of inheritance (including anticipated inheritance through the family) for everything except a modest family minimum would everywhere amount to a revolution. Meritocratic competition has modified the workings of inherited advantage, producing selective but increasing opportunities for the most talented and energetic to rise from below through preferment in schools and in firms.

The two principles of class and meritocracy – theoretically in contradiction – live in uneasy but peaceful coexistence. Their opposition to each other is weakened by the smallness of the stakes, or the narrowness of the range of alternatives, in the national politics and the national life of most countries: the ambitious upstarts are soon accommodated and assimilated, and often become the most enthusiastic champions of the ruling dogmas and interests. The tension between these two principles is attenuated as well by facts that the ruling political pieties leave unspoken: the primacy that the educational and examination systems of contemporary societies increasingly accord to a narrow set of analytical skills and the extent to which the facility for these skills may itself be partly inherited.

In the least unequal countries, and the ones most envied by other nations, the most advantaged have resigned themselves to seeing some of their children go down in the class hierarchy and some of the children of other classes come up. They know that more often than not they will succeed in reconciling inheritance and meritocracy. They secretly hope to turn contested class privilege into a set of commonly (but not universally) inherited advantages. These advantages appear to be rooted in both the inescapable division of labor and the inevitable differences among individuals.

The most common result throughout the world of this coexistence of class and meritocracy is a system of four main classes overshadowing the life chances of individuals and undermining the promises of democracy. At the top is a class of professionals, managers, and rentiers that concentrates in its own hands wealth and discretion – the power to do as it pleases, both on its own and by commanding others – even more than it concentrates income. Beneath it is a small business class, reliant on self-exploitation, most often through the mobilization of family labor. It is followed by a white-collar and blue-collar working class, working for a wage in specialized jobs under command, and seeking release from labor that is rarely valued for its own sake in the consolations of domestic life and popular entertainment. (In the United States workers with bourgeois identities call themselves "middle class," an example followed by an increasing part of the world's population, as the relative importance of large organizations in economic life continues to shrink.) They are educated in schools that have the acquisition of habits of obedience as their chief concern. At the bottom of the class system is an underclass, largely composed of racial minorities and foreign, temporary workers, and condemned to unstable, dead-end jobs in the shadows beyond law and right. In many developing countries, including the most populous, this underclass represents a major part of the whole population. It suffers from insecurity and deprivation, sometimes without bearing the additional burden of membership in a despised race, caste, or nation.

One of the most remarkable features of this class system, as it is now realized in the richer countries, is that the working class, the small-business class, and even the rank and file of the class of professionals, managers, and rentiers are both safeguarded against destitution and excluded from power. They are excluded from power not only in the sense of influence over government but also in the sense of having any significant say over their own workaday experiences and prospects. They often see themselves as stuck – waking up one day to discover that they are leading the only lives they will ever lead – and, in large numbers, they are stuck.

The central promise of democracy is that ordinary men and women will have a chance to become freer and greater. By the standard of this promise, the harm committed by the class system is not merely the failure to achieve more equality of opportunity; it is also the abandonment of ordinary humanity to a perpetual belittlement. It has been a long time since large masses of people around the world were rescued from this diminishment by the terrible devotions of war.

Against this background, a hopeful sign emerges. In many developing countries, people aspire to a modest prosperity and independence. They devote them-selves to a culture of initiative and self-help: studying at night, in the hope of bettering themselves and opening a business, they often gravitate, for lack of other ways of pursuing their ambitions, to the idea of running a small family business. The significance of this aspiration is, however, enlarged by the moral yearning that regularly accompanies it: the longing to have a bigger life, allowing not only for the material pleasures advertised in the TV commercials but also for the moral adventures narrated in the TV soap operas. Everyone wants to relive in his fashion the ordeal central to the European novel of the nineteenth and twentieth century: a person making a self by struggling against a context.

In the rich countries the appeal of the ambition to open a small business may be less strong, because more clearly identified with a distinct class and its limited opportunities. However, it weakens only because the search for a modest prosperity and independence and for escape from the confinement and humiliations of working life takes more diffuse and disoriented forms.

The Left committed no greater strategic mistake in the course of its history over the last two centuries than to elect the petty bourgeoisie as its enemy, or as its ally of convenience, and to define as its core constituency the organized industrial working class. Everywhere in the world this segment of the working class is a diminishing part of the labor force. Everywhere it is seen, and ultimately comes to see itself, as one more special interest among others, clamoring for protection and favor. The class that the Left abandoned became the social base of the political movements that defeated it. We contemporaries are, in large numbers, petty bourgeois now, by imaginative orientation if not by economic fact.

The interest that the Left rejected, supposing it wedded to selfish reaction, has now become the stand-in for a universal aspiration. That is so as much in the United States and Europe as in China and India. If progressives could meet this aspiration on its own terms, and provide it with a vocabulary of institutions and practices richer than the device of traditional isolated small business and with a standard of value more reliable than family selfishness, they would gain the most powerful of all allies, and remove a major cause of their historical defeats.

An agent: nations wanting to be different

Nationalism was one of the most unexpected and powerful transforming forces in modern history. Today it has become a dangerous diversion. Reinterpreted and redirected, it could become an opportunity for the advancement of progressive alternatives.

In human experience collective identities have drawn their power from their content. To be a Roman, for example, meant to live as the Romans, to follow the Roman way: an inherited structure of custom and sensibility.

Ever since the Western powers broke upon the world, seeking to put the rest of humanity in thrall to their empires, their interests, and their beliefs, a rivalry once confined to the West has become global. To develop the economic and military capabilities required for national independence, and to retain its cultural identity, each nation has had to give up a large part of its inherited idea of itself at the altar of this universal struggle – a struggle at once practical and spiritual. Each nation has had to pillage the whole world, in search not just of the best machines but also of the most effective practices and institutions – the ones that would deliver the greatest boost to national capabilities with the least proportional disturbance to the entrenched structure of privilege in the national society. This universal exercise in imitation and recombination has changed, slowly but relentlessly, the nature of national differences.

Its result has been to hollow out collective identities, including national identities, robbing them, little by little, of their bases in distinct ways of organizing society and of understanding the possibilities and the perils of social life. However, the waning of actual difference has not weakened the will to difference. On the contrary, it has aroused that will. As one nation becomes more like its neighbor, it affirms all the more desperately its distinction. This will to difference is ever more poisonous because the collective identities it worships are so deficient in tangible detail. When they were concrete they were also porous to experience and open to compromise. Now that they are abstract they become the objects of an uncompromising faith.

Against this poison there is only one antidote compatible with democratic and experimentalist ideals: to replace the sterile and potentially murderous rage of this frustrated will to difference with the collective capacity to produce actual difference. Thus, a program that can contribute to the overthrow of the dictatorship of no alternatives must not only respond to the universal aspiration of the ordinary working man and woman for more opportunity by which to raise him and herself up; it must also turn democratic polities, market economies and free civil societies into machines for developing distinct and novel forms of life. That countries determined to advance this ideal may have to tread some of the same institutional ground – ensuring the conditions for successful national heresy within the global economy, democratizing markets, deepening democracies, and empowering individuals – and share much now the better to diverge later, is one of the many apparent paradoxes of the present situation.

An opportunity: innovation-friendly cooperation

Another opportunity to advance a progressive alternative results from the diffusion of a new set of innovation-friendly cooperative practices. These practices are changing the character of production and learning in much of the world. They are headquartered in the best businesses and the best schools. Their hallmark is to moderate the tension that always exists between the two most fundamental imperatives of practical progress: the need to cooperate and the need to innovate. Will these new ways of producing and of learning, which promise so greatly to enhance our productive powers, remain confined to certain advanced sectors of production and of learning? Or will they become accessible to broad segments of society and to many sectors of the economy? On the answer to these questions depend our chances of realizing the vaunted goal of socially inclusive economic growth.

Reduced to its simplest terms, economic growth is the consequence of three sets of causes. In the short run, a crucial determinant is the relation between the cost of what it takes to produce goods and services and the gains to be achieved by producing them. In the long run, a crucial factor is the development and the practical application of knowledge. The most important species of this knowledge is the one that allows us to routinize as much of work as we can so that we can do that routinized labor according to a formula. Whatever part of labor we can bring under a formula we can in turn embody in machines amplifying our powers. We can save our time for those activities that are not yet capable of being reduced to a formula and embodied in a machine. We shift the horizon of our attention from what can to what cannot yet be repeated.

In the extended medium term, however, what matters most to economic growth as well as other aspects of practical progress is our ability to cooperate. Cooperation must be so arranged that it is hospitable to innovation – if possible, to permanent innovation – thus laying the groundwork on which we can quicken the practical application of knowledge and shift our focus from the repetitious to the not yet repeatable. Cooperation is necessary to the practice of innovation – whether the innovations be technological, organizational, social, or conceptual. However, every innovation also threatens the established form of cooperation because it disturbs the regime of prerogatives and expectations in which the existing form of cooperation is embedded. If, to take a simple example, a new machine threatens to put one group of workers out of work while benefiting another, the truce between the benefited and the harmed groups, or between them and their employers, is likely to break down.

The extent to which the imperatives of cooperation and of innovation interfere with each other is not, however, constant. The cooperative practices richest in promise of practical progress are those that can accommodate repeated innovation most easily. These practices evolve. To take hold and to advance, they depend on certain conditions.

It does progressives no good to present their proposals as pietistic constraints on the forces that drive practical progress; they need to find a way of anchoring social inclusion and individual empowerment in the practical organization of the economy and society and in the social logic of growth and innovation. Neither, however, should progressives repeat the mistake of the Marxists in believing that the requirements of practical progress will ultimately and necessarily open the way to progressive change.

We should always ask ourselves how we can take hold of those forces and redirect them to suit interests and ideals that transcend them. This problem presents itself to us today in a form we have barely begun to recognize. One way to begin approaching this problem is to place it first in the context of a puzzle about the practical failure and success of contemporary societies.

In the course of the twentieth century some countries did well at both market-oriented and "dirigiste" or government-led economic arrangements. They veered from one of these styles of economic management to another, as circumstances required. No country has been more wedded to the religion of the free market – and indeed to a particular version of the market economy, wrongly equated with its essential nature – than the United States. Nevertheless, when the national emergency of the Second World War demanded it, the country unceremoniously put this free-market religion aside. In its place it established the forced mobilization of national resources, the imposition of marginal tax rates that, at the top, were nearly confiscatory, and a free-wheeling coordination both among private firms as well as between private firms and government. The result was spectacular; GDP nearly doubled in four years. The circumstances of wartime were, to be sure, exceptional, but they cannot have sufficed to produce the capabilities that made possible such a response.

Many other countries, by contrast, have made a mess of both market-oriented and "dirigiste" solutions. They have tried almost everything, as far as the institutional organization of the economy goes, and failed at almost everything.

The contrast between market and command lies close to the center of two centuries of ideological debate for two hundred years. As an organizing principle of controversy, this contrast is dead or dying. Long before its death, this way of shaping ideological contests deserved to be resisted on two grounds.

The first reason for resistance is the failure of this traditional focus of ideological controversy to recognize that market economies, like representative democracies and free civil societies, can assume institutional forms very different from those that have come to prevail in the North Atlantic world. Cutting across the familiar ideological contests about how much space to give to the market is a debate – at least as radical in potential reach – about what kind of market economy should be established.

The second reason for resistance is that the choice

between market and command fails to address the puzzle of succeeding at everything or failing at everything, of which twentieth-century history has given such telling evidence. The societies that have succeeded at both market-oriented and government-directed arrangements are those that have been able to deploy a superior set of cooperative practices. Mastery of such practices has helped give them both the flexibility to move between institutional systems – more market-based or more "dirigiste," as circumstance may advise – and the ability to use each such system to best effect. These societies have learned to combine cooperation with plasticity: a way of working together that is, to the greatest possible extent, hospitable to innovation, including innovation in the forms of cooperation itself.

A species of these innovation-friendly cooperative practices has gained immense importance in the world. It forms the core of an experimentalist vanguardism that now distinguishes the best businesses and the best schools in developing and rich countries alike: in China, India, and Brazil, as well as in the United States, Japan, and Germany. The network of such vanguards of production and learning has become a commanding force in the world economy. They are in touch with one another, exchanging people, initiatives and ideas as well as products, services, and technologies.

Among the marks of these advanced, experimental practices are an attenuation of contrasts between supervisory and implementing roles; a consequent fluidity in the definition of the implementing roles themselves; a tendency to move the focus of new effort, as far as practical constraints may allow, to the frontier of operations that are not yet readily repeatable because we have not yet learned how to bring them under a formula; a willingness to combine and to superimpose, in the same domains, cooperation and competition; and a predisposition for groups engaged in the cooperative regime to reinterpret their group interests and identities – and to expect to reinterpret them – as they go along. These practices – not just the accumulation of capital or the refinement of technology – animate the vanguardism that is revolutionizing practical life. Cooperation of a special sort unlocks the transformative potential of technology and science.

Will the direct experience of this advance in co-operative and innovative capability remain confined to the happy few? Or will it be made to penetrate much of economic and social life? Will the richer countries continue to rely on compensatory redistribution through tax-and-transfer? Will developing countries continue to depend on the politically supported diffusion of small property and small business in the hope of moderating the vast inequalities resulting from the discontinuities between the advanced and the backward sectors of their economies? Or will we find ways to generalize in the economy and society the practices that are revolutionizing the advanced sectors? Are we doomed to humanize rather than to transform?

For all who are today committed to progressive alternatives the need to answer these questions is an opportunity as much as it is a problem. It is an opportunity to associate the struggle for such alternatives with our stake in practical progress, lightening the burdens of poverty, infirmity, and drudgery that weigh on human life. At the same time, it is an opportunity to connect a progressive program with the cause of the permanent creation of the new. The dictatorship of no alternatives will never be overthrown by a combination of narrow interests and impractical pieties.

For this reason we need to understand the conditions that support this species of innovation-friendly cooperation in society and culture and that favor its diffusion. Progressive alternatives will prevail only if they succeed in showing how to secure each of these conditions with the resources and within the limitations of contemporary societies.

The first condition is the avoidance of extreme, entrenched inequalities without, however, being committed to a rigid equality of circumstance. Inherited class advantage cannot be reconciled with democracy or justified by the consequences of in-heritance. However, it is less important that the individual be able to escape his class, or to see his children escape it, than it is that the structure of social division and hierarchy not tightly predetermine how people can work together.

The second condition is that people be equipped and empowered in such a way that the manner in which they receive their educational and economic equipment leave the greatest range of social and economic life open to experimental reshaping. The practical meaning of basic human rights rests on an apparent paradox. We make people's basic rights and capabilities secure against the swings of the market and the reversals of politics. We do so, however, in the hope that, thus equipped, people may thrive all the more in the midst of innovation and change. We take something out of the short-term swings of politics and of markets – the rules defining fundamental rights – and in that sense limit what can be changed. We do so, however, in the hope of making the scope for valuable change broader.

We need not accept any fixed inverse relation between the empowerment of the individual on the basis of fundamental rights and the plasticity of his social setting. If we are bold and imaginative enough we can have more safeguards and more plasticity at the same time. The traditional forms of private law and of political democracy may provide more empowerment for less rigidity than a caste system. However, they provide less than the alternative ways of democratizing markets and of deepening democracies that progressives throughout the world should now seek.

The third condition is the diffusion of an experimentalist impulse in society and culture. The chief source of this impulse must be a particular form of education, administered in youth and made available throughout a working life. The distinguishing traits of such a form of education are to be analytical and problematic rather than informational; to prefer exemplary selective deepening to encyclopedic coverage; to encourage cooperation, rather than isolation or authoritarianism, in learning and teaching; and to proceed dialectically – that is to say, by the exploration of contrasting methods and views rather than by appeal to a closed canon of right doctrine.

The fourth condition is the effort to loosen the dependence of change upon calamity, and to design institutions and discourses that organize and facilitate their own revision. Franklin Roosevelt had war and economic collapse as his allies in the project of reform. It should be possible to be changed without first being ruined. We must redesign our institutions and discourses accordingly.

A progressive alternative suited to the realities of contemporary societies must show how to secure these four sets of requirements, both as goods in themselves and as encouragements to the spread of innovation-friendly cooperation. It is a task that presents itself with equal force in richer and in poorer countries. It draws on interests that are as much moral as they are material.

It is useful to understand the point in its most general form before applying it to the circumstances of contemporary societies. We usually act and think within a framework of assumptions and arrangements that we take for granted. Occasionally, we try to change the framework. The distance between our ordinary context-preserving acts and our exceptional context-transforming moves is not constant. We can so shape our institutions and our discourses that they either shorten or lengthen this distance. We have reasons to shorten it, facilitating the piecemeal transformation of our contexts as a normal outgrowth of our everyday pursuits. Our reasons are many: to strengthen the freedom to experiment – especially to experiment with the forms of cooperation – on which all practical progress depends; to undermine the basis of every entrenched scheme of social division and hierarchy in arrangements and dogmas insulated against challenge; and to retain in the midst of our engagement with a social world our power to criticize, resist, and reform it.

What is ultimately at issue here is something that

goes beyond the search for socially inclusive economic growth and for broader and more equal opportunity. It is our ability to give practical consequence to the essential doctrine of democracy: faith in the constructive powers of ordinary men and women, and a commitment to lift them up, to make them greater.

The developing countries: growth with inclusion

The recent experience of developing countries teaches two overriding lessons. They are in only apparent contradiction. The first lesson is that countries grow, although often with dramatic increases in inequality, when they unleash market forces. The second lesson is that those that have grown most – China and, to a lesser extent, India – are the least obedient to the formula that has been pressed upon them by the governments, financiers, and academics of the rich countries.

The most successful developing countries are those that have been most prodigal in institutional innovations, especially innovations in the institutional definition of a market economy itself. They have also been the countries that have been most insistent on raising a shield to protect national heresy in development strategy and institutional organization. The shield has been made of policy initiatives that broaden the margin of maneuver of national governments. The winning formula has been: markets and globalization, yes, but only on our own terms.

Even the relatively successful heretics, however, have proved failures in what matters most: socially inclusive growth and individual empowerment. In China, hundreds of millions of people live in a purgatory of joblessness, insecurity, and fear. In India, the majority of the nation continues to work in the shadows of an informal economy, without rights and without hope. In China the affirmation of national independence remains entangled in a dictatorship that has ceased to believe in the revolutionary faith that it once used to excuse its acts of oppression. In India democratic politics has failed to translate the promise of the national idea into the reality of capability and opportunity for the ordinary working man and woman. All over the developing world, vast numbers of people, even when free from hunger, churn in a vacuum of law and of opportunity. They have already received the message: they know themselves to be godlike. However, they cannot stand up.

There is another way. It builds on the lessons of this recent experience, especially the successful but truncated achievements of institutional innovation and national defiance. Its working assumption is that developing countries cannot accomplish the goal of growth with inclusion within the narrow range of forms of a market economy, a representative democracy, and a free civil society now established in the rich North Atlantic countries. And although it must vary according to the conditions of each country and moment, the basic direction it signals is pertinent to a wide range of present-day circumstance. Four axes of change define this alternative program. Together, they suggest a direction, not a blueprint. For that is what a programmatic argument can provide: a direction and a series of next steps.

The first axis is the raising of a shield over heresy: the set of policies and arrangements enabling countries to turn to markets and to globalization on their own terms, and on terms that make socially inclusive growth at least thinkable and feasible. To raise such a shield today is decisively to reject the contemporary functional equivalent to the gold standard. The point of the nineteenth-century gold standard – it has been observed – was to make the level of economic activity depend on the level of business confidence. It thus tied the hands of national governments to the benefit of those who controlled financial wealth.

Today's functional equivalent to this dead regime is imposed on some submissive developing countries rather than adopted with alacrity by the richer economies. Its components are: acquiescence in a low level of domestic saving and consequent dependence on foreign capital; a low tax take except when a high tax take is needed to service a domestic debt that is itself a means for transferring wealth from workers and producers to rentiers; and as nearly unrestricted freedom of capital to come and go as local conditions may allow.

The practical result is to strengthen the need for national governments to court the international capital markets. However, this dependence, rather than being denounced for the voluntary servitude it represents, is embraced as an advantage. It is supposed to prevent governments from delivering themselves to the populist adventurism and irresponsibility that the custodians of the pseudo-orthodoxy fear these governments would otherwise be tempted to embrace. The shield raised over heresy is the decisive alternative to this shadow of gold.

A first element of which the shield must be made is an increased – even forcibly increased – level of domestic saving. The acknowledgment that saving is more the consequence of economic growth than its cause must be trumped by the strategic imperative of enjoying greater freedom to defy the financial markets. A forced mobilization of national resources may require mandatory saving – especially mandatory pensions saving – on a steeply progressive scale.

Higher saving is useless and even dangerous if it fails adequately to be channeled into production. Today the dominant ideas and even the accepted nomenclature make it impossible to address the way in which the institutional arrangements of an economy may either tighten the link between saving and production or loosen it, allowing much of the productive potential of saving to be squandered in a financial casino. The truth, however, is that even in the richest economies, production is largely financed by the retained earnings of firms. Only a small portion of the vast saving gathered in banks and stock markets has more than an oblique and fitful relation to the financing of productive activity.

The second element of the shield of heresy must therefore be an effort to tighten these connections, both within and outside the existing capital markets. The devices for such tightening include those that would accomplish the undone work of venture capital: for example, independently administered and competitive funds would be charged with channeling part of mandatory saving into emerging enterprise.

A third element in the shield of heresy is fiscal realism – a government determined to live within its means – even at the cost of renouncing for a while the countercyclical management of the economy. The role of fiscal realism in the shield of heresy is, however, the reverse of its function within the pseudo-orthodoxy now recommended by richer countries to poorer ones: to strengthen the power to develop along a divergent path.

The only way to ensure, in the short run, the high tax take such a fiscal realism requires, while minimizing its negative effect on incentives to save, to work, and to invest, is to rely heavily on taxes like VAT that are admittedly regressive: they fall disproportionately on tax payers who can save less because they earn less. The sacrifice of fairness in the design of the tax system may be more than compensated not only by the redistributive social spending it makes possible but also by the opportunity-creating potential of the larger program it may help support. Once the heresy is established, the focus of taxation can begin to shift to its proper targets: the hierarchy of standards of living (to be taxed by a steeply progressive tax on individual consumption) and the accumulation of economic power (to be taxed by a heavy charge on wealth, especially when transmitted by family gifts and inheritance).

A fourth element in the shield of heresy is a remorseless tactical opportunism in the treatment of the movement of money. The careful husbanding of national reserves and the imposition of stringent but temporary restraints on capital movements may be followed by complete convertibility of the local currency and by unrestricted freedom to move capital as circumstance may dictate.

To raise in this manner a shield over national heresy is to establish a war economy without a war: the forced mobilization of resources that allows petitioners to become rebels. The raising of the shield helps create the space in which a developing country can better equip the individual, democratize the market, and deepen democracy.

The second axis of a progressive alternative is to equip the individual. The guiding aim of social policy should not be to achieve greater equality; only the reorganization of the economy and of politics can make major contributions to that goal. It is to strengthen the capabilities of the individual. Education must therefore be the core social policy. Its organization can serve as a partial model for other public services.

The chief responsibility of education under democracy, whether in poorer or in richer countries, must be to equip the individual to act and to think now, in the existing situation, while providing him with the means with which to go beyond that situation. To challenge and to revise the context, even in little, piecemeal ways, is not only the condition for a fuller realization of our ideals and interests; it is also an indispensable expression of our humanity as beings whose powers of experience and initiative are never exhausted by the social and cultural worlds into which we happen to have been born. The school must be the voice of the future. It must rescue the child from its family, its class, its culture, and its historical period. Consequently, it must not be the passive tool of either the local community or the governmental bureau-cracy.

In its resource base the school must compensate for inequalities rather than reinforcing them; it should never depend on local finance. There must be min-imal standards of investment for each child and performance by each school. Local and national authorities must intervene correctively when these standards fail to be met. In its content education must focus on a core of general capabilities, and prepare the mind for engagement in an experimentalist culture. In its attitude to the class system it must stand ready to sharpen rather than to suppress the contradiction between class and meritocracy.

In societies in which the transmission of inherited advantage through the family remains a powerful force, no arrangement is more likely to arouse ex-citement and ambition than one that lavishes special opportunity and support on the most talented and hard-working students, especially when they struggle against disadvantage. Nothing is better calculated to undermine established inequalities, in the short as well as in the long run, than to form a republican counter-elite equipped to defeat and to dispossess an elite of heirs. This counter-elite may well be as self-serving as its predecessors. It may be the beneficiary of inequalities that are not so much more just as they are more useful. Nevertheless, its ascent will signal a new set of conflicts that can help a program like the one sketched here advance.

The shield of heresy will have been lifted in vain, and the empowered individual will have been left without adequate opportunity to use his energies productively, if a country fails to organize socially inclusive economic growth. In the conditions of the contemporary world such organization requires the present forms of the market economy to be remade.

We have been accustomed by two hundred years of ideological dispute to think that the choice before us is market or command, or a little of each. This way of thinking conceals one of the major problems of contemporary societies, the solution to which has now become decisive for the future of developing countries. It is not enough to regulate the market or to compensate for the inequalities it generates by resorting to redistributive tax-and-transfer. It is necessary to reinvent the market: to redefine the institutional arrangements that make it what it is.

In this effort there are two main tasks. The first task

is to establish the basis for a series of progressive, destabilizing advances on both the supply side and the demand side of economic growth. Each such advance stretches the limits of what the economy in its present state is capable of producing and delivering. Each therefore generates a small crisis, which can be resolved only by other advances on either the supply or the demand sides. Each adds something to the project of doing more by including more.

The result is to arouse a fever of productive activity, not by suppressing the market but by broadening opportunities to participate in it. We cannot broaden such opportunities to engage in market activity without simultaneously reorganizing the familiar institutional form of a market economy.

The second task is to impose on the creations of such feverish productive activity a rigorous mechanism of competitive selection. The two tasks, although conceptually distinct, can and must be performed simultaneously.

The progressive interventions on the supply side that are needed can most readily be understood through an historical example. The nineteenth-century United States, formed on the terrible anvil of African slavery, nevertheless created markets in agriculture and in finance that were more decentralized and inclusive than any that had existed up to that time. The contest over land and farming ended in the

creation of an agrarian system of unprecedented efficiency, based on strategic partnership between government and the family farmer as well as on
cooperative competition among the family farmers.
The struggle over the national banks resulted in their
dismantlement and in the creation of the most decentralized and effective scheme to place saving at the
disposal of the producer and the consumer the world
had ever seen.

This particular example may no longer be applicable to the problems of today but the principle it
expresses has lost none of its force. To democratize the
market in ways like this is now part of what must be
done in spades in every sector of every national
economy all over the world. What is useful everywhere has become urgent in developing countries.

The progressive intervention on the supply side
should therefore take the form of institutional innovations that radically extend access to credit, technology,
and expertise and that help identify, develop, and
propagate the local productive experiments and technological innovations that have proved most successful.
A presumption should weigh against the idea of a
lockstep evolutionary ascent that would require developing countries to become platforms for the traditional,
rigid mass production industry that is now in decline in
the richest economies.

It is a prejudice unsupported by fact to suppose the

practices of innovation-friendly cooperation and cooperative competition to be a prerogative of high-technology, knowledge-intensive production in the richest countries. The goal must be to spread these practices out of step and before their time; to help them become established even in sectors of the economy that we may regard as rudimentary by their very nature; and to favor their diffusion throughout a national economy without relying on a master plan imposed from above by the State.

Neither the American model of arm's-length regulation of business by government nor the northeast Asian model of formulation of trade and industrial policy by a central bureaucracy prove equal to this task. Its execution is instead likely to require a form of strategic coordination between public action and private initiative that is pluralistic rather than unitary, participatory rather than authoritarian, and experimentalist rather than dogmatic. Public support for private enterprise can be justified only by a spreading of opportunity: more opportunity for more economic agents on more varied terms. What may seem, when viewed statically, like governmental subsidies to private interests may turn out, when seen dynamically, to serve as moves in an effort to broaden a market by redesigning the institutional arrangements that define it.

A host of funds and centers of technical support

intermediate between government and private firms may play a major role in this work. And from the different types of relations such funds and centers may develop with their client firms, alternative regimes of private and social property – multiple ways of organizing the coexistence of stakes in the same productive resources – may gradually develop. Such multiple regimes of private and social property would then begin to coexist experimentally within the same national economy. The classic nineteenth-century form of private property, enabling the owner to do whatever he wants, at his own risk, with the resources at his command, should be one such regime. It should not be the only one. Why tie the productive powers of society to a single version of the market economy?

The reshaping of the supply side must have as its counterpart a tilt on the demand side toward higher returns to labor. No tenet of present economic thinking is more entrenched and more revealing than the view that returns to labor cannot rise above productivity growth; any attempt to make them rise faster will supposedly be undone by inflation. That this view – so similar to Marx's idea of convergence of all capitalist economies to the same rate of surplus value – must nevertheless be false is shown by the dramatic differences among countries at comparable levels of economic development, and with comparable endowments, in labor's share of national income.

The tilt upward in the real returns to labor is an indispensable basis for the deepening of a mass-consumption market. It makes possible a strategy of economic growth that treats exports and globalization as an expression of the same vigor that must also be manifest in a deepening of the internal market. The methods for achieving the tilt upward must be as varied as the circumstances of the developing countries. At the top of the wage hierarchy, for example, one technique may be gradually to generalize the principle of worker sharing in company profits. At the base of the wage hierarchy, it may often be best to provide incentives or even outright subsidies for the employment and training of the lowest wage and least skilled labor. At the middle of the wage hierarchy the most promising basis of advance may lie in a labor-law regime that, by automatically unionizing everyone, creates a bias toward inclusion of broad categories of workers in deals about wages and rights.

The arousal of productive activity through the widening of opportunity, on both the supply and the demand sides of the economy, must be followed at every turn by the radicalization of competition. In every sector of established big business, sweetheart deals between government and private interests must be undone, and "capitalism" must be imposed on "capitalists." The combination of fecundity in economic activity with an implacable mechanism of competitive selection is the recipe for rapid and persistent progress.

Reforms such as those described by these first three guidelines of a progressive alternative for the developing countries will never be the gift of an enlightened elite to a passive citizenry. They can go forward and take hold only in a climate of heightened but organized popular mobilization. They depend on a facility for the repeated practice of structural reform – reform of the practices and institutions that shape the surface routines of social life. They require that the raising up of the individual not have as its reverse side the rigidity of established practices and arrangements. They demand much more room for deviation and experiment in every part of society than now exists anywhere. Their overall effect is to loosen the dependence of transformation on crisis. They make change "endogenous" to social and economic life: redefining as a project what the classic European social theorists falsely supposed to be an established fact. They turn democratic politics into a machine for the permanent invention of the future.

Thus, a fourth axis of an alternative is the establishment of the institutions of a high-energy democracy.

One set of institutional arrangements must help ensure a continuing high level of organized popular engagement in politics. A cold, demobilized politics cannot serve as a means to reorganize society. A hot, mobilized politics is compatible with democracy only when institutions channel its energies. It is a goal that can be achieved as the cumulative and combined effect of many devices. One example is the extended freed access that political parties and organized mass movements should enjoy to the means of mass communication. Another example is the exclusive public financing of electoral campaigns and the banning of all use of private resources.

A second set of institutions must be designed to quicken the pace of politics. For example, the direct election of a powerful president may help undermine and override the agreements worked out among political and economic elites. However, a presidential regime must then be purged of the bias to impasse that it has in the scheme by which Madison in the American constitution devised a way to slow and to contain the transformative uses of politics: a table of correspondences between the reconstructive reach of a political project and the severity of the constitutional obstacles its execution must overcome. Simple innovations can invert this logic: for example, granting both the executive and the legislative branches the power to call early elections to break a programmatic impasse. Both branches would have to face the electoral test. A similar result can be achieved by a pure parliamentary regime so long as elements of direct democracy – including comprehensive programmatic plebiscites and direct involvement in policy making and policy implementation at the grassroots – prevent the degeneration of a parliamentary regime into a set of backroom deals, struck under the shadow of prime-ministerial dictatorship.

A third set of arrangements forming the institutional agenda of a high-energy democracy would vastly expand opportunities to try out, in particular parts of a country or sectors of the economy, different ways of doing things. As we proceed down a certain path through national politics we must be able to hedge our bets. The way to hedge our bets is to radicalize the principle that is expressed but left undeveloped in traditional federalism. Local governments or networks of business or social organizations should be allowed to opt out of the dominant solutions so long as in so doing they do not establish a form of oppression or dependence from which their members are then unable readily to escape.

A fourth component of the institutional organization of high-energy democracy should be the endowment and empowerment of the individual. He must have a basic package of rights and benefits that are entirely independent of the particular job he holds. As soon as economic conditions allow, a principle of social inheritance should begin to be introduced. Under that principle the individual would be able to draw at turning points in his life – going to university, buying a house, opening a business – on a social-endowment account of basic resources. Social inheritance for all would gradually replace family inheritance for the few. Moreover, a special branch of government should be designed and equipped to intervene in particular organizations or practices that entrench forms of disadvantage or exclusion from which the individual is powerless to escape by the generally available means of economic and political action.

A fifth part of the constitution of high-energy democracy is the attempt to combine features of representative and direct democracy in even the largest and most populous states. The means are much the same as would contribute to the first two parts – the heightening of the level of organized popular engagement in politics and the movement toward the rapid breaking of impasse through appeal to the general electorate. These means include the use of comprehensive programmatic plebiscites, agreed between the political branches of government, and the involvement of local communities, organized outside the structure of both government and business, in the formulation and implementation of local social and economic policy. The goal is not only to melt structure without disorganizing politics; it is also to render commonplace in everyday life the experience of effective agency.

This whole program, marking a direction of cumulative change in practices and institutions, places the demand for social justice and individual empowerment on the side of constructive energy and perpetual innovation. Its aim is not only to make a heartless world less harsh; it is also to serve as a practical expression of faith in our ability to reconcile the search for worldly success with the promises of democracy. Such a formula applies as well to the circumstances and to the prospects of the rich North Atlantic democracies.

Europe: the reinvention of social democracy

Social democracy – the most widely admired form of the advanced societies – has long been in retreat in its European home ground. Because Europe has represented in the eyes of the world the promise of a form of the market economy and of globalization more inclusive and egalitarian than the form associated with American arrangements and with American power, the future of this retreat is pregnant with significance for everyone.

The traditional commitments of what was once described as the "Rhineland model" – to safeguard workers against economic downturns, to protect small, especially family, businesses against big business, to defend the insider constituencies of firms against the short-termism of stock markets, have all been given up, little by little. They have been sacrificed for the sake of protecting what is rightly regarded as more valuable – the ability to negotiate "social contracts" that distribute burdens equitably the better to realize common gains and the preservation of generous social entitlements, made possible by high tax takes. The preservation of these entitlements has proven to be the last line of defense of social democracy. Everything else is the process of being surrendered – slowly but relentlessly – in the name of the merciless imperatives of fiscal realism, economic flexibility, and global competition.

Should progressives in the rich countries hold on to this now eviscerated historical model, awaiting the first chance to restore some of its traditional content? Or should they propose a more fundamental change of direction? The answers to these questions follow from an understanding of the failure of the historical compromises that have shaped European social democracies to address the major problems of European societies today.

Social democracy was formed by a retreat. It retreated in its formative period from the attempt to reorganize both production and politics. In exchange for this withdrawal it achieved a strong position within the domain of the compensatory redistribution of income. Politics and the economy – so the founders of modern social democracy believed – could not be reorganized in the circumstance of the time. They could, however, be humanized. Much of the humanization consisted in a successful effort to equip people with the means with which to defend themselves against the consequences of economic insecurity. Today, however, policies of retrospective compensatory redistribution cannot adequately address the major problems of Europe, or indeed of any of the advanced societies. Social democracy needs to reenter the two terrains from which it early withdrew: the organization of production and of politics.

The truth of this proposition may not be readily apparent. For there are at least two sets of advances – crucial to the future of social democracy – that may seem capable of being achieved within the limits of the historical social-democratic compromise. Considered more closely, however, these advances turn out to be mere preliminaries or bridges to a world of concerns lying outside the limits of traditional social democracy.

The first such advance concerns the provision of social services. The citizens of every social democracy pay dearly by high taxation for public services. They are right to demand that these services improve. The model of standardized services to be dispensed by a bureaucracy specialized in education, health, or welfare assistance is the administrative counterpart to a form of industrial production that has become old-fashioned: the production of standardized goods and services with rigid machines and production processes, on the basis of a starkly hierarchical organization of work and a rigid specialization of function.

The State should provide directly only those services that are too difficult, too expensive, or simply too new to be provided by private providers. These private providers, however, should not be just businesses. They should be whatever organizations or teams may emerge to do the work. It is not enough to await such an active and entrepreneurial response from civil society; it is necessary to provoke it, to nourish it, and to organize it.

The role of government in the provision of public services should be twofold. One role should be to elicit and to monitor the broadest range of provision from the private economy and from civil society. Arm's-length regulation is not good enough. Government may often need to be intimately engaged in attracting and even in shaping such projects. Competitive diversity in the provision of services should be both the aim and the method. However, profit-making business is not the only or even the most suitable agent. The other role of government in the provision of public services should be to act as a vanguard, developing experimentally new services or new ways of providing the old services. The guiding principle is neither bureaucratic imposition nor consumer choice in a market. It is experimental diversification on the basis of a loose set of associations between governmental and non-governmental initiatives.

The second advance that may seem compatible with the historical limits of social democracy has to do with the conduct of economic policy. Everywhere in the advanced societies those who see the chief economic charge of the State as the counter-cyclical management of the economy have been chastened. Monetary policy has been surrendered to central bankers skeptical of the benefits of playing with the money supply, while fiscal policy has been taken over by politicians who have learned that the costs of deficit finance may last longer than its benefits.

Will the call to fiscal realism be used, however, simply to win and maintain financial confidence, identifying the whims of the capital markets with the dictates of economic wisdom? Or will governments use fiscal prudence to free themselves from these whims? Fiscal realism is not a program; not even a program for macroeconomic policy. It is merely a precaution. Its justification is to broaden a freedom of maneuver that must then be used. It does not teach us how to use this costly freedom.

A government that has largely foresworn the countercyclical use of monetary and fiscal policy, determining to avoid phony money and to live within its means, nevertheless has an economic task of enormous significance: to see to it that the productive potential of private saving be more effectively tapped. Venture capital – the financing of emerging business – remains a tiny industry. It has failed so far to fulfill the hope that it would become the consummate expression of the role of finance in production.

In the rich as in the developing countries it is vital to recognize that the extent to which the accumulated saving of society serves production, especially new production, depends on the way the economy is actually organized. The role of the venture capitalist – to identify opportunity, to recruit people, to nurture organizations, and finally to finance them in exchange for a stake – all this must happen on a much larger scale. If the market as now organized will not do it, then the State must help establish the funds and the centers that will mimic a market, reproducing its features of independence, competition, and accountability. If national governments have steeled themselves with fiscal prudence, then let them use their resulting freedom to help tighten the links between saving and production, and to help fuel ambition and enterprise.

With such advances in the organization of public

services and of finance, however, social democracies would reach a frontier of problems outreaching the historical compromises that formed them. For the European countries now face three sets of problems that can be addressed only by initiatives requiring the very reorganization of production and of politics that social democracy abandoned in the course of becoming what it is today.

The first such problem is the narrowness of the social and educational base for access to the most advanced sectors of the economy: the sectors that are now the favored home of innovation-friendly cooperation and that have become responsible for an increasing part of the creation of new wealth. In all the advanced economies, such productive vanguards remain relatively small and weakly linked to the rest of the economy. The vast majority of people who are lifted above poverty are excluded from them as well as from the educational institutions that prepare people for them. In all the advanced economies such vanguards have close to a stranglehold on the practices of innovation-friendly cooperation, which otherwise flourish in elite sectors far removed from the production system, like experimental schools or universities, missionary churches, commando units, and symphony orchestras.

A byproduct of the relative smallness and isolation of the advanced sectors of production, responsible for such a large part of technical and economic innovation and for an increasing portion of the creation of new wealth, is the heavy burden placed on public finance. Inequalities rooted in the structural divisions of an hierarchically organized economy must be attenuated retrospectively by redistributive transfer, financed by a high tax take. Equity and efficiency turn into adversaries, and the State into Sisyphus.

We need a radical broadening of social and educational access to these productive vanguards and above all to the ways of working and thinking that make them what they are. Such a broadening must be combined with a great expansion of the area of social and economic life in which the advanced practices of productive and educational experimentalism take hold. Not only must the gateway to the existing advanced sectors be opened more widely but the methods of work and invention that flourish within these advanced sectors must be transplanted to many other parts of the economy and society.

The rich social democracies cannot accomplish these goals solely by governmental regulation of enterprise and reallocation of resources. Nor can they achieve them by waiting for the market, as it is now organized, to produce it. The American model of arm's-length regulation of business will not do it, and neither will the northeast Asian method of having a bureaucracy formulate trade and industrial policy from

on high. The social democracies need to develop a
model of decentralized coordination between government and private enterprise. The purpose of this
model should be the same as the governmental actions
that in nineteenth-century America helped create an
extraordinarily successful agricultural system: not to
trump a market, but to create one by broadening the
terms of access to productive resources and opportunities.

Two sets of initiatives are crucial: one, economic;
the other, educational. The economic initiative is the
generalization of the work of venture capital beyond
the traditional confines of the private venture-capital
industry. A set of funds and support centers intermediate between government and private firms
should do the work of facilitating access to credit,
technology, expertise, and markets. When existing
agents fail to do this work, such funds and centers
should do it themselves. A large part of their work
should consist in identifying and spreading successful
local practice and in accelerating innovation. They
cannot perform this mission unless, secluded from
political pressure and subject to competitive pressure,
they are able to reproduce and even to radicalize the
principles of a market.

The associations between such funds or support
centers and their client firms need not follow a single
model; they can go from an intimate sharing of stakes

and tasks to a relatively distant relation of funding and technical assistance, provided in exchange for equity. Here, as in the earlier, related proposals for developing countries, the different types of dealings between emergent firms and the organizations that assist them may contain the kernel of alternative regimes of private and social property – different ways of organizing the coexistence of stakes in productive resources – that should begin to coexist experimentally within the same economy.

Leftists should not be the ones who seek to suppress the market, or even merely to regulate it or to moderate its inequalities by retrospective compensatory redistribution. They should be the people who propose to reinvent and to democratize the market by extending the range of its legal and institutional forms. They should turn the freedom to combine factors of production into a larger freedom to experiment with the arrangements that define the institutional setting of production and exchange.

The educational initiative complementing these economic innovations should include the provision of a form of lifelong education focused on mastery of comprehensive practical and conceptual capabilities. Such mastery enables the individual to move from job to job and to participate in a form of production that increasingly becomes a practice of collective learning and permanent innovation. The school must not only equip the child with the tools of effective action. It must also endow the student with the skills and habits of perpetual, piecemeal experimentation. In every domain of thought and practice, however modest, it must teach people how to probe and to take the next steps.

People must be able to go back to school periodically, at the expense of both the government and of their own employers; no part of their basic social endowment is more important than a claim to continuing education. And here, as in the developing countries, the financing and the staffing of schools must remain uninfluenced by the unequal resources available to different localities.

This last precaution can be given more general form. The European Union is now developing according to the principle that economic regulation is centralized while social and educational policy remains local. Exactly the inverse of this regime should prevail. There should be expanding scope for economic experimentation on the ground. By contrast, a core responsibility of the Union should be to guarantee the endowment – especially the educational endowment – of all its citizens.

The second problem beyond the limits of the historical compromises that shaped social democracies is the weakening of the basis of social cohesion. The practice of compensatory transfer payments – the stuff of social insurance – is an achievement of unquestionable significance. It has saved hundreds of millions of people from poverty, indignity, and fear. However, it cannot serve as social cement. In all the contemporary social democracies people belong to social worlds that are fast moving apart. The residual meaning of social solidarity has become the movement of checks through the mail: resources flow, through the hands of the State, from people making money in the productive vanguards, for example, to people needing and spending money in the caring economy. The inhabitants of these different realms may know one another less – and therefore care for one another less – than the members of many a traditional hierarchical society.

Checks sent through the mail are not enough. The principle must be established that every able-bodied adult will have a position in both the production system and the caring economy: part of a working life or of a working year should be devoted to participating in the provision of care for the young, the old, the infirm, the poor, and the desperate. It is an effort that can be effective only if people receive the basic training their jobs may require and if civil society is organized – or the government helps it organize itself – to use such efforts to best effect. Social solidarity will then have a foundation in the only force that can secure it: people's direct exercise of responsibility for one another.

A third problem that cannot be addressed within the boundaries of traditional social democracy is the need to give people a better chance to live a big life, transfigured by ambition, surprise, and struggle. No anxiety must be more central to democracy, and therefore to social democracy, than the fear that progress toward greater prosperity and equality may be unaccompanied by an advance in the capabilities and in the self-affirmation of ordinary humanity. The reasons to want more are both practical and spiritual: to make better use of everyone's dormant energies and to establish in the mind of the ordinary man and woman the idea and the experience of their own power.

In the European homeland of social democracy this problem bears a special pathos. For vast numbers of ordinary people the occasion for being lifted out of the littleness of ordinary life has been war: sacrificial devotion has been associated with slaughter. Peace has brought stupefaction and belittlement. It need not, and it should not if Europeans are to succeed in raising the energy level of their societies for the sake of all their most basic material and moral interests.

Consider this issue of belittlement from a particular angle: whether having been born in a small country – and all the European countries are relatively small – it is possible to live a large life. Norway, for example, is a country sitting on a cushion of oil rents. It has room for maneuver, as – relatively to the rest of the world –

do all the more prosperous European societies. The Norwegian government could help prepare the willing elements of the Norwegian people to become an international service elite, taking the whole world as their horizon for a broad range of entrepreneurial, professional, and philanthropic activities. In the pursuit of such a project Norwegians would have much on which to draw in their national experience. The government – by the terms of this Carthaginian solution – would act as a master venture capitalist and instigator, helping spawn the broad array of organizations that would have to do the first-line work of preparation and support. On returning home, transformed by the experiences of the whole world, these missionaries of constructive action would change the tenor of national life. It is simply one example among many of how a problem considered to lie beyond the reach of reform may in fact be brought within it.

The direction of a program that oversteps the boundaries of social democracy in all the three directions I have described is clear. The reformers of European social democracy have not been mistaken to hope for a reconciliation of economic flexibility with social cohesion and inclusion. Their mistake has been to accept the established institutional framework as the template for such a reconciliation. They continue to require calamity to support reconstruction.

Their institutional dogmatism has helped prevent them from envisaging the majority constituency they might win for a transformation of society that, although gradual in its progress, might nevertheless be revolutionary in its outcome. It has kept them from meeting the popular dream of modest prosperity and independence on its own terms, and providing it with the tools with which to reinvent itself in more adventurous and magnanimous form. Above all, it has stunted their vision of the ideals to which their proposals can and should appeal.

The forces with the best chance to achieve and maintain political predominance in the near future of the advanced societies are those − whether right, center, or left − that most persuasively associate themselves with the cause of restless experimentation and energy. It matters to the future of these societies that they also be forces committed to the belief that the freedom of some depends on the emancipation of all.

The United States: hope for the little guy

There is not supposed to be a Left in the United States, at least not in the same sense or with the same force as there is a Left in the rest of the world. It is nevertheless vital to turn the debate about the future of the Left into an American debate.

In the first place, it is vital because the United States is not only the predominant power in the world; it is a power that is not in imaginative touch with the rest of humanity. The great ideological debates that shake the world today seem distant and dangerous fantasies when rehearsed within the United States, as the ideological contests of the nineteenth century echoed within Great Britain. The bias of Americans is that the rest of the world must either languish in poverty and despotism or become more like them. This failure of imagination is a source of immense danger. The only way to redress it is for Americans to recognize the fundamental similarity of their predicament to the condition of other contemporary societies: similarity in the range of the most pressing problems as well as in the character of the most pertinent solutions.

In the second place, it is vital because the distinction between the two faces that the rich North Atlantic world has shown to the rest of humanity is fast losing its clarity. As European social democracy hollows out its historical agenda in the pursuit of a supposed synthesis between European-style social protection and American-style economic flexibility, the hope of taking European social democracy as a point of the departure for the development of an alternative of worldwide interest weakens. The value of establishing the beginnings of an alternative inside the United States increases.

In the third place, it is vital just because the United States is not only the hegemonic power in the world; it is also the power whose ruling interests and beliefs are most closely associated with the emerging form of the global order. Globalization has very largely meant Americanization, not only in the realm of economic forces and political power but also in the domain of ideas and ideals.

A conception of human life and of its prospects has taken over the world. It is the most powerful religion of humanity today. This religion lies at the center of the historical aspirations of the Left. No country identifies more completely with this creed than the United States. How can it be that the country most fully identified with the doctrine central to the Left is the one that is supposed to have no Left?

The answer is that the United States accepts the religion in truncated or perverted form. Because it is the preponderant power in the world, this American heresy and its correction concern everyone.

The religion of humanity presents the self as transcendent over context: incapable of being contained within any limited mental or social structure. Not satisfied occasionally to rebel, it wants to fashion a principle that makes rebellion permanent, and renders it internal to social life, in the form of ongoing experimental remaking.

No institutional and imaginative ordering of social life accommodates all our strivings. The next best thing to such an all-inclusive order is the combination of experimental pluralism – different directions – with experimental self-correction – each direction subject to the condition that it ease its own revision.

The aim is the creation of a self that is less the plaything of accidental circumstance and the puppet of compulsive social routine; a more godlike self. Such a self is able to imagine and to accept other selves as the context-transcending agents they all really are. It can experience a form of empowerment untainted by the exercise of oppression and by the illusions of pre-eminence. To this end, society must equip the individual – every individual – with the educational and economic instruments he needs to lift himself up and to make himself more godlike.

This faith in self-construction goes together in the contemporary religion of humanity with a faith in human solidarity. At its extreme limit, it is the vision-ary conviction, belied but not destroyed by the terrors of ordinary social life, that all men and women are bound together by an invisible circle of love. In its more prosaic form, it is the historical insight that the practical benefits of social life all arise from coopera-tion and connection.

That form of cooperation will be most productive that is least bound by the restraints of any established scheme of social division and hierarchy and that is most successful in moderating the tension between the imperatives of cooperation and innovation. Every innovation – technical, organizational, or ideological – jeopardizes the present system of cooperation be-cause it threatens to upset the social regime of rights and expectations in which cooperative relations are embedded. We should prefer the way of organizing cooperation that minimizes this tension. It will generally be one that makes the endowments and equipments of individuals independent of the accidents of their birth as well as of the particulars of their position; that rejects all social and cultural predetermination of how people can work together; and that encourages the spread of an experimentalist impulse, harnessing confrontation with the unexpected to create the new.

The most valuable form of connection will enable people to diminish the price of dependence and depersonalization that we must pay for engagement with others. Self-construction depends on connection, and connection threatens to entangle us in toils of subjugation and to rob us of the very distinction that we can develop only thanks to it. There is a conflict between the enabling conditions of self-affirmation. To diminish that conflict is to become freer and greater, not by living apart but by living together while deepening the experience of self-possession.

Such is the twofold gospel of the divinization of humanity, in the name of which the torch has been set, and will yet be set, to every empire in the world. It is the message that should forever lie at the heart of the work of the Left. It can be advanced only through the remaking of both our arrangements and our sensibilities. It has been central to American democracy and to the form of globalization with which American hegemony is associated, and yet in that democracy and that globalization, misshapen and diminished.

One aspect of the perversion is a failure to acknowl-edge the extent to which the institutional structure of society is open to revision and the extent to which it holds hostage what people understand to be their interests and ideals. It has been a besetting myth of American civilization to suppose that Americans early discovered the basic formula of a free society, to be adjusted only rarely, under pressure of national emer-gency. The three great periods of institutional effer-vescence in the United States were the time of independence, the time of Civil War and the time of the mid-twentieth Depression and world conflict. Only then were they partly freed from the strangle-hold of institutional superstition.

This fetishism of the institutional formula, most completely manifest in the cult of the Constitution, is an extreme instance of a conformism that is now in danger of seducing the whole world and of defeating the essential goal of the Left. The greatest price that it has exacted from American democracy is failure to progress in the realization of the most persistent American dream – an American variant on what has now become a worldwide aspiration.

This aspiration is the dream of a society made for the little guy: a country in which ordinary men and women can stand on their own feet, morally and socially as well as economically, achieving a degree of prosperity and independence as well as the resources of independent judgment and the claims to equal respect that past societies largely reserved for an elite. In the initial decades of America's life as an independent country, this dream had a tangible and immediate expression: only one in ten of free white men worked for another man at the beginning of the nineteenth century. It is a commitment that has since proved unable to impose its stamp on the forces shaping American society.

Two institutional vehicles have carried the weight of this dream in American history. The first device has been the defense of small property and small business against great wealth and big business. The second device has been the appeal to the regulatory and redistributive powers of the national government. Neither instrument has prevailed against the consequences of the hierarchical segmentation of the economy. Neither has sufficed to make the dream real. To realize the dream further than those two vehicles can go would require reshaping the economic and political institutions of the country, and doing so without the aid of a crisis. It is a reformation that the vice of institutional fetishism denies to American democracy.

The other major perversion of the religion of humanity among the Americans lies in the imagination of the link between self-construction and solidarity. If the predominant tendencies of consciousness in American life have understated the extent to which society can be reorganized, they have also exaggerated the degree to which the individual can save himself without needing to be saved by the grace of other people. A little Napoleon who takes the crown, and crowns himself, has been the illusion that perpetually seduces them.

To this mirage of self-reliance turning into self-salvation Americans owe their common oscillation between an extreme individualism and an equal extreme collectivism (seemingly opposites but in fact reverse sides of each other), their attraction to the middle distance of pseudo-intimacy and cheerful impersonal friendliness in social relations (like Schopenhauer's porcupines moving uneasily between the distance at which they get cold and the closeness at which they prick one another), and their endless quest for ways to deny frailty, dependence, and death (even at the cost of a mummification of the self and mystification of its true condition in the world).

It is this idea of the self, and of its disengagement from the formative claims of solidarity, that the rest of humanity vaguely but rightly understands to animate much of the institutional formula the United States seeks to propagate throughout the world and to entrench in the arrangements of globalization. This idea deserves to be resisted, and it will be resisted, because it represents a gross misdirection in the religion of humanity.

Their misdirection has not, however, prevented Americans from excelling in the cooperative practices, and from advancing in the development of those innovation-friendly forms of cooperation in economic and social life from which we must expect the greatest contributions to the practical progress of mankind. To this skill we must credit their demonstrated ability to succeed under a broad range of circumstances and rules with equal success, as they did when world war required them to adopt arrangements and practices that were anathema to their official ideology.

They live under the most extreme class hierarchies of the rich democracies, yet they are second to none in denying the legitimacy of class and of its blight on equal opportunity. They have failed to equip the masses of ordinary men and women with the instruments of initiative and innovation, but they retain faith in the constructive genius of plain people. They surrender to institutional fetishism, however, only by according to their institutions a scandalous and powerful exemption from the experimentalist impulse that otherwise remains so powerful a force in their culture.

If only they could free themselves from their institutional idolatry and imagine more truly the relation of self to other, they could realize their dreams more fully, and correct them in the course of realizing them. Many of the intangible barriers that separate them from the imaginative life of the age and of the world would fall away. They would no longer be adversaries of the Left, even though they might not describe themselves as Leftists, because they would have joined the central current of the development of the religion of humanity. And it is the combination of this religion with the disposition to renew the restricted repertory of institutional arrangements to which the world is now confined that has come to define the identity and the work of the Left.

Today the focus of the problem in the United States is the absence of a credible successor to the New Deal. Roosevelt's settlement in the mid-twentieth century was the American equivalent to the social-democratic compromise and the last great experiment – however limited in scope and dependent on the favoring circumstance of crisis – with the institutions of the country. Yet its focus on the development of the regulatory and redistributive powers of national government, rather than on democratizing the market or on deepening democracy, and on economic security, rather than on economic empowerment, is no longer suited to the tasks of the day.

The failure of American progressives to offer, within or outside the Democratic party, an effective sequel to the Rooseveltian project has rendered them powerless to respond to the great downward changes that overtook American democracy from the 1960s on: increasing inequality in wealth and income, and most strikingly, inequality in the compensation of labor at different levels of the wage hierarchy; stagnant or decreasing intergenerational mobility among social classes; shrinking popular participation in politics; and diminishing engagement in associational activity outside the boundaries of family life. These inflections are American variations on shifts common to all the rich North Atlantic democracies.

Any Left proposal that can speak to the most urgent problems of the United States must supply remedies against these changes, and turn the response to them into an opportunity both to realize and to rectify the American dream. Such a response must in turn be informed by an understanding of how and why these changes came about. Consider the outline of such an explanation; it includes the slow time of economic and cultural change as well as the fast time of decisive political events. All these elements – even the uniquely American political episodes – are characteristic of circumstances in which and against which the Left must now work throughout the world.

The slow economic change, which took place during the later part of the twentieth century, was a sharpening of the hierarchical segmentation of the economy, accompanying a shift in the organization of production. As mass production declined, replaced, in services as well as in industry, by knowledge-intensive,

more flexible production, the core historical constituency of the progressives, unionized industrial labor,
shrank. The emerging forms of production placed a
premium on educational endowments that the professional and business class was best able to transmit to
its children. The elite schools trained students in
distinctive conceptual practices and social skills –
talkative teamwork and personal charisma, carefully
concealed under a veneer of pliant self-deprecation.
Such practices and skills were alien to the social worlds
and the public schools of the working-class majority,
with their emphasis on the alternation between organizational and intellectual conformity at work and at
school and off-time fantasy and rebellion. The synthesis of class hierarchy and meritocratic principle that
has come to characterize all the rich countries thus
finds support in the biases of production and of
education.

A shift in consciousness, not directly related to this
change in production, has nevertheless accompanied
it. Alongside the neo-Christian and post-Romantic
narratives of the mass popular culture, with their
formulaic versions of redemption through engagement and connection, and of recovery and ennoble-
ment, through sacrifice and loss, a contrasting set of
themes has won increasing space. In this neo-pagan
vision, exhibited in the game and reality shows on
popular television, as well as in some of the most

refined productions of the high culture, the protagonist seeks to triumph, by guile and tenacity, in an arbitrary world, bereft of human as well as of divine grace. He spins the wheel of fortune rather than embarking on an adventure of self-construction based on the acceptance of vulnerability. At the center of this neo-pagan dispensation is a wavering of hope: the hope – central to the contemporary religion of humanity – that the transformation of society and the transformation of the self can advance hand in hand.

In a setting shaped by these changes in production and consciousness, the political direction taken by the would-be successors to Roosevelt in the final decades of the twentieth century followed the path of least resistance. It was a path that helped aggravate the effect of the anti-egalitarian and antisocial shifts that were changing the country, and that helped disorient and disarm the progressive forces in their resistance to those tendencies. Yet it was a direction that wore the outward appearance of realism and prudence.

Under the Presidency of Lyndon Johnson, the very time to which in hindsight we can first trace the inflections, a social and racial orthodoxy that was to contribute to the undoing of the progressives first crystallized. Roosevelt's commitment to programs, like Social Security, responsive to the anxieties and interests of a broad working-class majority was replaced by a "War on Poverty" that targeted its benefits to a distinct minority of poor people and that circumvented the machines of traditional working-class politics in the large cities. It was a mistake that the architects of European social democracy had been careful to avoid.

Racial oppression was defined as a threshold evil, to be redressed prior to any attack on economic injustice and class hierarchy. This self-styled integrationist orthodoxy became the basis for programs, like race-conscious affirmative action, that antagonized many who might have participated in a project responsive to the needs and aspirations of a transracial working-class majority in the country.

In the succeeding decades, three connected sets of events reinforced the dissolving effect of these choices.

One was the attempt by the progressives to use judicial politics to circumvent political politics. This circumvention biased the emphasis of the progressive project toward reforms focusing on redefinitions and reallocations of individual rights rather than on reconstructions of institutional life. These were the reforms that an elite of judicial reformers could most plausibly undertake before being brought back into line by the balance of political forces.

A second series of events was the federalization of a "modernist" moral agenda (abortion being the cutting issue) embraced in large numbers by the secular, the urban, the educated, and the propertied in the name of the progressive cause but in defiance of the beliefs of many who were needed to move it forward.

A third succession of events was the reemergence of "sound-finance doctrine" – the primacy of financial confidence in the conduct of macroeconomic policy – as the successor to a Keynesian orthodoxy that no longer spoke to the circumstance of the day. No attempt was made to harness the achievement of financial confidence to any affirmative attempt to mobilize saving, in new ways and by new devices, for production, invention, and innovation.

These repeated compromises, retreats, and misdirections, reinforced one another. Their effect in deepening the antidemocratic inflections – greater economic inequality, restricted class mobility, less political participation, thinner social connections – was sealed by the principle that war trumps reform (unless by requiring full-scale national mobilization of people and resources it provokes institutional experimentation). They were not the unavoidable reactions in national politics to the economic and cultural shifts the country had undergone; they were only the responses that proved easiest to give, turning lack of imagination into fate.

It was the background of a conservative hegemony, repeating in many of its elements and presuppositions the conservative ascendancy of the late nineteenth century. The linchpin of this hegemony was the success of conservative statecraft in the United States in combining recourse to the economic interests of the moneyed classes with appeal to the moral beliefs and political skepticism of the white working class outside the large cities. It was then that in the United States, as in much of the rest of the world, the program of the progressives became the program of their conservative adversaries, with a humanizing discount.

The programmatic response the Left should propose to this circumstance in the United States must begin with two preliminaries, redefining the racial and social pseudo-progressive orthodoxies formed in the late twentieth century. This response should have as its core a political economy of democracy, democratizing the market by reshaping both the forms of production (including the relation of government to business) and the condition of labor. It must be extended through innovations encouraging civil society to organize itself outside both government and business, and energizing democratic politics.

The first preliminary concerns the relation between race and class. There have been four main projects for the redress of racial injustice in the United States. The best hope for advance lies in a certain way of combining the third and the fourth approaches while going beyond both of them.

The first approach was the collaborationist project

of Booker T. Washington, put forward in the decades following the Civil War. The solution proposed was to occupy a secure but subordinate position in the economy – the petty-bourgeois position of the small-holder, the shopkeeper, the craftsman – on the basis of modest property distribution and vocational training. The paradox, at once political and programmatic, is that even such a seemingly modest program requires (or would have required in its time) large-scale political and social mobilization, which, once aroused, would have demanded more than this orientation could ensure.

The second approach has been the secessionist project – withdrawal from American society, even return to Africa. It has proved to be a feint. Although its tone has traditionally been voiced in belligerent contrast to the sweetness of the collaborationist strategy, its practical expression has been the same: retreat not into a separate land but into an internal exile of small business under a leadership committed to impose, in the name of religious authority, petty-bourgeois norms of respectability.

The third approach is the integrationist project that would treat racial injustice as a threshold concern distinguishable from class injustice and prior to it. Its most characteristic expression has been affirmative action although its more fundamental work was the defense of civil rights for racial minorities. Its undoubted historical achievement has been the establishment of a black professional and business class.

However, it suffers from three defects. The first is that its benefits accrue in inverse proportion to the need for them: most to the professional and business class, less to the working class, especially of public employees; least of all to the underclass. The second defect is that it separates the black leadership from the mass of poor black people, accommodating them in the existing order as virtual representatives of those who are very largely denied its fruits. The third defect is that it offends the material and moral interests of the white working class, which reasonably believes itself to be the victim of a conspiracy of sanctimonious and self-serving elites, including the elite of those who claim to represent the downtrodden.

Confusing the struggle against racial discrimination with the social and economic advancement of a racially stigmatized minority, the integrationist orthodoxy achieves neither of these goals squarely. The alternative is to build on a fourth, reconstructive approach to the race problem and to reconcile it with the strong suit of the integrationist approach: its commitment to overcome the evil of discrimination on the basis of race. The keynote of the reconstructive view is to treat the problems of race and class as inseparable and to implement a political economy that deals with the evils produced by their combination. Its preeminent expression in American history was the short-lived work of the Freedmen's Bureau from 1865 to 1869, broadening economic and educational opportunity under the slogan "forty acres and a mule."

Individualized racial discrimination should be treated as a distinct evil, and criminalized. Active promotion of access to better schools, better jobs, and higher social position should be afforded on the basis of a "neutral principle": the entrapment of a group of people in a circumstance of disadvantage and exclusion from which they cannot escape by the readily available means of economic and political initiative. The fundamental criterion must therefore be class rather than race. It will nevertheless reach race by reaching class, without taint by the inversion of benefit and need, because of the racial bias in the composition of the underclass.

Race may nevertheless figure without imposing this taint. The combination of different sources of disadvantage – first among which are class and race – increases the likelihood that the disadvantage will prove hard to escape. That conjecture, however, must be tested against experience; and only insofar as it holds in fact should it apply as law.

If the reformation of the treatment of racial injustice, and of the relation between race and class, is the first great preliminary to a Left program for the

United States and in an American idiom, the second is the rethinking of how progressives should address the conflicting moral agendas in American society. At the turn of the twenty-first century the foremost fighting issue of the day was abortion, as a hundred years earlier it had been prohibition. It has become conventional to call these agendas traditionalist and modernist, religious and secular. In fact each of them expressed a response to contemporary experience, and each could be stated in secular as well as in religious form.

The decision by the progressives not only to espouse the modernist agenda, but to enforce it by federal power and federal law was a practical calamity. Together with the racial orthodoxy, it helped diminish the chances of winning the support of a supra-racial working-class majority for a progressive national project.

It was, however, not only a mistake in tactics; it was also a failure of vision. Both the contending agendas were deficient as bearers of the religion of humanity. One revealed the moral prejudices of a Christianity that had subordinated the heart to the rulebook, and that had struck a deal with cultural and social orders that it was the calling of a Christian to defy. The other carried the stain of a heartless narcissism and gratification, alien to the sacrificial impulse on which all hope for the divinization of humanity depends. If the Leftist had an interest, it was not to enforce one of these agendas against the other; it was to radicalize the conflict between them in the hope that from this contest something deeper and truer might result.

The means by which to accomplish both the tactical and the programmatic goal is to return to the states the decision concerning the issues in contest. The almost certain result would be divergence among the states in the relative weight they would give to each agenda, and the consequent deepening of the national debate. With respect to the star moral-agenda issue of the day, poor women who would need to travel from states forbidding abortion to those permitting it would be the greatest victims. The burden, however, could be lifted by the simple expedient of organizing to transport them to the permitting states, and paying for their transport. It is a small price to pay for the cutting of one of the Gordian knots that now threatens to strangle the progressive cause in America.

The heart of a Left agenda for the United States must be a proposal in political economy. The core concern, as in the reformation of European social democracy, should be to democratize the market economy. It cannot be belatedly to import into the United States the arrangements of a European social democracy that is now embarrassed on its home ground. As in the European setting, this democratizing project presupposes a mobilization of national resources for new productive initiatives: at the limit, a war economy without a war. Here as there a guiding aim must be readiness for innovation achieved by means that ensure socially inclusive empowerment rather than by devices that generalize insecurity and aggravate inequality. It is the only way to reverse the consequences of the hierarchical segmentation of the economy in the real circumstances of the rich North Atlantic countries.

The chief elements of this mobilization are: the raising of the tax take by reliance on taxes that are regressive in the short run but nevertheless progressive in overall effect by virtue of their place within a broader program; the forced increase of the level of domestic saving, especially through reforms to the private and public pension systems; and the creation of new linkages between private or public saving and production, both within and outside the capital markets as they are now organized. A brief word about each of these concerns will suffice to highlight the points at which the American circumstances deviate significantly from the European in the constraints they impose on the accomplishment of such goals.

No activist program of governmental initiative in economic empowerment can be carried out in the United States without a rise in the tax take. And no such rise in the tax take can take place without heavy reliance on the form of taxation – the transactions-oriented taxation of consumption in the form of the comprehensive flat-rate value-added tax – that is unequivocally regressive in its immediate effect. The attempt to increase overtly redistributive taxation elicits an economic and political reaction that overshadows and interrupts its vaunted progressive aims. The short-term acceptance of price–neutral regressive taxation, capable of delivering the greatest tax yield for the least economic disruption, can justify itself not only if it enables more redistributive social spending but also and above all if it forms – and is seen to form – an integral part of an effort to democratize economic and educational opportunity. In their attitudes to taxation the American progressives need to stop genuflecting to redistributive pieties that have served only to prejudice redistributive results. They cannot do so without braving the risks and the paradoxes inherent in transformative action.

Although no large country now saves less than the United States, none has been more successful in financing new enterprise. Yet in none is the relative disconnection between the trading of positions in the capital and equity markets and the effective financing of production more apparent. The measures for the broadening of economic opportunity on the supply side that are explored in the following paragraphs would have to be accompanied by efforts to expand the role of venture capital beyond the terrain in which it is accustomed to work. The principle of such an expansion is always the same: use the market when possible, and entities established by government but mimicking the market – or anticipating another broader and more pluralistic capital market than the one that now exists – when necessary.

If the realities of American economic relations to the rest of the world did not force an increase in the level of domestic saving, a project like the one I propose here would nevertheless require it. This increase could be achieved by forced mandatory saving through the public and private pension systems on a steeply progressive scale. It could be ensured as well by a tax that would give a progressive tilt to the indirect taxation of consumption: the sharply progressive taxation of individual consumption, falling on the difference between the total income and the invested saving of each taxpayer, and thus hitting what must always be the chief target of progressive taxation – the hierarchy of individual standards of living.

To democratize the market economy must mean much the same in the United States as it means in Europe and in other contemporary rich social democracies. It is a commitment requiring initiatives on both the supply and the demand sides of the economy.

The variety of instruments of economic vitality in the United States is such – with its longstanding decentralization of credit, its readiness for risk and novelty, its habits of practical ingenuity, and its absence of significant barriers to start-up business – that nothing short of the boldest supply-side initiatives would, by an apparent paradox, make a difference in this the most unequal of the advanced economies. That which in the European setting I defined as the maximum goal – to use the powers of government to propagate advanced experimentalist practices of production outside their favored and habitual terrain in capital, knowledge and technology-intensive sectors of the economy – should here be taken as the minimum one.

What the American federal and state governments did in the nineteenth century for the organization of what became the most efficient system of agricultural production in world history – helping to underwrite a system of cooperative competition among family farmers, forging instruments for risk management, and opening access to resources and markets – these tasks governments must now undertake on a larger scale and with a different focus. The scale must be the whole of the industrial and service economy. The focus must be the creation, through governmental and collective action, of functional equivalents to the preconditions of advanced experimentalist production and the propagation of the local organizational and technical innovations that have proved most successful.

Those equivalents are necessary because these pre-conditions are missing in much of even the most advanced economies. They include organizations that screen and enhance credit; that adapt advanced technology to more rudimentary conditions; that give people access to continuing education while they have jobs and re-skill them when they are between jobs; that provide instruments for the effective management of risk when such instruments are not made readily available by existing market institutions; and that support networks of cooperative competition enabling teams of technicians and entrepreneurs to pool resources and to realize economies of scale and scope. The diffusion of the most successful local practices is in turn most useful when it strengthens the links between advanced and backward sectors of the economy, and engages people in the habits and methods of permanent innovation and cooperative competition.

The agent of this institutional reshaping of the market economy cannot be a central bureaucracy guiding from on high. It must be a range of governmentally established and funded social and economic organizations that emulate the market, in competition with one another as well as with standard private businesses, with staffs rewarded for performance as measured by the very markets they help open up.

Their mission is not to regulate or to compensate. It

is to create markets for more people and in more ways. It is from the variety of their relations to the people and the firms with which they deal that one can hope for the eventual emergence of alternative regimes of property and contract. The market-oriented idea of free recombination will thus be generalized and radicalized by being imported into the institutional framework of the market itself. In its present dogmatic form it consigns the majority of working-class men and women to what has increasingly become a form of precarious busy work, sufficient to protect against poverty but not to empower and to enlighten. It therefore also condemns the would-be little Napoleon of the American dream to frustration and fantasy.

In the United States as in Europe, such progressive interventions on the supply side – less the regulation of the market than its reshaping – would have to be matched by progressive interventions on the demand side. However, rather than taking the form of monetary and fiscal boosts to popular consumption, this second order of initiatives would best address the position of labor. In no democracy, rich or poor, has the position of labor – its share of national income, its degree of internal segmentation, its level of organized power, influence, and security – degenerated more dramatically over the last forty years than in the United States. It is a circumstance not only unjust and disempowering in itself but also subversive of all other aspects of a program like the one advanced here. It destroys the link between the accumulation of wealth in society and the ability of the ordinary worker to enjoy the benefits of economic growth. Moreover, it arouses an impatient anxiety that is at least as likely to help the Right as it is likely to serve the Left.

To generalize the principle of sharing in the profits of firms; to strengthen the power of an organized minority of workers to represent the interests of the organized in the economic sectors in which they work while affording direct legal protection of temporary workers; to provide at public expense opportunities for lifelong education in generic capabilities as well as in job-specific skills; to spread, through public as well as private means, the most advanced, experimental practices of production, preventing their concentration in isolated economic vanguards; to subsidize through the tax system the private employment and on-the-job training of the poorest and least skilled workers; and to impose direct legal restraints on the aggravation of wage and benefit inequality within firms – all these are examples of instruments that, in their combined and successive consequences can help contain extreme disparities in the returns to labor and reverse the decline of the share of labor in national income.

The democratization of economic opportunity in the United States would achieve its full effect only within a broader program for the deepening of American democracy. This program must include the reorganization of the economic and institutional basis of voluntary action and the energizing of democratic politics.

No capacity has been more important to the success of the United States than the ability to cooperate; the antipathy of Americans to class privilege, maintained in the presence of a class structure whose force they are reluctant to acknowledge, and their faith in the power of ordinary men and women to make large problems give way to the cumulative effects of an endless flow of small solutions have helped them excel in the knack of working together under many different rules and in many different circumstances. The downward inflections of the late twentieth century, including as they did the weakening of voluntary association, have placed this great collective capacity in jeopardy.

The institutional fetishism that has always exercised so great an influence over American beliefs would have us suppose that the problem lies only in the spirit of association, not in its institutional vessel. There is, however, a problem with the vessel, and only a Left committed to institutional innovation can show how to solve it. Until they confront the inadequacies of the institutional setting of association, Americans will continue to call the spirit, and it will continue not to come.

The fiscal basis of voluntary action should be strengthened. One way to do so is to reserve part of the tax favor represented by the charitable deduction allowed to all philanthropic contributions. This reserved part should be channeled into public foundations, entirely independent of governmental influence and managed by people representative of different currents of opinion. Voluntary groups could apply to these public foundations for support as they now apply to private foundations. The rich would not be able to ride their hobbyhorses through private philanthropy without helping to open a space beyond plutocratic and governmental influence.

The social focus of voluntary action should be sharpened. No focus is more important than responsibility for taking care of those in need. The principle that every able-bodied adult should hold a position in the caring economy as well as in the production system creates an immediate challenge to civil society and to its capacity for self-organization. Society would need to organize, outside government and outside private business, to develop and apply this principle to best effect, in new forms of public service and community organization. It would be an expansion of the traditional American knack for cooperation for the sake of collective problem-solving.

The legal apparatus at the disposal of voluntary action may therefore also need to be broadened.

The traditional regime of contract and corporate law may not suffice. As an instrument of voluntary association, private law presupposes that the readiness to organize is already present. And public law sets what is done with private law within a mandatory framework, imposed from the top down according to a single formula.

The task of social law, neither private nor public, would be to incite the self-organization of society, outside both government and business, for the purpose of fulfilling responsibilities such as the responsibility of organizing people to take care of one another outside the family. For example, the law might establish a structure of neighborhood associations parallel to the structure of local government but completely independent of it. Thus, local society would be organized twice, within local government and outside it. Each of these forms of organization would bring pressure to bear against the other, neither duplicating its work nor accepting in its dealings with it a rigid division of labor.

Within such a program the reform of the basis of voluntary association would need to be complemented by the reorganization of the institutional basis of democratic politics. The cult of the Constitution is the supreme example of American institution worship. From it results the American preference for changing the Constitution by reinterpeting it rather than by amending it, as if any emergent vision of the political needs of the people would have to lie hidden within the constitutional scheme, waiting to be revealed by brazen oracles of the law.

The American constitutional order, however, confuses by design two distinct principles: one, liberal; the other, conservative. The liberal principle is that power be fragmented: divided among different branches of government and different parts of the federal State. The conservative principle is that a table of correspondences be established between the transformative reach of a political project and the severity of the constitutional obstacles its execution must overcome. The point of the conservative principle is to slow politics down, and to tighten the dependence of change upon crisis.

To Americans the liberal and the conservative principles seem naturally and necessarily connected. They are not. It is possible to keep the former while repudiating the latter. This goal could be achieved by combining two sets of reforms. One set would be designed to raise the level of organized, sustained popular engagement in politics. The other set would be calculated to resolve impasse between the political branches of government quickly and decisively, and to do so by involving the general electorate in the resolution of the deadlock.

This second set of reforms could include, for example, the use of comprehensive programmatic ple-biscites, preceded by national debate and mutually agreed by the President and the Congress. Such innovations could also provide for the right of either of the political branches, when faced with a program-matic impasse in its relation to the other branch, to call early elections. Although initiated by one branch, the early election would always be simultaneous for both branches. Thus, the branch to exercise the right would have to pay the price of the electoral risk. By means such as these, particularly if implemented in the context of reforms raising the level of popular political mobilization, the institutional logic of Madison's scheme would be reversed. From being a machine for the slowing down of politics, it would become a machine for its acceleration. In matters of institutional design, small differences can produce large effects.

The cult of the Constitution and the widespread failure to recognize any need to quicken the tempo of politics in the absence of national emergency would work together in the United States to leave any such proposal without supporters. The place to begin in the reformation of democratic politics in America is there-fore not a constitutional redesign favorable to the rapid resolution of impasse. It is the acceptance of reforms that would increase the level of civic engage-ment and education while diminishing plutocratic influence over politics: raising the temperature before quickening the tempo. Some such initiatives would provide for the public financing of campaigns. Others would broaden free access, on behalf of organized social movements as well as of political parties, to the means of mass electronic communication as a condition for the award of the public licenses under which the business of television and radio is conducted.

Seen as a whole, in the combination of all its parts, such a project of redirection and transformation for the United States may seem too all-encompassing and too ambitious to withstand the test of constraint in context. Yet it is composed of elements that are almost entirely familiar. Advance in some of its parts could go very far before hitting against the limits imposed by a failure to advance in others.

This program addresses a constituency that does not yet exist: a working-class majority able to transcend in its commitments racial and religious divisions. It does not, however, take the existence of such a constituency for granted. Its formulation in thought and its promotion in practice would help bring that constituency into existence. The project helps create the base; the base allows the project to go further. In all these respects it presents problems that are not uniquely American; they are typical of the difficulties to be faced by the Left in any contemporary society, richer or poorer.

In the United States as anywhere else such a project could come to life only in the setting of a larger contest over consciousness. In that struggle it would be necessary to challenge the American understatement of the room for institutional alternatives and the American exaggeration of the chances for private escape, through self-help and self-enhancement. Political parties and social movements are insufficient instruments in this prophetic work.

In quarreling over such beliefs we take the spirit of the nation as our object, given that the nation-state remains a privileged terrain for experiment with the common terms of life. The characteristic qualities of the American people are their energy, their ingenuity, their generosity, their practical good faith, their readiness to cooperate, and their sense that something is missing from their national and personal lives. This sense inspires their restless striving and their heart-sick longing. Their characteristic defects are their idolatrous attitude to their institutions, their failure fully to acknowledge the dependence of self-construction on social solidarity, their willingness to settle in social life for the circumstances of the middle distance, robbing them of solitude without affording them company, and their lack of imagination. They cannot realize more fully either their interests or their ideals without providing better occasions than they currently do for the cooperative skills and the sacrificial impulses on which all greatness depends.

Globalization and what to do about it

Such alternatives for richer and poorer countries require for their advancement a global order that does not suppress them by its very design. Globalization has now become the generic alibi for surrender: every progressive alternative is derided on the ground that the constraints of globalization make it impractical. The truth, however, is that, as the contrasting experiences of contemporary China and Latin America show, even the present global economic and political order allows for a broad range of effective response. Moreover, we have no reason to approach the established global economic and political regime on a take-it-or-leave-it basis. The question can never be only: how much globalization? It must also always be: what manner of globalization?

The overriding aim is a qualified pluralism: a world of democracies. The differences in form of organization and of experience in such a world should be limited only by the requirement that no society claiming to be free should make reform depend on crisis, or deny to the dissenting individuals and groups that may emerge within it the effective power as well as the formal right to challenge it. This power and this right will never be wholly secure unless the individual is free to escape the society and culture into which he was born. Greater freedom to cross national frontiers and work abroad is not only the most powerful equalizer of circumstance among nations. It provides individual liberty with a default safeguard.

The role of national differences in a world of democracies is to represent a form of moral specialization: humanity can develop its powers and possibilities only by developing them in different directions. A premise of such a qualified pluralism is that representative democracy, the market economy, and a free civil society lack a single natural and necessary form. They develop through renewal of the institutions that define them.

A reform of globalization will never be offered by an international elite of reformers to the grateful, well-behaved masses of ordinary men and women. It must be the result of a struggle rooted in what remains the most important setting of the search for alternatives: the nation-states and regional blocs of the world. For such a reform to be realized, many countries must take a direction that brings them into conflict with the established rules and formative compromises of the global order. The constraints imposed by the present order are unlikely to prevent any determined country from taking the first steps in the pursuit of alternatives like those I explore here. These constraints will nevertheless become intolerable as such alternatives are pushed further.

Today the societies with the greatest potential to be seats of resistance may be the continental developing countries – China, India, Russia, and Brazil. These countries combine within themselves the practical and spiritual resources with which to imagine themselves as different worlds. Their advantage as agents of world transformation, however, is no more than relative and circumstantial. Moreover, each of them has recently been inhibited, for different reasons, in its ability to make good on this potential for defiance. To succeed in their attempts at rebellion and reconstruction, they would need help not only from one another but also from Europeans and internationally minded Americans.

Reforms in the arrangements of the world political

and economic regime must then be demanded by nation-states that insist on reconciling their rebellious experiments with full engagement in that regime. The reforms would in turn facilitate the progress of the heresies. It is in this interplay between national deviation and global reconstruction that the best hope for humanity now lies.

The program of the progressives for the reform of globalization should include at least three elements: redesign of the global trading regime; redirection of the multilateral organizations – particularly the Bretton Woods institutions; and containment or transformation of the American ascendancy.

The emerging system of world trade is now organized on three principles, each of which should be radically revised. The first principle takes the maximization of free trade to be the commanding goal of the world trading regime. The almost unbroken record of dosage and selectivity in free trade that has accompanied the rise of all the richest contemporary economies is regarded by the ideologues of the present system as an archaic misdirection. Instead of such a qualified approach, there is an attempt to entrench as inflexible trade law what throughout most of modern history has been no more than a controversial and contested doctrine.

A corollary of the maximization of free trade is the minimization of opportunities to opt out of the general trade rules. The General Agreement on Tariffs and Trade was prodigal in such opportunities. The World Trade Organization regime to which it gave way has drastically restricted them.

The chief goal of the global trading regime should be to facilitate the coexistence of alternative development trajectories and experiences of civilization within the ample limits of a democratic pluralism. Free trade is a means, not an end. No open world economy will be secure that depends on the suppression of democratic experimentalism, including experimentation with the institutional arrangements that define both political democracy and the market economy.

A corollary of this contrasting principle is that countries should enjoy wide latitude in their ability to opt out of the general trading rules so long as such opt-outs are negotiated on the basis of corresponding loss of access to the markets of other countries. An opt-out may not be in the sole interest of the countries that exercise it; it may be in the interest of the whole world. Like the member states of the global order, the whole world has a stake in hedging its bets by encouraging more variety of national experience than this counterprinciple would allow if were not supplemented by opt-out rights.

The second principle of the present world trade regime is the effort to organize world trade on the basis of a particular, dogmatic view of how a market economy should be organized. The result is a drive to incorporate into the rules of the trading system the forms of private property and contract now established in the richest economies and to outlaw as prohibited subsidies a broad range of possible forms of coordination between government and private enterprise.

A market economy cannot create its own presuppositions, including its institutional presuppositions. From the standpoint of the abstract idea of a market it is entirely arbitrary where and how we draw the line between the permissible and the impermissible instances of association between the State and private firms. Nevertheless the confused ideas we so often mistake for economic orthodoxy regularly associate one particular way of drawing this line with both the nature of the market and the requirements of free trade. The narrower the room allowed to governmental engagement in the creation of new types of market – affording more opportunity to more people in more ways – the greater the likelihood that the distribution of comparative advantage in the world economy will appear to be a fact as natural, and as hard to change, as the distribution of climates.

The opposing principle on which the alternative should be based is a refusal to incorporate into the global trade regime the assumptions of any particular variant of the market economy, save such assumptions as may result from basic human rights. The applicable standard of such rights should evolve as humanity becomes less tolerant of oppression and according to the extent the global order turns into a world of democracies. This evolution should, for example, reflect pressure to universalize standards of occupational safety, to prohibit child labor, to guarantee the right to organize unions and to strike, and, more broadly, to ensure democratic participation in national life.

Within these limits, the trading system should not entrench one version of the accidental combination of rights we call property. Nor should it impose, in the name of the idea of intellectual property, the way of turning innovations into assets that the rich countries have come to favor. It should not outlaw as prohibited subsidies the use of governmental power to reshape markets as well as to overcome the inhibitions of relative backwardness. Market-making initiatives should not be confused with market-trumping allocations of resources.

The third principle on which the global trading regime rests is a selective understanding of what the idea of a free world economy means. A system is established under which capital is to be free to roam the world while labor remains imprisoned in the nation-state or in blocs of relatively homogeneous nation-states like the European Union. They call this selective unfreedom freedom.

The contrary principle should be affirmed that capital and labor gain together, in small cumulative steps, freedom to cross national frontiers. Nothing would contribute more to a rapid moderation of inequalities among nations than greater freedom of movement for labor. Nothing would go further toward accelerating a change that has for long, although unevenly, been happening in the world: the substitution of institutional and moral distinction – shared engagement in building a shared future – for generational succession as the basis of what a nation is.

To all the many problems that the strengthening of such a right would produce – in particular, the threat to the position of labor in the richer countries and the danger of reactionary backlash – the answer is always the same: to progress step by step. Temporary work permits must come before full social entitlements, and the right to join must be balanced by the power to exclude. The change of direction would nevertheless have tremendous impact on the character of the world order and on the nature of every state within it.

Reform of the global trading system should be accompanied by the reorientation of the multilateral organizations: in particular the original organizations of the Bretton Woods system – the International Monetary Fund and the World Bank. These organizations now serve as the long arms – harshly (the IMF) or softly (the World Bank) – of the program that the richer countries press on the poorer ones, and that the poorer ones accept only when they have been so improvident or so unlucky as to depend on the assistance of their would-be tutors and censors.

In a period in which many alternatives in development strategy and institutional order flourished these organizations might have reason to exert a contrasting pressure: to seek a basis of core common principles and commitments on which to establish an open global economy in a world of democracies. However, in a situation such as the one in which we now find ourselves – the dictatorship of no alternatives – their chief role must be to support the emergence of difference. They will be most useful to humanity if they act in contrarian fashion, seeking convergence when divergence prevails and divergence when convergence rules.

The principle should be established that insofar as these organizations have universal responsibilities they should have minimal powers. For example, the minimalist work of the IMF should be to help keep the world economy open in the face of occasional balance of payments crises and deep differences of orientation. Far from using trouble as an occasion to impose uniformity, it should help organize – or in the last resort, provide – short-term bridge loans or credit enhancements the better to support national experimentation.

To the extent, however, that the multilateral organizations are deeply involved – as public bankers, public venture capitalists, or public experts – in assisting and in helping to define national development strategies and national reform agendas, they should serve pluralism. The only sure way for them to serve pluralism is for them to become pluralistic themselves. In the exercise of these trajectory-shaping responsibilities, they should either be broken up into multiple organizations or transformed into shells or networks accommodating rival teams. Each of these multiple organizations or teams would place itself at the service of different strategies and agendas.

Such a scheme could be effectively implemented only if its financing were largely automatic. It might be funded, for example, by a worldwide surcharge on the most common and the most economically neutral tax in the world today: the comprehensive flat-rate value-added tax. If the world were wise and just enough to tolerate a modicum of redistribution, such a surcharge might be calculated at three or four rates, according to a country's per capita income. Call this tax the pluralism tax: a tax levied to help support the marriage of economic progress to institutional diversity.

Until a more genuine plurality of powers once again emerges in the world, neither the reform of the international trading system nor the reorientation of multilateral organizations will suffice to create a global order more hospitable to democratizing alternatives. For such a pluralism to prevail it is also necessary to contain the American ascendancy or to transform its character. At least since the Second World War every American government has struggled to subject the precarious framework of international organization to the ideological commitments and security concerns of the United States. Every American administration has stood behind the curtains of the international organizations and pulled the strings. For over a hundred years the unwavering goals of American foreign policy have been to exercise undisputed hegemony in the Western hemisphere and to prevent any other power from so consolidating its regional position in any other part of the world that it is then able to bid for global influence. Better American hegemony than any other that is now thinkable. But much better yet no hegemony at all. Better even – or especially – for the American people, who risk losing a republic to an empire.

The United States is a revolutionary power: its conception of its interests is as much ideological as it is practical. Its civilization represents a heretical variation on some of the central ideas of the West. Americans have wanted to exempt their own institutions from the experimentalist impulse that otherwise prevails in their culture. They have believed themselves to have discovered the formula of a free society, a formula to be revised only rarely and in the face of extreme pressure. They have thus frozen the dialectic between institutions or practices and ideals and interests that is indispensable to the improvement of society. At the same time they have given a central role to a conception of self-reliance that downplays our claims upon one another and that exaggerates the extent to which the individual, relying on himself, can make himself into a little king. Their conceptions of political democracy, of the market economy, and of a free civil society are faithful expressions of these beliefs.

All humanity has a stake in preventing this faith from being imposed, in the name of freedom, on the rest of the world, and in denying to its sponsors the prerogatives of Constantine. Only by circumscribing the force and by changing the nature of the American influence can we create a world situation more open to the national and international reforms that represent the best hope of a way forward today.

How can a broader pluralism of trajectories of development and experiences of civilization be reconciled with the fact of American predominance? To deny the fact of that predominance and to cling to the juridical fantasy of the equality of states is to renounce the work of answering this question.

Compare three traditions of international thought and practice in modern history: Metternichian, Wilsonian, and Bismarckian.

The Metternichian tradition has order as its formative commitment and the concert of great powers against efforts at subversion as its preferred method. Transforming present advantage into vested right, it seeks to bar the gates against revolution.

The defining aim of the Wilsonian tradition is to universalize national self-determination. However, it sees national self-determination as an instrument for the propagation of values and institutions closely identified with the great powers – or the great power – that supports the state system. It favors a pluralism of power, through its commitment to national self-determination. Yet it sees no incompatibility between such pluralism and its commitment to propagate the institutions and ideals of the sponsoring powers or power. Its principal method is international law and international organization, supplemented by wars that are also ideological crusades. Its program depends on the happy accident of coincidence between might and right; the rise of the United States to world power is the supposed providential fact on which its reasoning relies. It is therefore unable to admit any contradiction between the defense of this power and the interests of humanity.

The overriding concern of the Bismarckian tradition is to avoid the consolidation of any such hegemony, particularly its consolidation through war. It wants to prevent any of the great powers from crowding the others out, or from forcing them to choose between war and surrender. Abstracted from its original historical setting, it is defined both by its attachment to a plurality of centers of power and by its skepticism about the association between power and ideology. To achieve its ends, it seeks to draw great and lesser powers into shared understandings and practices of concerted action. Its preferred method is to concentrate on practices lying in a middle zone between force (exercised through war or threat of war) and law (anchored in ideology). From this fixation on the middle ground results one of its greatest strengths: its openness to correction in the light of experience and of changed circumstance.

The containment of the American hegemony in the interest of democratic pluralism requires a transposition and recombination of two of these three traditions. From the Wilsonian tradition we should take the commitment to national self-determination and human rights, freeing them from the institutional and ideological dogmatism that invites confusion between what one country preaches and what mankind needs. From the Bismarckian tradition we should take the commitment to a plurality of centers of power and the effort to advance this commitment through understandings among states, understandings articulated in a region midway between law and force. However, we should unburden this commitment to a plurality of powers from any reluctance to define moral and political limits to the national differences that should be tolerated in a world of democracies.

In this spirit, imagine a political-diplomatic initiative outside the relatively stultified United Nations system. Its relation to that system would be open-ended; to the extent it succeeded it would help bring the United Nations back to life. The basic partners in the initiative would be the internationalist current of opinion within the United States, the European Union, and some of the large developing countries (China, India, Russia, Brazil). The initiative would seek to establish a regime of relations between the United States and the middle-level powers with the following operating rules.

First, major issues of international security and reform are to be decided by a consensus among the partners. Consensus is defined as a marked preponderance of opinion among the United States, the European Union, and the continental developing countries. Democratic self-government is not a requirement for participation in this entente but neither is absence of progress toward democracy compatible with continuing engagement in its affairs.

Second, the partners of the United States in this entente acknowledge the fact of American ascendancy without affirming its legitimacy. The practical implication is that no threat to the vital security interests of the United States can be tolerated by the entente. Conversely, the United States serves as a co-guarantor of the multilateral regime.

Third, although at the limit the United States is free to act on its own understanding of its security interests, whenever it acts in defiance of the understanding of its partners in the entente, it pays a price. It leads them to draw closer together to circumscribe it. This ganging up of lesser powers against the United States is, however, the result that it has been the foremost goal of American policy to avoid. Thus, the regime benefits from a self-stabilizing mechanism.

Such a political–diplomatic construction represents an attempt to escape the dangerous contrast between the brute fact of American hegemony and the juridical fiction of equality of states. Deploying devices that are proto-legal rather than either legal or extra-legal, it has a vital attribute: it is capable of evolving.

At the heart of such a regime lies a bargain. Through the voices of the lesser powers the world recognizes the fact, not the right, of the American ascendancy. It does so in exchange for an advance toward global pluralism. Anxious to escape both the dangers of anarchy and the burdens of empire, the United States, in return, accepts a system that raises the price for unilateral American action undertaken in defiance of multilateral understanding.

Two conceptions of the Left

What does it mean to be a Leftist today? A preexisting idea must be realized in a new circumstance through a new project. The new project in turn requires the reinvention of the preexisting idea.

Two conceptions of the Left should now struggle for primacy. One expresses the orientation of institutionally conservative social democracy and of its continuing retreat from transformative ambition in richer as well as in poorer countries. The other animates, deepens, and generalizes a programmatic direction like the one outlined in these pages.

The first of these two conceptions prevails, although few of its votaries acknowledge it for what it is. It has two parts: only one of these parts is regularly made explicit; the other one usually remains in the shadows.

The part made explicit is the commitment to greater equality of resources and of life chances, to be achieved mainly through compensatory redistribution by tax and transfer. The main work of such redistribution today is to attenuate the income effects of the hierarchical segmentation of the economy; the primary concern is with inequality of income and of living standards. The apparent extremism of the commitment to greater equality coexists with the narrowness of the intended result – greater equality of income – and of the preferred means – retrospective correction through use of governmental transfers.

The part left in the shadows in this dominant conception of the Left is acceptance of the established institutional background of economic and political life. Experiments in institutional reshaping are associated with the calamitous political adventures of the twentieth century. The point is to sweeten what we no longer know how to rethink and to reshape. If there are great institutional changes to make, we do not know – according to this view – what they are. If we did know, we might nevertheless be powerless to bring them about and well advised to fear the dangers of any attempt to introduce them.

Many of the most influential political philosophies of the day theorize the combination of redistributive egalitarianism with institutional skepticism or conservatism. In so doing they confer a philosophical halo on social democracy. The philosophers agree for the most part about the end point: the rectification of classical liberalism by redistributive and institutionally conservative social democracy. They disagree only about the starting point: in what vocabulary is this pietistic and hopeless dogma best expressed, and on what assumptions is it best grounded. How could such window-dressing pass for thought?

It may seem strange that a redistributive egalitarianism, which when formulated abstractly may seem radical, should coexist with a craven acceptance of established arrangements. The apparent contradiction, however, reveals the real result: the unchallenged and unchanged institutional arrangements cut the theoretical egalitarianism down to size. The measure of economic equality that can in fact be brought about is the measure compatible with these arrangements. We know from historical experience that social entitlements work, but they work better to empower than to equalize. Insofar as they equalize, their effect is ancillary to such reforms as may broaden economic and educational opportunity.

The theoretical and extreme egalitarianism of this conception of the work of the Left, with its single-minded focus on material circumstance, serves as a consolation prize. We cannot become bigger; so let us become more equal. This substitution reverses the relation that should exist between the enlargement of human powers and the commitment to diminish extreme and entrenched inequalities, of circumstance as well as of opportunity. To enable everyone to enlarge those powers is our best reason to overcome these inequalities. We know we are doing little good, in exchange for certain harm, if our efforts to moderate the inequalities serve only to make it easier for us to bear the diminishment of our powers.

An alternative conception of what it means to be a Leftist replaces both elements of this fake egalitarianism. In the place of the institutional conservatism and skepticism it puts a succession of institutional changes and a practice of institutional experimentation. The point is to reject the choice between wholesale institutional change and humanization, through economic redistribution and legal idealization, of the established arrangements. The project that takes the place of this unacceptable choice is the democratization of the market, the deepening of democracy, and the empowerment of the individual. The practice that takes its place weakens the contrast between engagement in a world and action to change that world, so that we can better defy and transform while we engage.

The overriding goal to which this practice and this project are directed is to make us bigger, both individually and collectively, and to make us more equal, in circumstance as well as in opportunity, only insofar as inequality diminishes and confines us. The aim is less to humanize society than it is to divinize humanity: to bring us to ourselves by making ourselves more godlike.

The most primitive sense of this impulse to divinize humanity is the effort to equip our constructive energy, diminishing the contrast between the intensity of our longings and the paltriness in which we waste our lives. The poet Wordsworth described the problem in his pamphlet, "The Convention of Cintra," but he did not suggest the nature of the solution:

. . . [T]he passions of men (I mean, the soul of sensibility in the heart of man)—in all quarrels, in all contests, in all quests, in all delights, in all employments which are either sought by men or thrust upon them—do immeasurably transcend their objects. The true sorrow of humanity consists in this;—not that the mind of man fails; but that the course and demands of action and of life so rarely correspond with the dignity and intensity of human desires: and hence that, which is slow to languish, is too easily turned aside and abused.★

However, there is a solution − at least to some extent and in some sense. It requires a sustained set of

★ William Wordsworth, "The Convention of Cintra" in *The Prose Works of William Wordsworth*, edited by W.J.B. Owen and Jane Worthington Smyser, Oxford University Press, Oxford, 1974, volume 1, page 339.

changes in the organization of society as well as in the orientation of consciousness. Its benefits touch on our most fundamental interests. First, on our material interest in lifting the burden of poverty, drudgery, and infirmity weighing on human life; it lightens this burden by developing those forms of cooperation that are most hospitable to permanent innovation. Second, on our social interest in disengaging our cooperative relations from the restraints on predetermined social division and hierarchy. Third, on our moral interest in creating circumstances that enable us better to reconcile the conflicting requirements of self-construction: to live among others without surrendering to them our self-possession. Fourth, on our intellectual and spiritual interest in so arranging society and culture that we are better able to be both insiders and outsiders, and to engage without surrendering.

The enlargement of human powers, individual and collective, we should seek and prize is the combination of these four interests. The protagonists and beneficiaries are ordinary men and women rather than an elite of heroes, geniuses, and saints.

The ideal of equality plays a twofold role in such a conception: as a presupposition and as a practical requirement. As a presupposition equality means that we are all capable of becoming bigger and more god-like; the divisions within humanity are shallow and ephemeral. Particular nations or classes may pioneer insights, inventions, or arrangements that have value for all mankind. The particularity, however, will then belong to the plot rather than to the message.

As a practical requirement equality means avoiding extremes of privilege and deprivation: preventing the hereditary transmission of economic and educational advantage and disadvantage through the family from shaping decisively the life chances of individuals. It also means imposing limits on the benefits that will be allowed to accrue to individuals as a result of their inherited intellectual and physical endowments. How much and by what criteria? By no metric other than the evaluation – in the living circumstance – of the danger of entrapment in self-sustaining privilege, weighed against the benefits of flexibility, of opportunism, of free experiment in the project of democracy and divinization.

Such an evaluation will have all the controversial and paradoxical characteristics of action and intention in context. Any attempt to entrench a rigid equality of circumstance, or to adopt as a guiding principle the preference for whatever arrangements produce the greatest benefit to the least advantaged, will represent a wrong direction. Such an attempt perverts the effort that should rightly lie at the core of the program of the Left: the struggle to make the ordinary big by taking nothing for granted and by reshaping everything, only little by little and step by step.

There is one domain in which the combination of these impulses gains greatest significance and clarity: the reformation of the arrangements defining democracy. The institutional reimagination and remaking of democracy represents more than just another setting for experiment in the service of bigness; it reorganizes the domain of social life that most influences the terms on which we can reorganize all the other domains.

The project of developing a high-energy democracy is common to the proposals that the Left should espouse today for richer and poorer countries. It illustrates in its most general aspects the nature of the marriage between the two elements forming the second conception of Leftism – the practice of institutional experimentalism and the commitment to make ordinary people and ordinary experience greater by giving scope and equipment to its hidden intensity.

Democracy seen from this view is not only about popular self-government and its reconciliation with individual rights. Democracy is also about the permanent creation of the new. The collective practices for the permanent creation of the new are a point at which our most basic interests meet: our material interest in practical progress, our social interest in the subversion of predestination by class and culture, our moral interest in the reconciliation of the conflicting conditions of individual self-assertion, and our spiritual interest in engagement without surrender.

Five themes coalesce in the idea as well as in the institutional construction of such a democracy.

The first theme is the development of arrangements favoring a heightened, sustained, and organized level of popular engagement in politics. Politics with structural content, hospitable to the repeated practice of radical reform in the absence of crisis, must be high-temperature politics. To be fertile for the cause of democracy and for the program of the Left, high-temperature politics must be institutionalized rather than anti-institutional or extra-institutional. To this end, the political arrangements must favor whatever electoral regimes encourage the development of strong political parties, with well-defined programmatic profiles. It must assure political parties and organized social movements greater free access to the means of mass communication, especially television and radio. And it must weaken the influence of money in politics, for example by providing for the public financing of political campaigns and by restricting as much as possible the electoral use of private resources. In particular it must prohibit the use of private money to buy communication time.

The second theme is the bias toward rapid resolution of impasse among branches of governments, and the involvement of the electorate in its resolution. The point should be to turn constitutional government into a machine for the quickening of politics, not for its slowing down. It is a concern that carries particular force when the constitutional arrangements establish divided government, as they do under an American-style presidential regime. The solution is then to devise means that preserve the plebiscitarian potency of the direct election of a powerful president in a large federal State while equipping the regime with devices for the rapid breaking of deadlock on the basis of popular involvement: comprehensive programmatic plebiscites, agreed by both political branches, and early elections, called by either political branch. As they break impasse, such devices will also help raise the temperature level in national politics.

A pure parliamentary system, without separation of powers, may seem in no need of tools for impasse-breaking. Yet such a system may suffer from the functional equivalent to the programmed slowing down of politics that accompanies divided government: if society is very unevenly organized, the actual development of policy may degenerate into inconclusive bargaining among powerful organized interests. The remedy is to insist on initiatives that raise the level of organized political mobilization. It is to propagate through larger sections of society advanced practices of production and learning, not allowing them to remain arrested within isolated vanguards. And it is to establish social solidarity on the foundation of a universal responsibility to care for others.

The third theme is the determination to rescue people from such circumstances of entrenched disadvantage or exclusion as they may be unable to escape by the means of economic and political action that are readily available to them. This goal should be pursued both remedially and affirmatively.

Remedially the aim should be advanced by the establishment of a branch of government (under separation of powers) or of an agency of the State (under no such separation) equipped with both the practical resources and the political legitimacy to undertake a task for which the traditional Legislature, Executive, and Judiciary are ill suited. The task is to intervene in particular social organizations and practices that have become little citadels of despotism, and to reconstruct them.

Affirmatively the purpose should be served by assuring to every citizen a basic stake of resources as soon as the wealth of society, free from tolerance for extreme inequalities of circumstance as well as of opportunity, so allows. It is a matter of circumstance and experiment whether this minimum stake will take the form of a guaranteed minimum income or of a guaranteed social inheritance. Such an inheritance would be a social-endowment account, consisting of cashable resources on which an individual could draw at turning points in his life. The minimum guaranteed inheritance would vary upward according to the two countervailing criteria of special reward for demonstrated achievement and special compensation for demonstrated handicap.

As class privilege wanes in force, society must take care not to reinforce excessively those advantages that already result from the inequality of natural endowments. It should do so without embracing a dogmatic formula. Instead, it should multiply the range of recognized excellences, and subject to skeptical scrutiny the practical reasons to reward a particular excellence for sake of the supposed benefit to society (remembering that the expression of such an excellence is itself likely to be a source of both joy and power, requiring no further inducement). It must weigh such reason to reward as may survive scrutiny against the harm the aggravation of the preexisting inequality of endowments by the subsequent inequality of reward may do to the texture of social solidarity.

"Against the superior talents of another person there is no defense," wrote Goethe, "but love." The closest equivalent to love in the outer coldness of social life is the practical organization of the responsibility to care for others, nourished by the patient development of the ability to imagine other people's experience. To inform and inspire that ability must be one of the greatest concerns of education under democracy.

The fourth theme is the commitment to increase

opportunities for experimental deviation in particular places and sectors. No simple inverse relation holds between a strengthened ability for decisive options in national politics and an increased capacity for movement by particular localities or sectors in directions that diverge from such choices. We can have more of both, but only if we renew the institutional arrangements for the ordering of relations among the parts of a national state. It is in the general interest that as society goes down a certain path it should encourage the development of strong contrasts to the future it has provisionally chosen. In this way it hedges its bets.

To this end we should free ourselves from the prejudice that all sectors and localities must enjoy the same, constant power of experimental variation. When strong and broad support develops in a place or sector to opt out of some aspect of the general legal regime and to try something completely different, the experiment should be allowed, even if it imposes a cost on the collective whole. It should be permitted so long as the freedom to opt out is subject to later assessment and confirmation in national politics and so long as it is not used to establish new exclusions and disadvantages, steeled against effective challenge.

The fifth theme is the effort increasingly to combine features of representative and of direct democracy in even the largest states. Direct democracy does not supplant representative democracy; it enriches it. This fifth theme reinforces the first theme – the heightening of organized political mobilization. Moreover, it enhances the experience of agency that the Left should want to nurture in every part of social life.

The combination of representative and direct democracy can be promoted by the direct engagement of local communities in the formulation and implementation of local policy outside the structure of local government (for example, through a system of neighborhood associations); by organized popular participation in national and local decisions about the measure of experimental variation allowed in the organization of firms, in the regimes of contract and property and therefore in the terms on which capital is allocated and rewarded; and by the occasional use of comprehensive programmatic plebiscites preceded by extended national debates.

A high-energy democracy marked by these five ambitions will never emerge simply because a coterie of ideologists manages to persuade a nation of its virtues. It will be established only when people come to understand that they need such a democracy if they are to achieve the social and economic transformation they desire. They must want much more empowerment and opportunity than they now enjoy. They must understand that they cannot get them within the straitjacket of the established political institutions. No wonder that the need for a high-energy democratic politics will be most apparent in the unformed countries that suffer from extreme inequalities of opportunity and that bend under the weight of imported or imposed institutions. A larger life for the ordinary man and woman is what people must want, and find themselves denied.

Calculation and prophecy

The advancement of alternatives like these would amount to world revolution. It would not deliver world revolution in the form we have been accustomed by the prejudices of nineteenth- and twentieth-century thought to associate with the idea of revolution: sudden, violent, and total change. The transformation would be gradual, piecemeal, and generally peaceful. It would nevertheless be revolutionary on several counts. It would overthrow the dictatorship of no alternatives under which we now live. It would do so by breaking the limits of the restricted repertory of arrangements for the practical organization of society that is our most vivid experience of a collective fate. It would combine, as every revolutionary change does, a political and a religious transformation: a change both in the institutions under which we live and in the ideas about humanity that these institutions embody. The most important sign that we will have succeeded would be that we would have diminished the dependence of change on crisis.

That we have trouble in recognizing revolutionary alternatives for what they are is a direct consequence of the habit of misunderstanding directions as blueprints. A false dilemma paralyzes programmatic thought. A proposal that is distant from present ways of doing things is derided as interesting but utopian. A proposal that is close to established practice is dismissed as feasible but trivial. Lacking a credible conception of structural transformation, we fall back on a fake criterion of political realism: proximity to the existent. We fail to see what a programmatic argument rightly is: the vision of a direction and of the next steps. As we change in fact or reconsider in imagination our practices and arrangements, we revise as well our understanding of our interests and ideals. This thinking from the bottom up and from the inside up uncovers ambiguity in the midst of dogma and opportunity in the midst of constraint.

The idea of social alternatives remains caught within the slowly decaying corpse of the great evolutionary narratives of the last two hundred years of social thought with their now unbelievable ideas about indivisible systems succeeding one another by force of inexorable laws. Such narratives, however, have been followed by the rationalizing, humanizing, and escapist ways of thinking established in the contemporary social sciences and humanities. These tendencies of thought have denied us a basis on which to think programmatically. We should not wait to be provided with that basis by a transformation in theory; we should build as we go along, under the discipline of our efforts to define and to take the next steps.

A set of proposals like these is a rushing ahead – ahead not only of how contemporary societies are now organized but also of what our present understandings allow us with confidence to say. It must draw energy and authority from two distinct types of appeal: one, calculating; the other, visionary.

The calculating appeal is to recognized class and national interests. The two most powerful such interests are the petty-bourgeois demand for a condition of modest prosperity and independence, often identified with the traditional forms of small business or professional independence, and the universal desire to uphold and develop national distinction, usually identified with national sovereignty. People cannot realize these two sets of interests today, in richer or poorer countries, without changing the practices and institutions that have served, up to now, as their vehicles. They cannot refashion these vehicles, however, without revising their understanding of those interests.

The prophetic appeal is to a vision of unrealized human opportunity. It is not a prophecy that anyone has to invent. It is already expressed in the romantic popular culture embraced all over the world. The storylines of this culture are sentimental, formulaic variations on themes of the high romantic culture of the West, nowhere more fully articulated than in the European novel. The protagonists both find and develop themselves by struggling against their social fate. Even when they fail to change the situation, they succeed in changing themselves. They discover that they have infinities inside themselves; they raise themselves up to a bigger life. They are not so ordinary after all; not the hapless puppets they at first appeared to be.

In one direction this prophecy speaks to the desire for stuff: for consumption and material exuberance. Franklin Roosevelt said that if he could place one book in the hands of every Russian child it would be the Sears Roebuck catalogue. However, if accumulating things may be an alternative to connecting with people, the opportunities afforded by a higher material standard of living may also serve as a passage to experimentation with a broader range of human powers and possibilities.

In another direction this prophecy voices a higher hope. It is the hope that society will recognize and nourish the constructive genius of ordinary men and women; that, as a result, seemingly intractable problems will yield, one after another, to undaunted ingenuity; that the reform of society and culture will lift from our efforts at self development and cooperation the incubus of a rigid scheme of social hierarchy and division; and that none of us will therefore have to choose between surrender to subjugation and isolation from others, or between engaging with a particular world on its terms and keeping the last word, of judgment and resistance, for ourselves.

The basis of these hopes is an idea about ourselves: the idea that we are greater than all the particular social and cultural worlds we build and inhabit; that they are finite with respect to us, and that we are infinite with respect to them. There is always more in us – in each of us individually as well as in all of us collectively – than there can ever be in them.

No social order can provide a definitive home for the human spirit so understood. However, one order will be better than another if it diminishes the price of subjugation that we must pay to have access to one another. One order will be better than another if it multiplies opportunities for its own revision, thus attenuating the difference between acting within it, on its terms, and passing judgment on it from the outside, on our own terms. One order will be better than another if it enables us to shift the focus of lives away from the repeatable to that which does not yet lend itself to repetition: to the perpetual creation of the new. Not the humanization of society, but the divinization of humanity, is the message of this prophecy.

It is a message both enigmatic and impotent so long as it remains disconnected from the driving forces of society and bereft of ideas about the next steps to take. Possessed, however, of such connections and such ideas, its subversive and reconstructive capabilities become all but irresistible.

After the ideological and institutional adventures of the twentieth century, with their terrible record of oppression in the name of redemption, much of humanity may have reason to be wary of proposals to reorganize society. It may prefer to resign itself to small victories in the defense of old rights or in the achievement of new advantages. The discipline of ruling interests and ideas has allied itself with a skepticism that masquerades as realism, creating, all over the world, a semblance of closure.

This sense of an end to ideological and institutional contests is, however, an illusion fueled by a lack of imagination. The interdependencies of the world open up opportunities for reconstruction at the same time that they impose obstacles to straying from the prescribed path. The meaning of any national experiment that is identified as the flawed bearer of a powerful message about alternatives can now resonate around the world with sensational rapidity. Acts of defiance that seem impossible may, once practiced, seem inevitable.

For over two hundred years a vision of the ability of ordinary men and women to lift themselves up – to become not just richer and freer but also greater – has joined the savage contest of states, classes, and ideologies and the magnifying force of our mechanical and organizational inventions to set the whole world on fire. To our faithless eyes, unable to discern its glow in unfamiliar form, the flame may appear all but extinguished, or visible only as reaction, terror, and fantasy. It will nevertheless burn again, with a greater light. To what end our ideas and actions must now determine.

Index

ALSO FROM VERSO

False Necessity:
Anti-necessitarian social theory in
the service of radical democracy
Volume I of *Politics*
ROBERTO MANGABEIRA UNGER

Paperback   1 85984 331 X
$19/£14/$28CAN
792 pages • 6 X 9 inches

'Unger does not make moves in any game we know how to play ... His
book may someday make possible a new national romance ... It will help
the literate ... citizens of some country to see vistas where before they saw
only dangers ... see a hitherto undreamt-of national future.' *Richard Rorty*

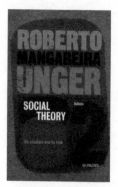

Social Theory:
Its situation and its task
Volume 2 of *Politics*
ROBERTO MANGABEIRA UNGER

Paperback   1 84467 515 7
$17/£12/$25CAN
256 pages • 6 X 9 inches

'*Politics* sours into the rarefied atmosphere of social theory, striving to realize
the highest aspirations of modernity itself...' *New York Times*

ALSO FROM VERSO

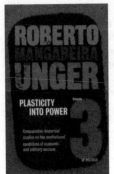

Plasticity into Power:
Comparative-historical studies on the institutional conditions of economic and military success
Volume 3 of *Politics*
ROBERTO MANGABEIRA UNGER

Paperback 1 84467 516 5
$17/£12/$25CAN
232 pages • 6 X 9 inches

'A philosophical mind out of the Third World turning the tables, to become synoptist and seer of the First.' *Perry Anderson*

Democracy Realized:
The progressive alternative
ROBERTO MANGABEIRA UNGER

Paperback 1 85984 009 4
$20/£12/$26CAN
310 pages • 6 X 9 inches

'Roberto Mangabeira Unger's project is breathtaking ... He is writing what may be the most powerful social theory of the second half of the century.' *Geoffrey Hawthorn*

ALSO FROM VERSO

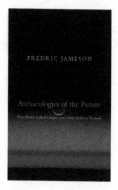

Archaeologies of the Future:
The Desire Called Utopia and
Other Science Fictions
FREDRIC JAMESON

Hardback 1 84467 033 3
$35/£20/$49CAN
480 pages • 6 x 9 inches

'There is no better example of a "Marxist scholastic" than Fredric Jameson.'
The Economist

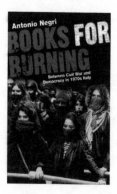

Books for Burning:
Between Civil War and Democracy in 1970s Italy
ANTONIO NEGRI

Edited by Timothy S Murphy
Translated by Arianna Bove, Ed Emery,
Timothy S Murphy and Francesco Novello

Paperback Original 1 84467 034 1
$25/£16/$35CAN
336 pages • 6 x 9 inches

PRAISE FOR *MULTITUDE*
'Far left thinking with clarity, measured reasoning and humour, major
accomplishments in and of themselves.' *Publishers Weekly*

ALSO FROM VERSO

Spectrum:
From Right to Left in the World of Ideas
PERRY ANDERSON

Hardback 1 85984 527 4
$29/£20/$40CAN
416 pages • 6 x 9 inches

PRAISE FOR *THE ORIGINS OF MODERNITY*
'... as lucid and patient an account of the idea of postmodernity as you could wish for.' *The Economist*

Critique of Everyday Life
Volume III: From Modernity to Modernism
HENRI LEFEBVRE

Translated by Gregory Elliott
Preface by Michel Trebitsch

Hardback 1 85984 590 8
$30/£16.99/$42CAN
208 pages • 6 x 9 inches

'A savage critique of consumerist society.' *Publishers Weekly*

'A brilliant example of how theory can be joined with experience to critique and better understand contemporary society.' *Frontlist*

MORE TITLES AVAILABLE FROM VERSO

Theodor Adorno
1 84467 500 9

In Search of Wagner
$18/£12/$25CAN

Louis Althusser
1 85984 282 8

Machiavelli and Us
$19/£13/$27CAN

Etienne Balibar
1 85984 267 4

Politics and the Other Scene
$20/£15/$29CAN

Jean Baudrillard
1 85984 462 6

Cool Memories IV, 1995–2000
$20/£13/$30CAN

Jean Baudrillard
1 85984 463 4

Passwords
$20/£13/$30CAN

Butler, Laclau, Žižek
1 85984 278 X

Contingency, Hegemony, Universality
$20/£15/$28CAN

Regis Debray
1 85984 589 4

God: An Itinerary
$35/£25/$52CAN

Ernesto Laclau
1 85984 651 3

On Populist Reason
$26/£15/$38CAN

Francisco Panizza, ed.
1 85984 489 8

Populism and the Mirror of Democracy
$25/£15/$36CAN

Jean-Paul Sartre
1 85984 485 5

Critique of Dialectical Reason
$23/£18/$34CAN

Susan Willis
1 84467 023 6

Portents of the Real: A Primer for Post-9/11 America
$23/£15.99/$36CAN

Ellen Meiksins Wood
1 84467 518 1

Empire of Capital
$15/£10/$22CAN

ALL VERSO TITLES ARE AVAILABLE FROM:

(USA) WW Norton **Tel:** 800-233-4830. Alternatively, please visit www.versobooks.com

(UK AND REST OF WORLD) Marston Book Services, Unit 160,
Milton Park, Abingdon, Oxon, OX14 4SD
Tel: +44 (0)1235 465500 / **Fax:** +44 (0)1235 465556 / **Email:**
direct.order@marston.co.uk

(AUSTRALIA AND NEW ZEALAND) Palgrave Macmillan, Levels 4 & 5,
627 Chapel Street, South Yarra, Victoria 3141
Tel: 1300 135 113 / **Fax:** 1300 135 103 / **Email:** palgrave@macmillan.com.au

Macmillan New Zealand, 6 Ride Way, Albany, Auckland
Tel: (09) 414 0350 / **Fax:** (09) 414 0351

Credit cards accepted

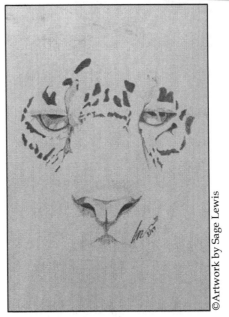

©Artwork by Sage Lewis

It's going to happen to all of us —

it's just a matter of which day and how.

While we're here, why not

slow down and pay attention?

There's a true gift in being completely present —

where angels play.

In between the sounds of life and death

lies a sacred space called peace.

Dip your heart into every single moment.

I double dog dare you!

~ Sage

WHERE ANGELS PLAY
What Other Angels Are Saying...

"Having personally witnessed Sage's unfolding and her connection with Great Spirit since the day she was born, I wholeheartedly recommend reading this book. You'll laugh and you'll cry, but most of all you'll be inspired to be a better YOU!"
- Stephanie Frank, Behavioral Analyst, Author, Educator

"I have been fortunate to have a front row seat in witnessing the love and compassion that flows from Sage's beautiful, intuitive heart - a heart that sees and feels deeper than most of us. I encourage you to follow her stories and let her lead you into the dance of life." **- James Schattauer**

"I was lucky 30 years ago to be Sage's therapist and she my client. As all of us who know Sage realize, she of course became my therapist and I her client. I have never had such fine therapy in my life! Sage has love and perfect kindness for every being on this planet and any planet. Thank you, Sage, for writing another spiritual book to help us along our journeys."
- Joan Elliott Gray, Certified Clinical Social Worker

"Sage is my Life Coach, Spiritual Guide, Animal Communicator and friend. Knowing her has truly changed my life!"
- Karen Carter

"Her name says it all; she is profoundly wise. I've learned more about life, love and myself through Sage's teachings. I'm so very grateful." **- Cheryl Filip**

"Sage was there for us when our dog, Christopher, transitioned. Her competence and wisdom on behalf of our four legged loved one was a huge comfort."
- Cynthia Winton-Henry, Cofounder of InterPlay

"Sage is an amazing intuitive spirit. She helped me understand the importance of communicating with our pets as they are naturally open to receiving us. My soul dog and I had a deeper connection during his transition, and without Sage, this would not have happened."
- Pam Gaber, CEO and Founder, Gabriel's Angels

"Sage is a wise teacher and a remarkable voice for the animals. When you learn from Sage, you open to your own wisdom. When you read Sage's words, you read her heart. When you sit with Sage, you sit with the miracle of all that you are."
- Lynn Baskfield, M.A., Equine Guided Coach and Educator; Owner, SpiritDance Coaching

"Sage Lewis is a remarkable human being who has dedicated her life to understanding the energy and power of love and its capacity to heal when we open up to it. Like many of us, Sage has experienced grief and loss. Her newest book, Where Angels Play, is a love story -- a story of love leading the way in whispers and whimpers." **- Rosie Senjem**

"Sage has been my coach, mentor, friend, colleague, and companion on this spirited journey called life and the one who always, I mean always, makes me laugh. Her stories of mystical experiences and the lessons she's learned never fail to inspire me, challenge me to go deeper, to choose love, and to remember joy." **- Laura D'Ambrosio**

"Sage and I have been on a journey of the soul for eight years, and at important points I like to celebrate with a haiku:

> Laughing crow flies on.
> Guiding me toward the light.
> What wonders await?"
- Rich Hardin

"DON'T GRIEVE.
ANYTHING YOU LOSE
COMES 'ROUND
IN ANOTHER FORM."
- RUMI

WHERE ANGELS PLAY

Life, Death and The Magic Beyond

SAGE LEWIS

Published by Dancing Porcupine LLC
303 East Gurley Street #121
Prescott, AZ 86301

©2019 by Sage Lewis
www.DancingPorcupine.com

First Edition: © June 2019
Printed in the United States of America

ISBN: 978-0-578-52929-5

FOR
ANGELS
EVERYWHERE.

THANK YOU.

WHERE ANGELS PLAY

Life, Death and The Magic Beyond

SAGE LEWIS

TABLE OF CONTENTS

INTRODUCTION

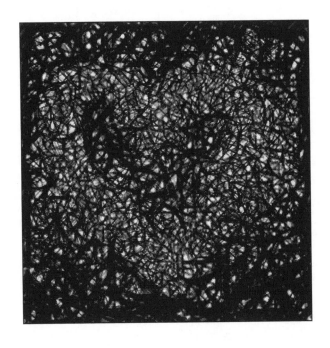

"PERHAPS THEY ARE NOT THE STARS,
BUT RATHER OPENINGS IN HEAVEN,
WHERE THE LOVE OF OUR LOST ONE
POURS THROUGH AND SHINES DOWN
UPON US TO LET US KNOW
THEIR SOULS ARE AT PEACE."
- ESKIMO LEGEND

"It's like a split – two parts that were together split apart – kind of like walking through a curtain but you leave some things behind that don't matter anymore.

Nothing hurts.
There's no fear.
No worry.
No anxiety.
No reactivity.

It's like all the good and easy parts are the only things that get through the curtain, and then everything feels easy. I remember fighting to get through the curtain because I could see it, and I couldn't get through it. It felt frustrating at times.

There were moments those last few weeks where I could feel things separating slowly in their own time, but then after a while I felt like I had some say in it. I decided at the end to rip off the Band Aid® fast and make things split apart quickly. I was done.

I had seen through the curtain many, many times but it was like I was leashed to a pole and couldn't get there.

Finally, the last release, when I fell apart from myself, was like I was colored dust running straight ahead and nothing was stopping me.

It was really cool." – Java

JAVA (11/2/00-3/2/13)

PREFACE

RUSHING INTO ACTION, YOU FAIL.
TRYING TO GRASP THINGS, YOU LOSE
THEM. FORCING A PROJECT TO
COMPLETION, YOU RUIN WHAT WAS
ALMOST RIPE. THEREFORE, THE
MASTER TAKES ACTION BY LETTING
THINGS TAKE THEIR COURSE.
- LAO TZU

It's so cold out that it feels like I can see my breath even before I even get outside. Getting in my car, I head toward the highway to make my way to the nearest food cooperative to get something organic that costs more money than something that's not. I can afford it. I work hard and earn a healthy living.

Setting my plump grocery bag in the passenger seat, I notice a bunch of bright yellow organic bananas peeking out to say hello. I tuck them back in, turn up the heat, and switch the dial over to public radio.

Nearing home, I spot a woman standing on the off ramp, wearing less than half of what I have on, and carrying a cardboard sign that's been handwritten with a black marker. "Need money for food – God bless" She's not wearing any mittens, but she's wearing a smile.

I have a decision to make. Will I choose love or will I choose fear? Love says, *Dig into your heart, Sage, and let her see into you.* Fear says, *I hope the light turns green so I don't have to stop and have eye contact.*

How we choose to live our lives is no different. In every moment, we have a choice whether to choose love or choose fear, and to act or react. Will we be held back by our inner critic or saboteurs - those nasty little voices that tell us we're not good enough, not rich enough, not pretty enough and so on? Or will we swat at those voices, persevere and move forward?

It takes courage to live a life of love – to move fears out of the way one by one, walk through them, kick them to the curb and stay true to your life purpose. Our purpose is to live from a place of essence – pure spirit.

Who are you when nobody's looking? Who are you when everyone's looking? Are you living your life from essence or are you trudging through your days with an inner critic on your shoulder? What would your life be like if you swatted all those inner critics away and lived from love? What are you waiting for?

As I dug deeper into my heart, I smiled back at the woman on the off ramp, reached into my grocery bag and grabbed an organic banana. Rolling down the window, I reached out and shared a spirit-to-spirit glance that I'll never forget with a woman I probably won't ever see again. It was love.

In one single moment she shared her entire essence with me. We were two strangers living very different lives in that moment, yet there was no barrier between us because we truly saw one another. Grasping the organic banana in her mittenless hand, she raised it up to the sky like the Statue of Liberty and squealed with exuberance at the top of her frostbitten lungs. "GOD BLESS CALCIUM!!" she yelled up to the sky, as her smile etched itself forever in my heart.

Potassium. Calcium. Love.

Same thing.

This is a true story of life, death and the magic beyond. If you're freaked out about dying (or living), then quickly shut this book right now, pass it along, and make it easy on yourself. If you've made it to this sentence, keep going.

I have enough gray hair to remind me of the life that's passed before me – a life filled with joy, despair, delight, apathy, ecstasy and every other color of the rainbow. I have lived an amazingly colorful life, had a number of glimpses of death, and have delved into the glorious playground of the magic beyond.

When I felt my grandmother's hand on my chest the week after she died, I felt curious, frightened and comforted. She shared a vision with me that same night during my dreamtime - showing me some stitching on a familiar apron that she had worn in the past. I didn't understand, and I didn't know where to go with it, so I shut it out.

When my father showed up at the foot of my bed the night after he died, I held it inside and wondered if it was real. When the animals started talking to me, I thought I was nuts. For years I dove deep into the unseen - questioning, wondering, and most of all, feeling alone. Not everyone sees, hears, feels, smells and tastes the unseen, but I was connecting deeply with all that magical place where angels play. I'm not alone.

Over 50 million people have telepathic communications with the other side. I've been told that what we need in order to communicate to the animals, plants, trees, rocks, stars, moon, ocean, loved ones, etc are three things. 1) Believe it's possible. 2) Have a desire to communicate with other beings. 3) Trust.

Trusting takes the longest. I've been on this road of telepathic communication since the early 90s when I first tried to "listen" to my greyhounds after reading a lovely book about animal communication. When it didn't work easily and immediately for me, I gave up. Years later, it happened when I stopped trying and surrendered. That's usually how things go.

I have learned to slow down to the place of holding still and paying attention, because that's where the whispers show up. When I heard my dog, Java, walk up the stairs the night *after* she died, I fully trusted.

Our lives are filled with magical and mystical experiences. Sometimes we notice, and other times we forget. May this story remind you of what you've forgotten along the way, and guide you back home to that glorious place where angels play. Tag, you're it!

SAGE & REGGAE

ACKNOWLEDGEMENTS

"LIFE IS EITHER
A DARING ADVENTURE
OR NOTHING."
- HELEN KELLER

This book has been in the works since a few weeks after my dog, Java, died a natural death at home after months of heartwrenching and heartwarming hospice. Her death ignited life. Java had fans worldwide asking when the sequel was coming out about her life, her aging and her death. Thank you to everyone who has asked. You lit a fire in me to write again and to love even more deeply.

Thank you to my soul dog, Java, for inspiring so many through your incredibly exuberant life, your graceful aging, your dignified death and your wisdom and antics from the afterlife. Thank you for coming to me, staying with me, allowing yourself to let go of your last breath in my arms, and for continuing to come to me in a variety of wonderful ways from the other side. You will always be a part of me.

To our sweet, sweet dog, Reggae. Thank you for showing me that it is possible to love again, and to love even more deeply. You are an absolute delight in my life, and I cherish every moment I have with you. Thank you for showing me that there are balls to be found on every walk if we pay attention and that everything has life – even sticks, water and seemingly dead tennis balls that are half chewed and buried. I love you more than I thought I ever could.

To my animal guides and teachers in the spirit realm. You know who you are, and you help me to know who I am. Thank you for showing up so completely and clearly – over and over and over again. I am deeply humbled and eternally grateful.

To all of my dear friends, family and human and animal clients along the way. You have helped me to become a better person.

To my father, Michael Lewis, my former husband, Gerard Brillowski, and my grandmother, Fern Anderson. Thank you for helping me become more of who I am, and for coming to me so sweetly and gently in the moments preceding and following your deaths. Each one of you has helped me in your own unique way to realize that there is more out there than what we can see. Thank you for inspiring me to trust myself enough to support others in connecting with their deceased loved ones, and for continuing to show up.

Dad, thank you for helping me realize that it's never a bad idea to drive five hours just to see the sunset at the Grand Canyon, and to go after every single thing I want in life. You have taught me to never give up. Gerard, thank you for teaching me compassion for alcoholism, and igniting my inner drummer. Your light shines inside of me, and I'm grateful. Grandma Fern, thank you for reminding me over and over that I'm a precious being, and that good cookies don't burn.

To my beloved Mom, Karen Lewis. Thank you for allowing me to hold your hand through my entire life, and through your incredibly beautiful and sacred death. Thank you for coming through to me so clearly the months before your death, for gifting me a poem during my dreamtime the night before you died and for continuing to show up from the afterlife in beautiful and comical ways. You have taught me the value of living one day at a time, the power of will, the incredible power of motherhood and that smiling is all it takes to make a friend.

To my sister, Stephanie Frank. You have inspired me beyond words. Your resiliency is palpable, and your love and connection are necessary for me to thrive in this world. We are soul twins who were born at separate times, and I adore you so much. I will always look up to you from wherever I am. Always.

And to my very patient, understanding, creative, hilarious, deep diving husband, James Schattauer. Thank you for exploring life, death and the magic beyond alongside me - day in and day out - no matter what. I love you so, so completely.

©Artwork by Sage Lewis

"WE ARE LIKE STARS –
STARS IN THE SKY.
THE DARKER THE NIGHT,
THE BRIGHTER
WE WILL SHINE."
- DAVID NEWMAN

XXVI

Chapter One

BLUE STAR WOMAN

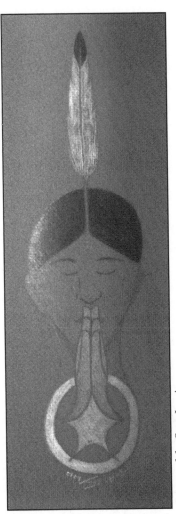

Stars shine. That's what we do. As much as we try to blend into the world around us, our light shines like high beams on the highway – making it uncomfortable at times for oncoming traffic. We just can't help it. Beams of brilliance pour from every cell in our bodies – reminding us of our greatness, our spirit, our home in the cosmos. We shine so brightly, and then begins the journey we call life.

I am a Star Being – a person whose source of entry into this world came blasting through an infinite ball of fire in the sky however many gazillion years ago. For me it seems normal to be made of stars. They sparkle no matter what's happening, and they feel like home.

I remember lying in bed when I was a kid – thinking about the Earth and how it seemed like a snow globe with a rounded top that was filled up with a bunch of things inside that you could shake up and watch settle. I could never figure out how we didn't fall off the edges if the Earth really *was* round. Sometimes I still can't comprehend it. As a highly sensitive person, it makes total sense that living on a spinning sphere can cause some internal upset.

For as long as I can remember, I've looked up – toward the sky, toward the sun, the moon, the stars – toward that feeling inside that I call home. I have reached for the stars - literally and figuratively - my whole life, and never really felt a need to explore more about it. For some reason, there was always a sense or knowing that the stars felt familiar. Like family.

When I was a little girl, I was completely convu.
that the night sky was created by a dark rooftop over
the rest of the planet – kind of like an indoor football
stadium with holes poked in it where the light could
shine through. I used to lie on the grass in our backyard
on many summer nights and just look up – pointing at
one bright star that I knew from wherever I was.

Sirius. The Dog Star. Home.

"WE'RE ALL HERE TO WALK

EACH OTHER HOME."

- RAM DASS

For my 40th birthday, I decided to give myself the
gift of a five-day spiritual immersion into shamanism
at Omega Institute in Rhinebeck, New York. Hank
Wesselman (www.SharedWisdom.com) was giving
his Visionseeker 3 training, and after reading his
Spiritwalker series of books it was time for me to dive
in heart first.

A pilgrimage of sorts, I was ready to learn more
about who I was and where I wanted to go. So, I
boarded a plane and headed East. After a plane, train
and taxi ride, I found myself in a gorgeous setting that
was ripe for spiritual growth.

Morning yoga was followed by a vegetarian breakfast and then I headed into the woods with 30 other spirit seekers to bang on a drum and to journey into non-ordinary reality for a few hours. Then a mid-day break for a dance class, more vegetarian food, more drumming and journeying, more food, more journeying and lots and lots of dreaming before repeating it all again the next day for 10 hours. This non-ordinary reality quest went on for five solid days, and there was nothing ordinary about it.

What that means in everyday language is that I was trying to find myself. My method of choice to come home was using the shamanic drum journey to connect deeply on a spiritual level with teachers and guides in the spirit realm. The job of those teachers and guides was to help me gain direct revelation, to find guidance, direction, balance, and harmony. I was hooked.

I had gone through a divorce seven years prior, had moved to a new state for a new love and then watched that relationship change form very quickly. I was on a journey. Literally.

Shamanism is the oldest spiritual practice dating back to 50,000 years ago in Siberia. The word shaman means "he or she who sees with the heart." There are medicine men and women in every culture who use the sound of the drumbeat, rattle (or singing, breathwork, dancing, plant medicine) to go into a deep Theta brainwave state or trance in order to connect with Divine guidance. The work of the shaman or shamanic practitioner is to help restore harmony within themselves, others and the planet around them.

There's no sign-up sheet to become a shaman. And, honestly, if there was one, I don't think anyone would sign up. It's hard, hard work. People are either born into shamanism through indigenous culture, are appointed by an indigenous family member or tribal member as a shaman, or are chosen through near death experience/s.

My story is the latter – a head on car accident on a crystal-clear starry night that became a catalyst for deep spiritual awakening and healing through a near death and out of body experience. After facing what I knew to be my Higher Power, I knew there was something more out there that was guiding me forward and I was curious.

"WHAT DOESN'T KILL US
MAKES US STRONGER."
- FRIEDRICH NIETZSCHE

Mother Earth resonates at the same level of hertz that the drum creates during a shamanic journey. You've heard of the heartbeat of Mother Earth? When we go into a Theta brainwave state, we are in complete coherence with the pure spirit of Gaia – the Great Mother. No wonder it feels so amazing to be connected with nature during a drum journey. And just being in nature creates oxytocin (the love chemical) which allows us to relax and feel blissful. Who wouldn't want to connect with your inner la-la-land!?

Having begun my spiritual practices in shamanism many years prior after the car accident in 2000, I strapped my drum to my back during the five-day training and off I went into the woods to sit in a huge yurt surrounded by the sights, sounds and smells of nature.

One by one, the journeys got deeper and deeper – diving into where souls are created, the Akashic records and connecting with a star to find out what you could about the star. Connecting with a star? I was so excited about the possibility of connecting with a star that I don't really remember the instructions.

As the drumbeat began, I found myself moving into an altered state very quickly. Soon after, a large ball of blue and green energy undulated in my mind's eye and I saw a dolphin move through my virtual landscape. Far off in the distance, a star started to show itself and I heard a voice say to me,

"You are the granddaughter of this star."

I asked for the name of the star and heard Cyon and then saw Sirius – the Dog Star who was my teacher, guide and friend in the night sky ever since those days of lying on the grass in the backyard when I was little.

As the drumbeat continued, I found myself deepening into the journey, and feeling weightlessness in my body. After a short while, I couldn't feel my body, as I became the star, become the dolphin and become the ball of blue green undulating energy.

With the next exhale, I began to hear the callback beat – bringing me back into my body, back onto Earth, back into the yurt out in the woods at the retreat center, and back to the reality that I had just left to go star searching.

Where had I gone? What had I seen and experienced? I was curious and yet there was also a sense of complete peace and knowing.

Our teacher, Hank, began to ask the students if anyone would like to share their journey with the rest of the room. As somewhat of a newbie, I decided to stay quiet and listen as people shared their mystical experiences one by one. My journey seemed simple and concise in comparison, and really not much to share so I kept quiet. Well, I kept quiet until I heard Hank speak what felt like directly to my soul.

He shared that the Dogon people of Africa believe that the Star Beings came here on the backs of whales and dolphins. These Star Beings come from dual stars – two colors mixed together. Star Beings are people who were sent to this world to feel deeply and to help others feel deeply as well. They are very sensitive beings and are often told that they are overly sensitive.

They have trouble with violence and seldom watch the news, and they shine.

My jaw dropped and my heart swelled. Most of my life I had felt like a misfit. I had been told I was overly sensitive, overly emotional, and I wondered why I couldn't be around violence, the news or anything that was upsetting to me. At the same time, I have been stopped by complete strangers on multiple occasions to have them share with me that I sparkle, I shine, and that I have beautiful eyes – eyes that were blue when I was born and turned green when I was five. Yep, blue and green – just like the star in my journey.

After everyone filed out of the yurt, I waited for a private moment with Hank and then I approached him to tell him about my journey.

"I've been waiting for someone like you. You have just affirmed what I have been told." He said with a sly grin peeking through his grey beard.

Now two jaws were dropped.

As I headed back to my cabin, I felt more like myself than I ever had and fell soundly asleep that night feeling like I had aligned fully with my true North. I had come home.

The next morning, I headed to the internet café to see if I could find some information about the star, Cyon, that showed up in my journey. I had never heard of it, but trusted what had come in my vision, and I trusted that my favorite star, Sirius, would guide me.

I have learned that a good shamanic journey leads to another journey, another journey, another journey. Wow, was I on a journey!

As I narrowed down my search, I noticed myself holding my breath and my eyes fell open in a state of amazement. Before me in real life internet images was the star Procyon – a small star that found its place in the night sky right next to my favorite star, Sirius. Procyon (Before the Dog) was a double colored star, just like the Dogon people of Africa had talked about, and had been in existence since before Sirius came into view. No wonder I've spent my entire life looking up!

A few hours later, I found myself back in the yurt, banging on a drum after lunch with a circle of 30 others and going deep into trance again. With each drumbeat, I fell deeper and deeper into myself and closer and closer to my connection with all that existed.

Shamanic journeying has been a spiritual practice of mine for longer than I have been doing it in real life. It's a practice that has felt like home since the first time I returned to it - the year I had my first out of body and near-death experience during my car accident.

There's an alignment that happens when the body, mind and spirit all come into a place that feels like one. For me, it happens when I allow myself to go into this journeying state to connect with the Great Mother,

Great Spirit, the plants, animals, trees, rocks, mountains, stars and all that exists and has existed. It's the place that is between the places and the place that is everything.

So, with the drums becoming louder and louder, and stronger and stronger, I found myself going deeper and deeper into a trancelike state. Behind me, I felt a strong presence and saw a man in my mind's eye who was at least 7 feet tall and wearing a white head dress and full regalia. His energy was strong and powerful, and I could tell he was there as a teacher for me as he held his energy strongly behind to hold me up. I found myself turning around to see who was there, but when I turned, there was nobody to be seen other than the unseen that I was feeling and knowing.

Drums continued to rise in ecstatic thunder as the Chief behind me told me to look in front of me. With eyes closed and hairs standing on end, I saw a very clear vision before me of a woman staring straight into every part of my soul. She had long black hair parted down the middle and one single, thin braid down her back. Her chocolate brown skin and dark brown eyes were an elixir of gentleness and power, and she stood at least 8" short of my 5'10" frame.

Her soft gaze went into mine, and mine into hers as we stood looking through one another until we became one. The drums thundered wildly as the Lakota Chief held me up from behind – the white feathers on his head dress bouncing in ecstasy, as I heard the cry of medicine songs surround me with healing and familiarity.

Focusing my energy forward again, I heard the Native American woman in front of me speak as clearly as the star I had come from.

"You're Blue Star Woman." She spoke softly with reverence and humility.

"Yes. I AM." I replied.

Chapter Two

DANCING WITH LIFE

"LIFE IS WHAT HAPPENS
WHILE WE'RE BUSY
MAKING OTHER PLANS."
- JOHN LENNON

Light attracts light. It also allows us to find our way in the darkness. And, just as the dark of night can feel unsettling and scary, so can our dark night/s of the soul. Our work is to recognize and find compassion for both the light and dark within ourselves and others, and to deepen our practice of feeding the light and moving through and releasing the dark. Easier said than done sometimes.

Walking the planet as Blue Star Woman felt like a secret – like I was coming out of the darkness and into the light and nobody knew except me. Kind of similar to when it's your birthday and nobody really knows unless you tell them. That feels like a secret, too.

For such a long time I didn't really know who I was, and now that I had a name and a location for my place of origin, I moved more fully into my power. I felt alive, and for the first time I felt fully accepted and whole. I felt like I was more in my true essence than I had ever chosen to allow before. I was sparkling.

In the past, I mostly fought with myself – feeling an array of frustration and that's about it. More like an explosion rather than a sparkle. In essence, I was numb to what I was truly feeling. When I felt sad, I showed frustration. When I felt angry, I showed frustration. When I felt confused, I showed frustration. When I felt frustrated….you get the idea.

Joy seemed like the only feeling that was real, and yet at the same time I can remember feeling afraid that it would get taken away so I downplayed it.

Having grown up in a functioning dysfunctional family, I became aware at an early age that expressing emotions was not the norm for kids in families like ours. It took me many years to figure out how to crack the loyalty code:

DON'T TALK.

DON'T TRUST.

DON'T FEEL.

"Let it roll off your back." and, "It's not worth crying about." were phrases I heard many times as a child. But what happens if you *aren't* able to let it roll off your back? And what if whatever I was crying about *did* feel worth crying about? As a Cancer, I cry easily about anything, so can you imagine how confusing that was as a child? What happened was that I became funny at a very early age. My humor diffused almost anything in our family, and yet it was a coping mechanism for what was being unaddressed.

My parents were kind, extremely funny and very generous and loving, and yet there was an undertow of alcoholism that went unaddressed for most of my life. It was completely reasonable to be happy, yet anger, fear and sadness were not as supported. Add on top of that being a Cancer Sun with a Pisces Moon, Gemini Rising, a Star Being and a highly sensitive person. I was my own rainbow.

I remember the first time I owned my anger, fear and sadness as an adult through working with a wonderful therapist when I was around 32 years old. Through creative visualization, she took me deep inside the colors, shapes, sounds and textures of all of the emotions I had been unable to connect with up until that time. My first image of anger was red, yellow and orange – like a lava lamp of fire – and it sounded like my Dad's voice. Low. Loud. Direct. Booming. Hot.

When I crawled inside of the anger blob, it was warm and gooey, and not scary at all. In fact, there was a comfort of being truly inside the anger rather than *being* the anger. I felt surrounded and supported and felt completely at peace around anger. That's a big feat. As women, we are not taught to be angry unless we want to be called a bitch or be judged as irrational. But anger has a wonderful fuel of its own. It helps us to realize what really matters and what's worth fighting for. Anger is passion without a rock on the balloon.

When I moved on to the visualization with sadness, it was very simple. I saw a watercolor painting of blues, purples and greens and then I *became* the watercolor. Melancholy. Sad. Tears. Release. Very easy for a highly sensitive, sappy Cancer. Next!

On to fear….

When I first saw the image of what fear looked like it seemed insurmountable. There before me was a huge steel ball with spikes coming out of it – huge like the size of a house huge. Behind it was a glorious clear blue sky which felt incredibly confusing.

My brilliant therapist told me to go inside of that huge steel spiked ball of fear, and I felt my resistance. In reality, I told her that it was impossible to get inside of the fear. As any good therapist or coach might respond to the word "impossible", she challenged me and told me to get inside the ball of fear however I possibly could. So, I did.

Finding my spiritual welding mask and a big torch, I seared my way through the metal as if it were a big ball of butter. Within no time, the larger than life steel spiked ball was cut in half and fell to its death. What came next changed the course of my emotional life.

The ball of fear was completely empty inside.

Nothing.
Kaput.
No fear.
Fearless.

I felt kind of disappointed when there was nothing inside the steel ball because I had made fear out to be some huge gremlin that was in charge of my entire life. Now what? It's like opening a box of Cracker Jacks® and you dig and dig but there's no prize. In actuality, the prize of receiving nothingness was that now I had the courage and strength to be in charge of my own life and to take responsibility and make choices rather than allowing fear to rule my choices. Thank you, fear.

©Artwork by Sage Lewis

An old Cherokee is teaching

his grandson about life:

"A fight is going on inside me," he said to the boy.

"It is a terrible fight and it is between two wolves:

One is evil – he is anger, envy, sorrow, regret,

greed, arrogance, self-pity, guilt, resentment,

inferiority, lies, false pride, superiority, and ego."

He continued, "The other is good – he is joy, peace,

love, hope, serenity, humility, kindness, benevolence,

empathy, generosity, truth, compassion, and faith.

The same fight is going on inside you –

and inside every other person, too."

The grandson thought about it for a minute and then

asked his grandfather: "Which wolf will win?"

The old Cherokee simply replied,

"The one you feed."

Throughout my life, I've fed both wolves and noticed the outcome. When I feed the wolf of darkness, fear, anger, sadness, judgement, rage and hatred, I create more of the same. And when I feed the wolf of light, love, peace, kindness and joy, well, the result is absolutely magnificent.

Light creates light. Dark creates dark. There's a thing called mirror neurons where we take on the emotions of those around us. That's why it's so hard to be unhappy around happy people, and so hard to be happy around unhappy people. The brain and heart are affected as are all the cells in the body.

Dr. Bruce Lipton shares in his book, *Biology of Belief*, that every thought, feeling, belief and emotion goes out into the quantum field. We create our reality in every moment by what we think, feel and believe. Since the Universe, God, Great Spirit is always listening on some level, we get exactly what we say we want and what say we don't want.

Gregg Braden writes in his book, *Secrets of the Lost Mode of Prayer*, that our DNA is affected by our thoughts, beliefs and feelings, and also that the DNA of any living beings within 50 feet of those thoughts, feelings and beliefs are also affected. That means that when I choose to think, feel or believe from a place of fear, I'm creating fear in the cells of any living being within fifty feet of me. That's a lot of humility and responsibility.

In his book, *Messages from Water*, Dr. Masuru Emoto shows the correlation between what words we choose to say or think and how they affect the molecular structure of water crystals. Love creates a lovely image and fear creates a not so lovely image. The list goes on and on. What we say, how we act, who we're being – it all has an immense impact on our health, other beings and the health of the planet.

We have a very important job to do while we're here on Earth School.

Choose love, no matter what.

IT'S BETTER TO LIGHT A CANDLE
THAN TO CURSE THE DARKNESS.
– T.S. ELLIOT

My Mom always told me that there will be one dog in your life who is like no other. Java was that once in a lifetime dog. She came in with a bang, lived with a bang, and exited with a bang. Whenever she appears through a visit from the afterlife, she shows up with an even bigger bang that's like a brightly lit candle in the darkness. Java was a big bang of a boom – fiery, joyful, powerful, intelligent and passionate. She was a dog who went after what she wanted and lived every single moment to its fullest – even up to her last exhale.

When Java and I first met, there was an immediate soul connection between us. It took many years for me to find out, but Java and I came from stars that were right next to each other in the night sky. She was from the star, Sirius (The Dog Star), which is the next-door neighbor in star neighborhoods to my star of origin, Procyon (Before the Dog).

Java and I danced on the planet together like stars glimmer brightly on a clear night. We sparkled, exploded, laughed together, shared secrets, played ferociously and shined a very bright light on one another for many years. Our relationship shined a light on the bigger issues we had to overcome karmically – reactivity, fear, leadership, self-esteem, letting go, trust, faith – just to name a few. And, just as the whales and dolphins had their connection to the stars and all that shined, both Java and I had our own connection with the whales and dolphins, too.

Stars captivate, explode, shoot and create wonder. They make us stop in our tracks to imagine and dream about what has been and what is to come. When we look up, we look out into the expansiveness of possibility. And when we look out we begin to look deeply within.

Let's take a breath together…

We humans are interesting creatures – we seek and search and find things in all sorts of places to help us make sense of why we're here and what the heck we're supposed to be doing or being while we're here.

There was a time in my life when I used to wonder what my purpose was and why I was here. Now I don't think about it anymore. I live it. I know I'm here to become a better human being, and to learn, grow and be of service.

As much as I've tried to put my life into a neat little box, it just doesn't fit like that. In fact, life and living, it seems, is more like a huge finger painting that gets messy fast and cleans up easily.

"WHY WERE YOU HERE?"

- SAGE

"TO SHOW YOU WHAT'S POSSIBLE."

– JAVA

Java once called our time on Earth, "The Factory" – a place where we move from one thing to the next in small little bits – creating something larger that the smallness we think or feel. As we move through our day, we can become methodical and mechanical – pushing our smoothie cup across the counter morning after morning without much thought or feeling put into it. We can't forget to put love on the list - even if we *are* working at a factory.

The Factory reminds me of the classic *I Love Lucy* episode with the chocolates on the conveyer belt. When the scene opens, Lucy is relaxed and feels confident in her ability to do her job well. This is how we enter this world when we're born. We innately know what to do – breathe, eat, sleep, drink, play, love, potty, repeat.

Soon after we leave the incredible warmth and safety of our mother's womb, we learn fear. In the 60s, when I was born, babies got hung upside down and slapped as soon as we came out so that the doctors knew our lungs worked. That is a very bad idea, and I'd like to know who thought of it.

We learn to be fearful, and to cry out in order to get our needs met. Once our needs are met, we're happy again, and then it's back to love and bliss. After time however, the voice of fear creeps back in and often gets louder. And just like Lucy, as the conveyer belt begins to speed up, so does her stress.

What if I fail?

What if I get in trouble?

What if I get fired?

As the nervous system escalates, the brain fritzes out while unpleasant thoughts, feelings and chemicals race through our minds and bodies. In response to our fear, we usually create a response that involves harming ourselves - or someone or something else - so that we can have the illusion of feeling better. It doesn't work for long..

In Lucy's case, she fills her body with the chocolates so she can keep up with the speed of life. I wonder what would have happened if Lucy had stopped for a moment, taken a breath, and said to her boss,

"I'm not able to work as fast as what's required of me right now and still be in my integrity. I enjoy being of service, and I am needing more space in order to do my job well."

Not a very memorable episode. Can you imagine?

We often capitalize on stressful moments and laugh at or judge people who are enraged, acting out, or falling all over themselves with a lack of awareness. We get a kick out of "The Factory" breaking down and falling apart, and somehow society gives brownie points for being busy.

I wonder what might happen if society gave awards for stillness and authenticity. What if vulnerability and was the only distracting drug we could medicate ourselves with? Can you fathom the shift in the planet if we all chose to say it like it was and be totally transparent? When I taught elementary school, I had a kid tell me that I looked like I was wearing my Halloween costume. It was April, and it was delightful.

I still espouse to the belief that animals are our greatest teachers. They eat when they're hungry, they only drink water (versus caffeine, alcohol, soda, tea etc.), they rest when they're tired and they play and move when they feel like playing and moving.

Food.
Water.
Rest.
Play.

They don't push themselves to go on a diet or go to the gym, and they don't compare themselves to other animals. They just do what they can do to balance themselves naturally, and when they are out of balance, they let us know and hopefully we humans will do something to support a better balance.

Animals go through their lives with no material possessions and have no need for money. I find this fascinating. I was watching two deer walk through our backyard one day and had this epiphany of the brilliance of simplicity. They create their own homes with the resources that are already available to them, and they adjust to whatever the next new normal is – often without issue. Because we have chosen to domesticate animals, we have a big responsibility to provide care for them.

I was thinking awhile back how odd it really is that we connect an apparatus to a dog's neck or body and then string a piece of leather or canvas from their body to ours and walk them through their life like this – connecting us to them as if to say to the world,

"This thing is mine."

Like they're a purse, or personal property, I notice I can laugh about the absurdity. I also notice the grief. I, too, am a person who puts a dog on a leash and takes them with me as *my* dog.

If I was an alien coming down to Earth I would seriously wonder what was going on. I'm noticing more and more within myself the desire to free the animals back to their animal nature. I have the same desire of freedom for myself.

"FREEDOM'S JUST ANOTHER WORD FOR NOTHING LEFT TO LOSE."
– KRIS KRISTOFFERSON

Breath is life. We come into the world with an inhale and we leave with an exhale. When we hold our breath, we hold our life. When we breathe shallowly, we live shallowly. I've often found it to be a fun exercise to breathe in and out with the animals.

Have you ever exhaled with the power of a humpback? Or taken a few breaths with the deliberate slowness of an alligator? Or mirrored the rapidity and unevenness of a dog who is dying in your arms?

Notice your breath right now. Just stop, and take a breath. Now notice your desire to keep reading and not breathe. Go back and take another breath. I'll wait....

It's quite a profound thing to breathe. I watched my dear friend, Kevin, breathe for years and watched his breathing become labored, and labored and labored from ALS. I watched him need support for breathing, watched him becoming aware of his change in breathing, and held space with his family and friends while he let go of his last exhale.

This breathing thing is really something.

Keep doing it.

Chapter Three

DANCING WITH DEATH

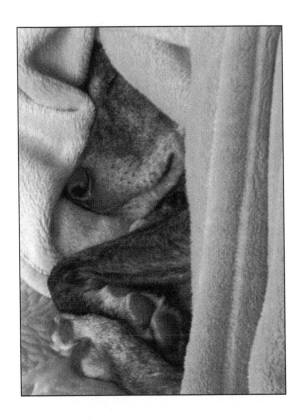

"EVERY BREATH IS SACRED.
EVERY STEP IS HOME."
– JAMES SCHATTAUER

I didn't think Java was going to die. I mean, I knew it would happen sometime, but I couldn't believe it when she refused to eat her dinner. Java had never refused food in her life – ever.

A month before her 12th birthday, Java skipped her first meal. She had just lost a close dog friend, and hadn't had any prior issues that we knew of, so I figured it may have been grief related. There's nothing like a swift shift to get a person to go into high gear.

Within a day, I scheduled an ultrasound and blood tests and was calling "Team Java" together – a core group of holistic veterinarians, chiropractors and healers. I knew something was off with her, and although it might seem extreme to rush into testing the day after a dog doesn't eat, Java was a dog who I knew like the back of my heart. What I didn't know at the time was that my house was squeezing the life out of both of us – one breath at a time.

Carbon Monoxide is a silent killer. I knew this intellectually, but I just thought it happened to other people. It took months to figure out why she wasn't eating, and why she was throwing up and having seizures. When I finally found out what was going on, I was crushed. A routine annual furnace check uncovered the truth on a freezing cold winter morning.

"You have lethal amounts of carbon monoxide in your house. I've quarantined your furnace. You're lucky to be alive." He said to me as his voice quivered nervously.

I will never forget the sobering words the furnace man shared with me as he came up from the basement that morning with his face as white as a ghost. My appointment was the first call of the day, which is why our lives were spared. With the amount of carbon monoxide that was in the house that morning, and the furnace kicking on at 6:30am, we would may very well have been dead if the furnace had stayed on one more hour.

I did something that night I had never done before – dug into my depths of vulnerability and reached out for help from my circle of family, friends and clients. With thousands of dollars in vet bills accruing, I was now facing a brand-new furnace purchase in the middle of a Minnesota winter.

With tears streaming from my weary green eyes, I took a deep breath and sent out a mass email - offering my clients a dollar-a-minute animal communication special in exchange for any support for my rising bills. I felt humiliated, humbled, grateful, embarrassed and very, very raw. The outpouring was absolutely off the charts, and I was freed in less than 48 hours from my financial strain. What I learned is that it's okay to ask for help, and it's okay to be totally vulnerable. Sometimes people just want to be asked so they can give what they've been wanting to give.

Java stopped eating because carbon monoxide kills a dog's sense of smell, and her food dish was in the room above the furnace. When beings can't smell, they don't feel a need to eat. In hindsight, that wasn't the only cause of her decline, but it certainly added to it.

Her first ultrasound showed a large mass on her spleen that I was told had been there for some time. I immediately wondered if it may have happened the winter before when she ran after a squirrel, fell and slid on the ice in the back yard until she hit the boards like an exuberant hockey player. She came out of that incident with a slight limp that day, so I gave her some Arnica, iced it and we moved on. Once I heard about the mass on her spleen, I felt guilty for not taking her to the vet that day and wondered if it was my fault for being a bad dog owner. Shame and guilt can be challenging energies to overcome, and my mind began to reel.

I remembered that Java also had a mast cell tumor removed from the top of her head at age 11, and wondered what else may have been lurking in her system. And when she was somewhere around age 11, Java ate two – yes, two - shamanic drums. Although she was taken to the vet, x-rayed and induced to vomit out the grapefruit size deer hide from the drums on both occasions, I wondered if she may have had undiagnosed digestive complications from her wild moments as a budding percussionist.

Java was a dog who had regular vet appointments her entire life, chiropractic and alternative care, and was seemingly healthy (as far as I knew) until the day she stopped eating. I am certain that the carbon monoxide poisoning sped things up for both of us on all levels. It takes facing death to truly appreciate life.

While I was frantically watching my 67-pound soulmate in a dog suit lose a pound of flesh a week, I was noticing my anger, fear and guilt rising up.
What if I had only.... (fill in the blank)?

It wasn't a matter of *if*, it was a matter of *when*. I really thought Java would stick around until about the age of 14, so I kept kicking myself for being the cause of her decline. I kept trying to figure out why this was happening, and what I could do about it. What did I do wrong?

Java was a dog with dignity, power, grace, grit and great majesty. She was somewhere between a queen and a roller derby athlete. I knew I was going to do anything in my power to help usher her into her death with the same majesty and dignity that she emanated in her life.

Java finally stopped eating anything on her own the last two months before she died. Having trained in animal hospice, I assisted her with feeding multiple times a day for those very sacred eight weeks.

Oral syringes became a fixture on my counter, and I made smoothies for her with anything that would detoxify her liver, build her blood, support her adrenals or just plain prevent her from losing a pound a week. It also gave me something to do to feel useful.

We were in the dance together, and some days it was a very frustratingly painful dance, and other days it was filled with the sacredness of love and peace. I remember really wanting her to eat, and it wasn't until I actually let go of the desire that I was able to find the sacredness of love and peace. Until then it was mostly frustration and pain for me, and gratitude and acceptance for Java.

Then there was the oxygen. Thank goodness for having a reactive dog who was accustomed to a headcollar and muzzle in her life, because it came in really handy when she needed an oxygen mask to support her in hospice. Oxygen counteracts the effects of carbon monoxide poisoning, so with the help of a local veterinarian, I received a prescription for an oxygen tank and a child sized mask.

Another vet taught me how to administer sub Q fluids, and then there were multiple reiki sessions, Tellington TTouch® sessions, energy work, prayer and Bentonite clay and Castor Oil packs to detox her liver. Java was very well cared for, and my business was running well, and yet I was losing ground personally.

My relationship with my heartner, James, became very strained. At the same time, I was finding myself strained in my relationship with myself. Only a few months prior, we had taken James' dog, Sophie, through a natural death, and our family wasn't yet finished grieving. Sophie's hospice process was a shocking year and half long and had also taken its toll on our relationship. From the fire into the fire, we headed straight into hospice with Java just one week after Sophie's death.

My spiritual practices were coming into play as I was continually being tested to find balance and practice impeccable self-care. With a house to take care of and a business to run while living alone, I was exhausted. Yet, looking back, I wouldn't have traded even one moment for the gift of hospice care with Java.

True hospice means that we support a being in having as peaceful of a transition as possible, and it's not for the faint of heart. There will be judgment, and there may be a lot of it.

People may ask, "Why would you allow your dog/cat/aunt/father etc. to suffer like that?"

You might get unsolicited advice or get reprimanded for your choices. What really happens when death knocks on the door is that we ourselves are suffering so we want to put an end to our own suffering by doing something to relieve the suffering.

We judge, blame, defend, justify and distract ourselves with anything that we believe will relieve the pain because we're afraid of feeling. When we're afraid, we go into fight, flight, freeze, faint or fool around, just like the animals do. Finding stillness and taking a deep breath until the next *yes* presents itself is an option that works well for me when I'm suffering. I used to run toward, away from and in circles until my therapist asked me,

"Have you ever thought about holding still?"

When our beloved animal companions are nearing death, we know that euthanasia is an option we have available to us. However, in my many years of connecting with the animals, I have never had an animal ask if they could be euthanized. It's not in their vocabulary, and some animals don't understand mortality and death. I've also never had an animal be upset about being euthanized when a person does make that choice.

If an animal is in great distress or extreme pain from injury, or they are not supported fully through hospice and are anxious or in pain, then there are certainly cases where euthanasia may be the kindest option for everyone. Death is a personal dance.

When you are trying to make a conscious decision about life or death, I encourage you to ask yourself,

"What is the next thing that will bring me peace?"

The animals know how to die. They are really great at it, and therefore, they are often far more peaceful then we are as they move into aging and finally let go of their bodies.

Animals adjust to the next new normal, which for some of them may be a loss of continence, loss of eyesight or hearing, loss of mobility and change in eating and drinking habits. They may also have to adjust to the range of emotions that move through family members as grief takes on a life of its own.

Many animals (and humans) also start to leave their bodies before they leave their bodies – hovering up above to relieve themselves of pain, anxiety and distress. When they get closer to letting go, they let go of their spirit more and more until the final thread releases and they are fully free.

Look into anyone's eyes and you can tell how much life and light is there. I saw it with Java. I saw it with my ex-husband. I saw it with my Mom. I will see it in myself and my husband someday, too. The light starts to dim in the ego/right eye and there is a clarity that emerges in the soul/left eye.

While Java and I were deep into hospice, and deep into another frigid Minnesota winter, we had been naively unaware of the carbon monoxide levels that were rising in our home.

I've been told that the symptoms of carbon monoxide poisoning mimic menopause symptoms – dizziness, headaches, crankiness, lethargy, insomnia and forgetfulness. Yes, we had multiple carbon monoxide detectors in our home, and they even had functioning batteries.

What I've since learned from the fire department is that unless you purchase high level, expensive digital carbon monoxide detectors that plug into the wall and have a battery backup, they may go off sporadically from dust collecting on the sensor. My detectors were the round smoke alarm/carbon monoxide combo and went off once that winter while I was baking cookies. I did what most people do – waved a towel at the alarm until the sound went off. I didn't know any better.

As the vets were doing their darndest to figure out what was up with Java, I was feeling like a normal perimenopausal woman in her late 40s. Carbon monoxide can dissipate in the blood within minutes once there is fresh air in the bloodstream, so, every time we left the house, Java and I both got fresh air and all of her blood tests came out normal – until the end.

There's something else that's really unique about carbon monoxide and gas leaks in general. Leaks attract ghosts. When there are gas leaks in a building, there is an entry point for spirits to visit. I didn't know this at first, but I soon found out firsthand.

Backtrack to the Winter Solstice and Java was about 2-1/2 months into hospice at this point. We hadn't found out yet that the furnace was leaking carbon monoxide into our home, and we were doing what many Midwest people do in the winter – staying inside and turning up the heat.

We went to bed on this particularly freezing cold Minnesota winter night as we usually did – snuggling up together under the covers. Java always dove under head first when the lights went out, then came out of the covers at some point - panting profusely when she got too hot. Either that, or she kicked the covers off with her back legs when she was too hot. I realize now that for many years Java and I fought about the covers all night long. On. Off. On. Off. Under. On top. Repeat.

During the dark and cold of the night I awoke from a great startle to see the ghost of a hooded man standing over the top of me on the bed. He looked to me to be about 7' tall and was wearing a long, black cloak that was covering most of his face. His energy was very dark, and it felt incredibly real. Someone *was* standing over me. In between waking and sleeping, I was absolutely frightened beyond belief as I watched the black cloaked man move his left arm up slowly as he pointed a long silver steel rod with a sharpened red tip directly at my throat. I was facing the Grim Reaper.

I couldn't breathe.
I felt paralyzed.
I *was* paralyzed.

Then something rose up inside me – something bigger than myself. Call it jaguar medicine or the will to live or hell no. Whatever it was, it was huge. This was NOT going to be the time for me to die!

With all the power I could muster up from every ounce of fire in my body, I made a huge and violent swipe with my left arm across the ghostlike image of the Grim Reaper and he disappeared into the silence of the night. Looking over, I saw Java lying on the floor looking up at me. She was surrounded by what looked like a hazy brown cloud of who knows what kind of energy – maybe the carbon monoxide - and I noticed I felt groggy and foggy as I tried to make out what was happening.

Heart pounding wildly inside my frame, I turned my head to the right toward the bedroom door and saw the tip of the long, steel, silver rod with the sharp red point coming around the corner at me again. I rose up in bed with the power of a silver back gorilla beating wildly on her chest, and screamed at the ghost-like image at the top of my lungs,

"GET THE F#@K OUTTA HERE!!!"

It left for good, and somehow I fell back asleep. The next morning, I did what most people do with a visit from the Grim Reaper. I posted it on Facebook and asked if anyone else had ever had a visit. Surprisingly, three other people responded right away that they too had been visited that very night by G. R. as well. I guess he'd been making the rounds!

Now, I was really curious. What was the link between the Grim Reaper and Winter Solstice, and why was G. R. coming for other people, too, that night? At this point in time, I still hadn't known about the carbon monoxide poisoning in our house, but I found out later that there is a direct link between carbon monoxide, and the Grim Reaper. Makes perfect sense.

I would love to see what people type into their Google search engine when they're looking up crazy information. I think my search went something like this: "Grim Reaper+sharp steel rod at my throat+red tip+winter solstice." I was shocked at what came up in the search.

There is a phenomenon called Sleep Paralysis that happens when someone is being affected by carbon monoxide poisoning and gas leaks. If a person is lying on their back, the breathing shifts, and there is a sense of not being able to move. That's what had happened to me.

Another search showed me that the Winter Solstice is the time when the zodiac moves from Sagittarius to Capricorn. Capricorn is ruled by Saturn, and Saturn is associated with....you guessed it, the Grim Reaper.

Oh, and Jesus.

Chapter Four

LOVE PREPARE ME

"LOVE PREPARE ME,
TO BE A SANCTUARY,
PURE AND HOLY, TRIED AND TRUE,
WITH THANKSGIVING, I'LL BE A
LIVING, SANCTUARY FOR YOU."
- TRADITIONAL

Java died a peaceful natural death at home on March 2, 2013 around 4am during a huge blizzard in St. Paul, Minnesota. A part of me died that morning, too, as I held her familiar body while she birthed herself through death and new life. The dolphins had come for Java during a vision only a few days prior.

"We're here to take you home." they said to me on behalf of her.

They were ready to take her back home to be with the other dolphins and whales, and to return her spirit to the star she had come from - Sirius, The Dog Star. She was ready to transcend. I was resigned.

Java's death was as powerful and dignified as her life. For almost three weeks I had been staying downstairs with her to help keep her safe and comfortable and to prevent her from falling on the stairs. Earlier in the day, I had come home from a massage to see her collapsed in the living room with a small pile of vomit next to her on the floor. Looking at me with eyes that only a dog human knows, I called the vet and we talked about next options for her hospice journey. The vet asked if she wanted me to have her come over and gave me some suggestions. I told her that I would be okay, and I hung up the phone and cried. A little bit of oxygen and some fluids in her body, Java was able to settle more fully and she began to walk around the house and rally a bit.

She and I rested for some time together on the floor – touching our hands and paws together and sharing stories of the past and present. Then I met James at a restaurant for a quick dinner.

As Great Spirit works, James and I had a stressful dinner date, and my anxiety of wanting to go back home made our time together even more challenging. I felt like I was pulled in two directions, and at the same time, all I wanted to do was be alone with the dog I had spent 12-1/2 years with as a single pet guardian. I was deep in my own process of letting go of a beloved companion, and at the same time, navigating a fairly new human relationship.

James and I went back to my house to try to find more connection and solace as a couple, and Java greeted us at the door with her tail wagging. Sitting down on the floor next to her, James and I could feel the strain as we cared for Java together and tried to find more peace between the three of us. Animals feel energy, and at one point, Java leaned over and plopped her paw on James' hand as if to say,

"Enough already!"

She had always been a great referee, and the last day of her life was no different. James decided to go back to his house for the night to get some sleep and allow the dust to settle a bit more before coming back the next day, and I decided to snuggle up next to Java in the living room for the night again.

Throughout our almost two full years of hospice care with both of our dogs, James and I had learned a lot about ourselves and one another. We had also learned a lot about hospice, and had been working together as a team for such a long time with our dogs as the focus. With Sophie dying and then going right into Java's hospice, our relationship had deepened and we were also experiencing extreme caregiver fatigue.

James and I kissed each other goodnight and trusted that the stress of the evening would dissipate with a good night's rest. He told me to call him if anything changed, and I assured him I would stay in touch.

Snuggling up on the floor next to Java's now 48# frame, I started to do some circular TTouches all over her body, and told her how much I loved her and how much I was going to miss her when she was gone. She was weak and hadn't been getting up much in those few hours and I could tell she was getting closer to letting go of herself. Java and I stayed connected for what felt like forever, and then I fell sound asleep with my hand resting gently on her back.

About two hours later, I was awakened from my slumber by Java shrugging my hand from her back. Scooting herself away from me, I noticed a gentle tug in my heart as I released my physical connection from the body I had known so well for so many years.

I've heard that the last to go is our sense of hearing, and that touching any being at the end stages of their life can actually keep them more in their body. I wanted Java to be able to let go easily when she was ready, so, I got up and moved myself to the couch nearby and fell back into a really deep sleep.

Another few hours passed, and I was startled awake by the feeling of Java's nose pressing gently into the middle of my back. Waking up with surprise, I turned over to see her standing up next to the couch with a look on her face that told me she needed to go outside. God bless her for this last expression of dignity, because she made it as far as the kitchen before she vomited and finally collapsed. Me, I didn't have dignity. I freaked out.

Up until this point, Java had been able to walk on her own except for two short collapses – one earlier that day, and one from weakness before I started to feed her with an oral syringe many weeks before. Seeing her fully collapse on the floor was really challenging for me, and I was aware of the karma that she and I shared as I felt myself in my aloneness. I noticed myself starting to clean up after her as the bright lights in the kitchen showed that the carpet was never going to be the same again. I noticed myself rushing and feeling nervous as Java raised her head up to look at me with eyes I knew were letting go.

For whatever reason - probably because it made me feel more comfortable - I lifted her up and carried her back into the living room and rested her on her dog bed. I noticed myself still wanting to help in some way, so I offered her some water. She refused, and I offered her food. She refused, and I offered her oxygen, and scooted her withered body away from me until her back was completely facing me.

I laid next to her without touching her for what felt like forever, and drifted in and out of lucidity. Listening to the sound of the slowness of her breathing, I found my own breathing starting to match hers to bring more comfort to myself. A low moan melted from her vocal chords like a river of grief, and then began to turn into a puppy like whimper that sounded like distress. Reaching over, I began to stroke her velvet soft ears with some Ear TTouches to bring more comfort to her and to me. She quieted down, and we had another short visit to dreamland together.

When someone is dying, there is a sacredness in the air that's palpable. I can't really tell if the air gets lighter or denser, but what I do know is that something else enters the room. There's a sense of timelessness and weightlessness that only the heart knows how to navigate.

We might hear a clock tick one second at a time, when before we didn't even notice that there was a clock in the room. We notice the world around us far more fully than we did before death starts to knock at the door, and we come more into that place of oneness with all that exists. When the veil thins, so does our perception of right and wrong and good and bad, and we become. Yes, we become.

Let's take another breath together...

Java woke me up one last time with the sound of one final fiery retch coming up and out from the depths of her soul. Reaching over with all the courage and love I had created in my 12-1/2 years with her, I held her listless head up and away from her vomit. With my right hand, I supported her wise and graceful spirit under her beautiful, brindle and now white muzzle. Gently placing my left hand on her strong and courageous beating heart, I could feel the magnitude of my death doula training coming into action - birthing her through her death and onto what and where was next.

Something rose up inside me, and I started to sing, sing, and sing in the darkness of the night like the song was singing me.

"Love prepare me, to be a sanctuary, pure and holy, tried and true, with thanksgiving, I'll be a living, sanctuary for you."

I sang it again, and I sang it again, and as the last verse wavered and wiggled in my vocal chords, her last exhale wove its way through the gigantic lump in my throat. She was dying, and now we were both letting go.

As her head, became heavier and heavier in my right hand, her heartbeat - still filled with strength, power and fire – continued to pound with passion under my left. Stillness filled the air as my heart became filled with something I still can't explain other than *more*.

With one last quiet *baboom* the once beating heart of the dog I had known as Java let go completely underneath my hand. Her mouth opened and closed one last time - ever so slightly and slowly like a fish out of water - and then it closed forever. Just she and I, Great Spirit, and the darkness of night.

She was done.

Death is a curious thing. There's so much life in it that it's almost a shame to call it death – like something isn't there anymore, yet at the same time it's like everything is there. I felt stronger than I ever had before, and more present than I knew was even possible. There's an energy that happens in the air during the time of dying that is almost indescribable by words.

After a few minutes, I removed my hand and heart from underneath her head, and rested her lifeless yet powerful body fully on the blanket below her. I felt the stillness and connection between us as I noticed I was now the only one breathing life into the room.

"She's gone." I said, as I exhaled into the phone while James took in an inhale of sadness and regret on the other end.

Silence filled the space between us, as we adjusted to the new shift in our family. When death strikes, life becomes more sacred.

"I'll be right over." He said.

The blanket beneath Java's body was a colorful fleece of vibrant hot pinks, yellows, blues and blacks that she had claimed as her own since she was a puppy. It was a gift from a dear friend, and one of many blankets in her lifetime that were complete with her signature "L shaped" rip from grabbing it with her teeth to pull it wherever she needed it most.

As I waited for James to arrive, I sat in the stillness and silent sacredness of my life and death with Java and allowed my mind and heart to do what it needed to do.

Sitting on the floor next to Java's body in the darkness, I heard a familiar voice remind me to keep documenting the process as I had been doing for months. In the pitch black of night, with only one candle lit in my spirit filled home, I took a photo of Java a few moments after her body let go and her spirit had begun or continued its journey home.

I gasped in disbelief, and also immense belief, as I looked at the photo I had just taken. What I saw before me was a large translucent bubble of white light about 4' in diameter that was hovering directly over Java's seemingly lifeless body. A few more photos over the course of the next 20 minutes revealed what I can imagine was Java's spirit floating around our house. Perfect that she chose to move closer to the refrigerator.

Grasping my yellow Hopi gourd rattle in my right hand, I took another breath. Preparing myself to help release Java's spirit completely to the other side, I noticed a feeling of immense grief welling up inside of me. Taking in a deep breath, I knew the work before me was bigger than I had experienced in the past, as a huge invitation to release her completely rose up inside my chest. I wailed more than I ever had before, as I felt my heart being pulled and stretched in every direction.

"HOW WILL WE CONNECT
AFTER YOU DIE?"
- SAGE

"LISTEN MORE DEEPLY."
- JAVA

When someone dies, we have a choice. We can hang on or let go. There is a tiny silver thread that connects us all in some way through the web of life. In my experience with dying and death, there is a deep, deep letting go that can happen with both the person or animal who is dying, and also a deep letting go (or hanging on) from the person who is staying behind. The dance changes form and becomes a much healthier, freer and more loving dance as we move toward letting go. And, it's hard work.

When we fully let go of the silver thread that connects us, we are able to give a gift to the spirit of the deceased. By letting go fully, we can allow them to free their soul from the need to be attached to this world, and at the same time free the loved ones they have left behind. This world is dense, and when we or someone we love lets go of their density, there is an immense freedom in returning to the Oneness of all. Easier said than done.

Shaking my rattle vigorously and with the utmost intent over Java's body in my living room that cold, wintery morning, I felt grief and loss arise from every cell in my body – as if I was purging the depths of our relationship from every crack and crevice in my heart. It was the intensity of an amazing orgasm, but not nearly as pleasurable. In fact, it hurt like hell.

I wailed.
I chanted.
I rattled.

My heart collapsed and I let go completely. An expansive sense of peace fell over me as the sun began to rise, and the lightness of the morning began to peek through the blinds. Java's body lie in state next to mine, and as I noticed my breath going in and out, I felt her spirit was now running free among the stars.

James joined me at her side as the sun began to shine on our hearts, and the two of us held one another and cried a river of sorrow, regret, gratitude and great relief.

It can take up to three days for the spirit to fully release from the body, so allowing the body to lie in state for that time period can support a full release to the other side. Yes, three days. Get the dry ice, and be ready for an amazing experience! Having already hosted a shorter vigil for James' dog, Sophie, five months earlier, we were ready.

Preparing for a three-day vigil was pretty simple in the depths of winter in Minnesota. James was by my side in the wee hours of the morning to support sacred ceremony. Then, two dear friends came over to help us move through our grief and help prepare Java's body for the three-day vigil.

With the quiet of the morning and the sacredness of the night still in our hearts, I sat in ceremony with one of Java's angels who had come to help us. She and I did a shamanic journey on behalf of Java that morning, and smiled when we both received the same information from Java. Java had shared with me that she wanted her body to be covered in daisies when she was going to be transformed by the fire. She also told my friend that she wanted a vase full of daisies at her vigil.

As the morning unfolded further, the four of us found ourselves filling three large garbage bags with fresh snow from the back yard. Lifting Java's body up and placing the bags of snow under her favorite blanket in the living room where she had passed, we carefully laid her body back down with grace and reverence in the same position that she had died.

I remember feeling so much energy coursing through my veins in the moments and hours following Java's death. After having spent two months feeding her with a syringe multiple times a day - and the worry, the anger, the fear, the sorrow that went along with it - I felt like I had also been released to run free.

The day was pretty simple at our house the day she died. We continued creating an altar surrounding her body, and started to contact friends and fans. Java had touched so many hearts worldwide, that there was an outpouring of condolences and people wanting to stop by to make one more connection.

Heading to bed that night, with Java's body in state in the living room, I asked Great Spirit to allow her to come to me in my dreams if she wanted or needed to. And then I fell into a deep slumber entwined with my beloved, James, next to me.

Night became morning, and as we awoke, James turned to me and said,

"I heard Java walk up the stairs last night."

"Me, too." I replied.

When the veil is thin, anything is possible. The sound of Java's footsteps on the stairs at bedtime had been a familiar sound for 12-1/2 years. Why wouldn't she make the same choice in some form or another on the night she died?

We can either believe we are making stuff up, or we can believe in the power of the unseen. I have learned to believe in the latter.

I had seen and felt so many spirit-filled images in the night and days following my father's death and also my grandmother's death. And now, hearing the sound of Java's paws on the carpeted staircase the night of her death, I became fully convinced. When the veil is thin, and we listen more deeply, we can hear, taste, smell, feel and see the whispers.

Quiet the mind.
Open the heart.
Shhhh!
Listen.

When beings die, there is often a release of fluids – vomit, urine, feces. All three are really common. With Java, she was anything but common. Although she did have a bout of projectile vomit about an hour before she died, in the moments after her passing there was nothing coming out of either end. Well, not until we picked her body up to move it for the first time.

Every few hours, for three full days, James and I lifted Java's body up to change the snow underneath. Then we set her back down - in the same position of her death - on the colorful blanket with the L shaped rip she had created during her life.

The first changing of the snow we lifted Java's body up gently and with respect with the colorful blanket lying underneath her like a hammock. Then we placed her body in the same position just a few feet away from where she died, while we refilled the ice/snow bags with fresh snow from the backyard. Hooray for Midwest blizzards! Picking her body back up with the blanket hammock, we set her back down atop the snow to keep her body from smelling up the joint. I know you were wondering.

When we lifted her up and set her back down onto the fresh bed of snow filled bags, I noticed a drop of blood on the blanket. It was hiding itself conspicuously underneath her right nostril and had dripped onto the blanket at some point after her death.

One drop of blood was all that had come out of her body after her death. And get this. The drop of blood was in the shape of a heart. I can't make this stuff up.

Noticing the states of mortis along the way during the vigil – a stiffening, and then a pliability and back to a stiffness then pliability - was fascinating and at moments a bit comical. It's not easy to lift up a 48-pound body who is not cooperating.

When someone dies we are often very quick to get rid of the body as soon as possible. But keeping Java's body in state in the spot where she let go of her last breath was an unbelievably sacred experience. James and I spent time creating an altar around her body with flowers, cards, gifts and toys, which allowed not only for the two of us to grieve more deeply and privately, but also for so many people who loved and cared for Java to come by the house to grieve themselves over the course of the three days.

On the eve before Java's cremation was to take place, my house became filled with a myriad of friends who had loved and cared for her. Twenty or so drummers gathered in ceremony to help drum and chant Java's way on to the next world, and a few drummers bathed me in sacred drum washes to help me grieve more fully. I wept. I laughed. I released some more, and so did everyone else.

Java's altar became filled with roses, more cards, letters, photos and lots of memories. And then a miracle walked in.

Remember the woman who graciously came to my side to share in ceremony the morning Java died? Well, here she was in my living room, carrying the most gorgeous arrangement of daisies in a cobalt blue vase. Draped over the neck of the vase was a silver necklace with a tiny cobalt blue star dangling playfully.

At first I was completely speechless, and then I asked her how she could possibly have known about my connection as Blue Star Woman. She responded with confidence and curiosity because she didn't know what I was talking about. Up to that point, only a very few select people who had gathered in sacred ceremony with me had heard about Blue Star Woman. Now before me was this magically connected woman who proceeded to tell me that Java had told her what to buy for me.

"I just walked through the florist and listened. Java told me to tell you that the necklace was for you." She said.

With tears flowing from my eyes and a wealth of gratitude in my heart, I sat down and told her the entire story of how Blue Star Woman had come about. Now there were two of us who were shocked and also not surprised. Great work, Java!

Grief has a life of its own. So not only did this vigil allow James and I to grieve the loss of our dear friend, Java, it also allowed us and everyone else who attended her celebration to grieve more of what hadn't been grieved yet. We grieve for ourselves, we grieve stuff that happened in the past, we grieve for others and we grieve for the world around us.

Near the end of the night, one of Java's dearest human friends, Luna, walked up to me with a drum in her hand and a smile on her face. Luna was in utero when she had first met Java, and had on many occasions been a part of Java's care team with her parents.

At the tender and curious age of four, Luna wasn't fully understanding a vigil for a dead dog, but I noticed her mother explaining that Java had died and that she was still a part of Luna's heart.

Looking straight into the innocence of Luna's eyes, I waited for her to share with me what I knew were words that were formulating. I took a breath and smiled back while the words flowed like a Rumi poem that is etched in memory forever.

"Java is in my body!" She said emphatically, while she placed her sweet little four-year-old hand on her beautiful, big heart.

Yes, she sure is. Mine, too.

Chapter Five

FEEDING THE FIRE

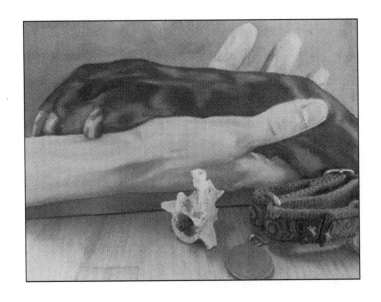

"ALL I AM,
I OFFER TO YOU."
– FROM MERE GURUDEV
BY KRISHNA DAS

The drumbeats subsided as night became ready for dreamtime, and all of Java's local fans said their goodnights and goodbyes.

James and I headed upstairs to bed for the final night of Java's vigil - knowing that her body was scheduled to be cremated in the morning. We were as ready as we knew we were.

For three full days and three full nights, Java's body lie in state in my living room in the exact spot she died. Changing the snow filled bags beneath her became its own ritual, and I was grateful we were almost done. The house was beginning to smell, and my heart was beginning to find peace.

It was incredible to feel so many colors of grief and relief during Java's vigil. With visitors coming, being alone with her body, and James and I sharing sacred ceremony, we were able to dive into a pool of grief that was full of the depths of pain and joy. Hooray for our friends who were totally game, because not everyone is up for walking into a house with a dead dog in the living room!

When someone dies, we have choices. We can hurry up and get the body out of there, or we can slow down, honor the body and spirit and allow ourselves, and others, to fully grieve. It's not easy to grieve fully, and it's also very, very necessary.

After spending time in animal hospice training, James and I chose to slow down and expand our ability to grieve and release completely. Cremation was next.

Waking up on cremation day, we were greeted by a full-blown Minnesota blizzard that had obviously been scheming all night long. With streets unplowed and sidewalks completely full of fluffy white snow, I wondered how we were going to get Java's body to the crematorium. When there's a will, there's a way.

As the morning unfolded, James and I began to collect items from Java's altar to bring along to her fire transformation ceremony. There was the cobalt blue vase of daisies she had requested along with the blue star necklace that she had told a friend to buy for me. I put on the necklace, then I packed some sage, sweetgrass and tobacco along with the Porcupine medicine card from my animal totem deck.

I pulled a few salt and pepper hairs from my head, while James cut some of the same from his beard. Then we added our hair into an envelope with a few distinct white hairs from just inside Java's left ear. These precious items that bound us together in sacred ceremony were now going to go into the fire along with her well used up body.

I can imagine that some people might run the other way around cremation, but James and I were running straight into it. We had found a wonderful place that was willing to allow us to bring Java's body to the crematorium ourselves, and to stay during the cremation to drum and play her favorite music.

There is a ritual we did with my Jewish grandparents when they died, where we drove past the synagogue on the way to the cemetery. The doors to the synagogue were open as an invitation to honor the dead and remember their goodness on the way to their final resting place.

Java was now ready for her processional. With hats, mittens and a shovel in tow, James and I created a sacred path from the front door to the back of my car so we could carry Java's body out with grace. Lining the path with red roses (which look absolutely stunning in a blizzard, by the way) we prepared the back of my car to receive her body with reverence, grace and intention.

With the hatch of the car left open for receiving, we headed inside the house to place Java's body onto a homemade gurney disguised as a long folding table. With James on one end of the makeshift gurney table, and me on the other, we were preparing our hearts to take her body out of my home for what would be the last time.

In true Java form, she had other divine plans that day which included lightheartedness and laughter during what could have been a very serious moment. As James and I somewhat clumsily placed Java's very pliable body onto a somewhat slippery table, we lifted it up with a 1-2-3 and headed toward the front door – verbalizing who should go this way or that way, and who needed to lift up or down so she didn't slide off. It was like moving a couch except it was sacred and it wasn't supposed to be funny.

When we got to the door, James and I were challenged to communicate much more clearly so we could get the table through the threshold without disaster. Just as we were ready to move her body gracefully through the doorway, Java's floppy paw opened up and pressed against the door frame – preventing us from going any further. We immediately burst out laughing, and as I moved her paw back out of the way, we noticed the sound of a large engine coming around the corner.

We continued to wrangle her somewhat balanced body through the doorway, as a garbage truck drove down the street and stopped directly in front of my house. We were halfway out the door, so with laughter in our hearts, and wide stares from the garbage truck people, Java's processional continued to the back of my car – not the garbage truck. Dark, dark humor, that girl.

James and I giggled like two little kids in church who weren't supposed to be laughing as we slid her body into the back of my Volkswagen hearse. Laying her atop the brightly colored fleece blanket that had been her resting place the past three days, we adorned her brindle body one last time with red roses and white and yellow daisies and then we shut the hatch.

Navigating unplowed streets, we drove Java's body past one of her favorite places on the way to the crematorium as part of our ritual – a way to allow her to have one last visit at her own private dog park. As a dog who spent much of her life reacting in fear to the world around her, I had become creative in how I allowed her to get her exercise and stimulation.

An industrial office park near my home served for years as Java's private dog park. Open green spaces and buildings that were occupied by workers allowed for a lot of spaciousness, privacy and safe walks together for years. Here we were, one last romp in the snow.

We parked in the parking lot and opened the back of my car as if to allow Java's spirit to take one last glimpse at all the memories we had created over the years. Then we headed slowly through the blizzard to transform her body through fire.

True hospice with the animals means supporting them through their life, their aging and their death in a way that allows for them to let go naturally and peacefully. For over 5 months, I had supported Java with a variety of tools so that she was able to let go easily on her own and at home. We were blessed.

Maybe you've been in that place before or maybe you'll be there sometime in the future – that place of needing to decide what's next. It's no different than anything else in life. You just wait for the next yes to appear, and it will.

When we got to the crematorium, James and I were greeted kindly and with sympathy by the business owners. They helped us move Java's blanket and her body onto a sturdy gurney and they wheeled her inside the building. I've learned to slow down, and to encourage others to slow down. Although we were there for a task, Java was my dog, and she was special to me and many other people.

I wanted these cremation specialists to get an image of the dog they were about to cremate, so James and I invited them to sit down in the conference room, while I gave them a signed copy of my JAVA book. We shared stories about Java for some time, and as everyone's hearts softened even more, we wheeled her body into the room with the fire.

What I learned through this process is to ask a lot of questions and to ask for what you want. Throughout Java's life, she loved listening to Krishna Das who is a beautiful kirtan singer with a voice that is as rich as the earth and as pure as gold. Java would often lie in front of my stereo and fall sound asleep anytime I played his music.

For Java's transition from body to bones, I wanted to honor her spirit with live drumming and her favorite Krishna Das song. Explaining this to the owners of the crematorium definitely moved them to a new level. They had never had anyone want to participate this much, and yet they were very touched and very open.

Rolling her gurney up to the cremation chamber, we could hear the fire roaring wildly from behind the steel door, as I felt the fire in my heart roaring wildly alongside it. James and I created one final altar on top of Java's chest made of roses, daisies, tobacco, sweetgrass, sage, the hairs from each of us, and the Porcupine medicine card from a deck of animal totem cards.

Porcupine medicine is that of playfulness and innocence, and it was Java who helped me name my business, Dancing Porcupine, many years ago by stomping on the Porcupine card during a Tellington TTouch® Training. Porcupines are misunderstood creatures who, when respected, are quite docile. Just like all of us, Java had been misunderstood in her life. It only made sense that the Porcupine medicine card would be transformed along with her body.

James and I gently placed our hands on top of Java's broad chest, and kissed her body goodbye one last time. Our hearts ripped wide open as the cold steel door exposed the blazing hot fire inside. Staring back at us was an invitation to go deeper.

If you've never placed a body into a cremation chamber after a three-day vigil, get ready to be a little surprised and amused. Remember when I told you about all the states of mortis along the way? Well, Java's body was like a cooked noodle and not very easy to manipulate or navigate. Not surprising that Java would get one more laugh out of us before we rolled her body into the white-hot flames and closed the door.

When one door closes, another opens. As James and I drummed, and drummed and drummed our way through our grief, there were new doors that were opening in our hearts. The smell of fire and mystery filled the air while in the background, my Krishna Das CD played Mere Gurudev over the cremation place's sound system. Our heart doors cracked open as wide as the huge watermelons that Java had loved so much.

MERE GURUDEV
- SUNG BY KRISHNA DAS

I offer these flowers of my faith at your feet,

Whatever I have, you have given to me,

and I dedicate it all to you.

I have no love, nor do I know you.

I don't even have the strength to worship you,

But this mind of mine,

this body of mine,

My every atom is dedicated to you.

You are the only one

in my heart and my thoughts.

You are the one who I call out to.

Now make me your instrument....

all I am I offer to you.

Within about an hour of drumming, listening to Krishna Das, and crying our hearts free, Java's body was transformed and so were our hearts. Nothing felt the same anymore. Nothing. As the steel door to the transformation chamber opened, I heard James ask the owner if he could have one of Java's teeth. I was touched by his innocence and his curiosity and courage.

The owner of the crematorium responded that he could wait to crush her bones until we looked for her teeth, and my heart skipped a beat. You mean we could keep her bones just as they were without crushing them? I had no idea that bones were crushed during a cremation, and I felt elated to be able to honor the organic process.

With Java's bone fragments intact (and yes, we found a few teeth), we headed back to the car with a cardboard box of cremains labeled "Shadow" instead of Java. I'm not sure why Shadow's box was empty and free for us to use, but it was the right size for Java's cremains and maybe Shadow didn't need it anymore. Hooray for recycling!

It felt surreal to enter a building with something or someone larger and end up with something or someone smaller. Placing the box in the back of the car felt painful and totally weird, as we made our way back through the blizzard to land in front of my house.

With Shadow/Java's cardboard box held in reverence and sorrow, James and I headed through the shoveled path toward my house – passing the majestic salute of red roses that were stuck in the snow and still holding vigil. As I entered the front door, I asked Java what she wanted me to do with her cremains.

"Gift them to people I love who love me." She spoke clearly and confidently. "You know who they are."

Yes. I do.

Chapter Six

LISTENING
MORE DEEPLY

"THE HEART
IS MEANT
TO BE FELT."
– GREAT SPIRIT

My ex-husband died unexpectedly the next day. It wasn't a matter of whether he was going to die or not, it was a matter of which day.

March 6, 2013 was the day that Gerard and Great Spirit picked for him move on to a place that was much easier and far more peaceful for him to navigate.

As an angst ridden creative, Gerard spent his life living every single moment as if it were his last. For him there was no day but today, and each day for Gerard was measured in seasons of love, in midnights, in sunsets and cups of coffee. He was an incredible drummer with a heart of gold, and also a man who struggled with alcoholism until the day he died.

Gerard and I first met when I was 12 and he wasn't. He was a counselor at a music camp that I attended in the summertime, and for six years I looked forward to seeing him at camp. The kids called him Mr. Brillo, and he sported wild new wave 80s hair, mismatched clothes and a smile and spirit that could fill an entire room. Gerard was fun and beyond funny.

When I turned 19 and he was 24, we both became counselors at the same music camp and then started off on our way together as a couple soon after. Pitchers of beer, playing darts and pinball became our Saturday night ritual as Bonnie and Clyde met Syd and Nancy met Kurt and Courtney.

Our time together was wild, fun, deep, funny and challenging. After 15 years together, and no change in his ability to let go of practicing alcoholism, it was time for me to let go. I wasn't willing to stay in a dysfunctional marriage anymore, and yet my heart was unbelievably broken.

I used to think that I was the only person on the planet who was affected by someone with alcoholism. What I learned is that one of every two people is affected by someone with alcoholism, and one of every eight adults is an alcoholic. There are six people a day who die from alcohol poisoning – drinking too much too fast. Once I started to talk about alcoholism, I realized how common it is. Misery loves company.

With Gerard, I knew that staying in my marriage the way it was would suck me down the drain. With his inability to move into recovery, it was an ultimatum. Me, or alcohol. He chose alcohol and I chose me.

Most people I've talked with have had really challenging divorces. Gerard and I were blessed with a really easy one. We both had the ability to be able to talk about our needs and our feelings, and to share our wishes for uncoupling. Our disengagement was filled with tears and understanding, some laughs and a lot of peace. Nobody goes into a relationship wanting to navigate substance abuse. And nobody gets married wanting to get divorced.

Gerard and I stayed connected over the years and checked in with each other once in a while to catch up and reminisce. We remained friends and had done our healing work, so when we connected via phone or in person it was often filled with the laughter that had brought us together. Yet the thread of his substance abuse never seemed to dwindle, and I remember the moment my heart moved from anger to compassion.

It was like a pendulum inside me swung from one place to another, and rather than being angry at alcoholism for stealing away someone I loved, I chose the path of understanding, peace and letting go.

For me, compassion is a feeling in my heart that mixes understanding with empathy. My heart feels soft when I go into a place of compassion and I can understand the suffering that someone else is going through without getting hooked.

Being married and divorced to Gerard gave me the incredible gift of compassion. He was a brilliant man, with a brilliant spirit and a brilliant heart. I miss him.

"I'VE LEARNED THAT WE SHOULD ALL BE UNBELIEVABLY IN LOVE WITH EACH OTHER. BEYOND THAT, IT'S JUST A MISUNDERSTANDING."

– GERARD BRILLOWSKI

Ironically enough, I was leaving a dance class when I got the voicemail from Gerard's second ex-wife. Just seeing her number come up on my phone told me volumes, but when I listened to the message, my heart sank. Today was the day.

It seemed that Gerard had been found unresponsive on a couch with a bottle of vodka lying next to him. He ended up dying from poisoning himself by drinking too much alcohol too fast. Curiously, I had never seen or heard of him drinking hard liquor in the 27 years that I knew him.

He was able to be revived enough by the EMT's to get to the hospital for more support. When I got the call, it was about 12 hours later, and he was put on life support. The doctors said he was quickly declining and my heart felt like parts of it were sinking along with him.

I knew in my bones that he would have hated to have been on life support, and I remember feeling both sad and angry about the choices that were made on his behalf. Gerard was the type of guy that liked to do things his own way, and he didn't like anyone to tell him what to do or how to live. He lived and died to the beat of an 80s new wave drummer.

When someone you love is dying, there is a choice. Be with them, or not. With the depth of connection that Gerard and I had for 27 years, it wasn't even an option not to be with him.

Calling the hospital from my car, I got more information from the doctors about Gerard's condition and prognosis. They told me he was stable yet fading, and I began heading home to pack to go to his side. If we can do nothing more than hold someone's hand while they're dying, we are offering a really great gift.

It was a six-hour drive to the hospital in Geneva, IL from my then home in St. Paul, MN, and I was ready to make the trek. Phoning James, I told him what was happening and my desire to drive to Illinois to hold Gerard's hand while he died. James was completely supportive, which was amazing, and it also said so much about his beautifully open and accepting heart.

By the time I got home, the hospital called back to tell me that Gerard had taken a turn and would be gone before I got there. I was absolutely crushed, and felt the blood in my heart falling swiftly to the bottoms of my feet. Then I sat still, and I took a deep breath.

Java's cremains were sitting in a bowl near me as I slumped into the couch. Losing two beings that I loved felt like way too much for one week let alone one day.

My beloved, James, drove over to my house to be with me and to hold my hand while we waited for Gerard to let go of all that he had been holding onto. That's a really good beloved.

As I punched in the Pink Floyd station on Pandora, Gerard's absolute favorite music, I remember a painfully sober feeling washing over every cell in my body. It was finally happening. He was dying completely.

All of a sudden "Shine On You Crazy Diamond" busted its way into the midst of another Pink Floyd song, and I knew it was a message. Pandora doesn't normally have songs that interrupt another song, but here was one of Gerard's favorite Pink Floyd tunes slicing in like it was pushing its way through. He was indeed shining on, and man, was he a crazy diamond!

I took a deep breath and smiled at the magic of Great Spirit in the form of Pink Floyd and walked up the stairs to go to the bathroom. As I neared the top of the stairs, I heard Gerard's voice ring through as clear as if he were standing on the top of the stairs next to me.

"I feel like an angel!" I heard him say, with a lightness and joy in his voice that I knew existed within him.

The phone startled me out of a Pink Floyd buzz five minutes later, and as I walked to pick it up, I let out another long exhale. I could feel in my heart that he was gone, and as I picked up the phone, the voice of his second ex-wife confirmed that Gerard had died a peaceful death just a few minutes before. With many loved ones at his side Gerard let go into the wind with one last exhale and a really loud cymbal crash.

I knew that Gerard was now going to be an angel for not only me, but for many hearts he had touched in his short 51 years on the planet. God bless everyone who gets to die a peaceful death – especially anyone who has lived a less than peaceful life.

The next day, I headed to Chicago, with Java's cremains in my car, to gather with friends and loved ones to honor Gerard's life. I couldn't imagine leaving her cremains at home and I couldn't imagine not going to Chicago.

Stopping at a coffee shop along the way, I walked in the door as Harry Belafonte's "Day Oh" came on from the house speakers. That was one of Gerard's classic songs when he and I played in the steel drum band together. To this day I have never heard that song played in any establishment, let alone a Midwest coffee shop. It was a wink from the other side for sure.

Grief has a life of its own. If there is one bit of advice about grief that I would like share, it's this. Grieve in any way you need to and for as long or as short as you need to. Grief doesn't wear a watch, and it's different for everyone. Kick, scream, cry, get an ice cream cone, wear your mother's t-shirt to bed for six months, bang on a drum, write, cook, suck your thumb, paint a picture, repeat. It's unique for each one of us, and it's so incredibly important for us to grieve. It's how we heal ourselves, one another and the planet, and it's how we heal the world.

On my way to Chicago, I stopped to sleep for the night and chuckled at bringing Java's cremains into the "No Pets Allowed" hotel. She would've loved that. She slept on one bed and I slept on the other. For the first time in many years, she didn't hog the covers.

I spent time that night talking with some of the guys that were in the steel drum band with Gerard and I for ten years. For ten years we traveled in a van together all over the Midwest, Colorado and Germany to share our music and frivolity, and now the man who had made it all happen was gone. We shared some tears together and shared stories that made us crack up until our hearts were full of the joy of Gerard. And, then I fell sound asleep.

Waking up in the morning, I started to gather my thoughts and my heart as I walked over to the hotel coffee pot in my room. As I started to pour the water into the reservoir, it emptied all over the counter. When I went to wipe it up, it was like it just kept coming out all over the place. There was water everywhere and then some, and I was curious how it had happened. I finally got it under control with a pile of hotel towels – giving up on making coffee – and sat down on the bed.

Then, I began to search for something on my phone, and my phone began to fritz out. It was doing things it had never done before like scrolling on its own without me touching it and locking up when it had never locked up before. Then a light went on.

Gerard was a clown when he was on the planet – like a real clown with a bright red clown nose, clown makeup and a clown name. He was Barney Bailey when he was a kid in Baraboo (say that three time fast), and his inner clown was definitely messing with me from the other side.

Spirits will come through however they can to get their point across. In his life, Gerard was not only a clown, he was a musician, an entertainer and a prankster. Although he was super funny in his life, I wasn't about to have him messing with me after his death. So, I told him very firmly to stop coming through to me as a prankster, and that if he wanted to connect with me from the other side he needed to come through in a kind a loving way.

Within moments, my phone started working, and so did the coffee maker.

Chapter Seven

GOING HOME

"WE'RE HERE
TO TAKE HER HOME."
-THE DOLPHINS

It is said that home is where the heart is, but what if we are not in our bodies anymore to have a physical heart and we get to choose where home is?

Java had come from the stars by way of the dolphins, and now they had come to take her home. A pod of thousands of dolphins arose in my mind's eye weeks before her death to share their wisdom that home was near.

After Gerard died, and Java died in the same week, I noticed inside of me that I was searching for a new place inside of myself called home. Letting go of some familiar and comfortable identities and titles, I began to search. Death can create a fruitful opportunity for more life.

Over the next few months, I found myself creating. I created ample space to grieve, ample space for my clients, ample space to foster my current relationship with James, and ample space for my heart to unfold into a place that felt tender and raw and totally new.

When someone dies, whether it be human or animal, there is a state that is called the Bardo or in between state - that place where beings go to figure out where they are and what's next. I liken it to a lobby at a doctor's office. You know you're going to the next place, but you have to wait and read old magazines first, and then wait for your name to be called.

It's during this Bardo state that those we've lost can often feel far away or even non-existent. In my own experience, everyone's Bardo state is different. I'm the type of person who chooses direct experience in order to gain most of my insight. Some people believe it can take a few months for a being to reconnect with loved ones on the planet. I say it takes as long as it does or doesn't.

It took only a short while for Java to start showing up for me, and the first sighting was in a dream. When Java was young, maybe 2 or 3 years old, I did what's called a Power Animal Retrieval on behalf of her. It sounds powerful and it is.

We are all born with a power or divine light. In the shamanic tradition or belief system, we have a guide who comes into this world with us. It may be an animal, a plant, a spirit in human form, a fairy, a rock – some entity whose job it is to help guide and support us.

I came into this world loving tigers more than anything on the planet. In fact, when I was only four years old, I tried to convince my parents that I promised I would take care of a tiger if I could please, oh, pretty please, can I please have a tiger?! As much as I begged, I couldn't convince my parents, but my love of tigers has never dwindled.

Along the way, we can lose our power in a variety of different ways. We can give it away or it can be taken from us. Our work is to maintain or reclaim our true power and reconnect with our own divinity. When we are in our power, we feel full of energy and feel powerful.

The work of the shaman or shamanic practitioner is to restore that power. I like to think of it like an oil change and tune up for your car. If you want your life/car to run smoothly, you have to maintain it. Get rid of what's not working for you, and fill yourself up with love and light. Keep your feet (tires) on the ground, your engine fine- tuned, and know when to press the gas and the brakes with grace and ease.

Power Animal retrievals involve a shamanic journey of some sort whether it be through drumming or rattling, or working with plant medicines or plant spirit medicines. Bottom line, it requires connection to become connected, so when we connect fully with our Power Animal and/or Spirit Guides, we become infused with the power that has always existed within us but we maybe had forgotten along the way.

The shamanic journey I had done on behalf of Java years prior had me going into that non-ordinary reality place through a drum journey to access an animal guide who would support Java in maintaining her power throughout her lifetime. We can have more than one animal teacher and spirit guide, so this was one of many teachers that Java received along the way.

During the power animal journey for Java, I went into a place in nature in my mind's eye, and soon after saw an image of a large moose walking directly toward me. I asked if it was a power animal for Java, and felt a strong yes in my heart. I could feel, see, smell and merge with this moose, and ask for guidance as well. When we go into a deep theta brainwave state, there is so much wisdom available to us when we take the time to listen deeply.

Asking for the spirit of the moose to return with me on behalf of Java, I cupped my hands over my heart and came back from the journey with the essence of moose medicine held gently in my hands and heart. Blowing the essence gently into Java's heart chakra and crown chakra, I shook my gourd rattle around her entire being as if to seal the moose medicine into her spirit forever. At the young age of 2 or 3, she had the power and wisdom of the moose as a teacher and guide along her side.

When we dream, we are connecting on some level with the unseen not unlike in the shamanic journey. In shamanism, everything is real, so we pay attention to our day dreams and our night dreams. As long as I can remember, I have had a very vivid night life. As a kid, I used to walk in my sleep, talk in my sleep, and my dreams have been colorful and powerful my entire life. The dream that came to me after Java died was profound.

The dream began with an image of myself lying in a train car that was stopped. All I could see was the four walls of the train car, but the top was wide open. Crystal clear blue skies sparkled above me like a crisp fall day in the Midwest – the type of day that is perfect for the first football game, raking leaves, apple pie and walking hand in paw with someone you love.

I often have lucid dreams – dreams where I am aware of the dream and can make choices during the dream. So, finding myself on the floor of the train car, unable to see outside of the four walls and just the sky above, I became curious. As I pulled myself up from the floor, I walked over to a wall of the train car and noticed a ladder. Climbing up the ladder, I could feel my body filling with anticipation and excitement as each step brought me closer to clarity.

Nearing the top of the train car, I was able to peek just over the edge of the wall to see what was outside of this metal box I had found myself in. Standing before me, in a field that spanned farther than I could see, were at least 300 peaceful moose. Some were grazing quietly and others were walking slowly.

What was most incredible to me was that they were each wearing a gigantic gold bow around their neck, so the image was not only expansive and sparkly, it was also unbelievably ecstatic. I knew that Java had made it to the other side, and that she was giving me a multi moose wink to let me know she was doing great and that all was well in her world. What an incredible, incredible gift she had given me in the dreamtime.

The dead come through however and wherever they can - sights, sounds, smells, feelings, hunches, touches – anything that will help us to know we are connecting with them. We might feel the temperature change as we walk through a room or we might feel a presence on the bed as we move into a slumber. Maybe we see a flash of something out of the corner of our eye, or song that connects us randomly presents itself.

For many months to follow, Java came through to me in the form of a smell. It was something like a combination of essential oils and death. Not necessarily the most pleasant of smells, but it was very obvious and it stopped me in my tracks every single time.

Sometimes I would smell her unique smell in the middle of a store, or while I was driving, or anytime I wasn't thinking of her specifically but she wanted to make sure I stayed connected in some way. When I asked her why she didn't come through in words, pictures or feelings like everyone else had done through my life and career, she responded,

"Because you wouldn't have believed me."

Bless Java for pushing the envelope and for making me a better medium.

Gerard also continued to come through in a variety of ways after he died. He showed up pecking at the church window in the form of a little yellow bird during his funeral, and he showed up one day in the form of our special song at a grocery store amidst music that was not even nearly the same genre. He shows up mostly in the form of sound and music, and it has always been something that has stopped me in my tracks. Nothing subtle from him either.

As part of my own grieving process, I began to honor Java's wish of dividing her cremains by gifting dear friends and family one at a time with a personal note that was channeled from Java. Along with the personally channeled note was a single bone fragment nestled in a small cardboard box that was decorated with a specific photo of her just for that person.

I was the last to receive a gift from Java. I honored one very large and distinct spinal bone by placing it on my altar – not knowing when or how I was going to release it, but knowing that at some point I would. I knew in my heart that the dolphins had called her home, and that what she had gifted me would return to the ocean one day.

And then there was the gift I gave myself. With the help of a local drum maker, I created a heart shaped bone rattle with an elk antler handle and filled it with 12 bone fragments – one for every year that she had lived – and lined it with rabbit fur. As a hunting dog by nature, Java would have loved to have killed a rabbit and ripped the fur off. Maybe she did while I wasn't looking.

Alongside the bone fragments inside the rattle was a small turquoise bear and a ¼" piece of quartz crystal. These sweet and sacred trinkets had been gifted to Java along the way in her life and I had used them as decoration for one of the drums I had made for my shamanic practice many years before.

The turquoise bear and quartz crystal were also the only pieces that were left from the cremains of my handmade drum that Java killed. Yes, she ate two shamanic frame drums in her lifetime, and the vet made her spit them out.

Death also makes us think about what really matters. As someone who has not enjoyed cold and snow for most of my adult life, I was ready to make a leap. I wasn't in a place of wanting to settle anymore in my life, and living in the Midwest was settling. My family had moved to warmer climates years prior, and now with the deaths of two beings I had loved dearly, I was re-evaluating my life.

I've learned that if we get clear on the "what by when" the "how" will present itself. The how is just fear, so if we can whack the fear, we can move forward. I wanted to whack the ice and snow and to head toward home – the place of the whales and dolphins – the Pacific Ocean.

The only thing that had been in the way was fear, and now I felt fearless.

Chapter Eight

SUNNY SURRENDER

"LET HAPPINESS FILL THE ROOM
THAT LIFE GIVES YOU." - JAVA

I got crystal clear. As a Madison, WI native who had chosen to live in the Midwest for all of her 46 years so far, I was done freezing my ass off. Done.

The winter after the year that both Java and Gerard died would mark my last full Minnesota winter of shoveling myself out of my house for 6 months straight. I wasn't sure how I was going to swing it, but I knew what I wanted and I knew I wanted it by December 1, 2014.

What by when minus the how equals power.

How was I going to do it? What about my relationship with James? What about my house? What about my friends and clients and.....?

Fear has a life of its own. A friend of mine once told me a great acronym for fear – Forgetting Everything's All Right. The other one I love is Fuck Everything And Run! Fear can make us fight, run away, run toward, run in circles, freeze, faint and fool around – just like it does with the animals. I was determined to choose to remember that everything was alright.

With a heart navigating grief, James and I took one of what would be two amazing trips to Northern California to check out the area and see how it felt. I had one dear friend who lived in the area, some family and some community possibilities. And, I had Mother Ocean. She was enough of a draw for me.

As a water sign, and a Star Being, the ocean is home for me. It really didn't even matter where I was living as long as I could at least drive to see the ocean, touch the ocean, taste the ocean, smell the ocean and become the ocean.

With the help of one amazing life coach and two therapists, I started on my way to making sure I was making a clear decision for myself, and not choosing codependency. I knew that if I stayed in Minnesota any longer my spirit would shrivel and die. That's not good for stars to fizzle out prematurely.

It was helpful to have a partner who also wanted to leave shoveling behind and head out on a new adventure. And yet, with him having more than half of his life and career in Minnesota, and family still in the Midwest, it was definitely a big leap for him.

Me on the other hand, my Mom and sister were in the Southwest and my Dad was in the afterlife, so moving somewhere else for me wasn't held back by family. Minnesota didn't feel like home to me, and I had created a business that was completely mobile and he had not. Hello, creative tension!

With the "what by when" as clear as a bell, I began to trust. I trusted my relationship would be and become whatever it needed to be in our highest good in order to move both of us forward in life. I trusted that I would be living in California near the ocean. I trusted that my house would find a new person to live in it and my mortgage would be paid by someone else.

Our first trip to Northern California turned out to be more magical than we could have imagined. I was in the area to teach a Tellington TTouch® Training for Dogs and their People, and we happened to have one free day on the trip. James and I were staying in the East Bay at an Airbnb and woke up to one free day to create in any way we wanted. Looking at a map, I pointed to what looked like the end of the earth and said,

"Let's go there!"

Where *there* was, was a tiny little piece of land jutting out into the ocean within driving distance. It seemed like a worthy day trip adventure, and we were both up for a day together of exploring. We looked to see what we could find out about this little piece of land, and after looking online at one photo of an old barn with a huge peace sign on the front I knew that this end of the earth destination was what was next.

We hopped in the rental car and found ourselves weaving and winding on the glorious roads of Marin County. Noticing a number of cars parked on the side of the road, we stopped at a market to see what was happening and what we might be missing. It was Valentine's Day and we enjoyed the gifts of hot pink, red and white that were filling the market and our hearts. Our sacred journey kept us open to whatever messages might come our way as we wove our way to the end of the earth.

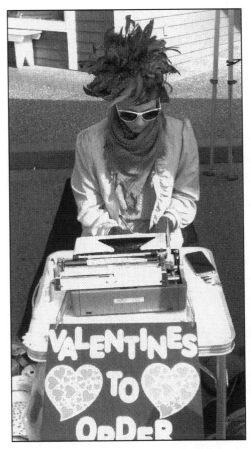

Walking up to a booth at the market, we were amused by a very colorful, young woman wearing a hot pink and purple peacock hat of feathers and dressed in a long bubble gum pink gown from the early 1900s. She was sitting behind an old typewriter with a sign draped in front of her that read, *Free Love Poems.*

James and I walked up with our squeaky-clean Midwest smiles, and eagerly asked if she would please write a poem for us. Since they were free, she of course said yes, and then she asked us what we were dreaming about. She asked what we wanted to manifest and what we wanted to create in our lives.

We shared with her our dream of leaving the brutal winters of the Midwest and heading to a warmer climate, and as we held hands tightly, we shared our dream of deepening our lives together as a couple.

She nodded her head as her feathery hat bobbed up and down, and told us to walk around the market for a little bit while she created a unique poem just for us.

Finding the cookie decorating booth for five-year-olds, we sat down and decorated our own Valentine's Day cookie with little eyebrows raised next to us on the picnic table. Big kids are not supposed to decorate cookies, I guess, but we did. We passed a booth with baby goats, and then the one with spinach and kale, and finally couldn't resist sitting on the curb to have the best donut on the planet.

Fifteen minutes passed, and we went back to the colorful bubble gum dress woman to see what had come from our dreams and desires. She read the poem aloud to us with the peacock feathers in her hat bouncing along playfully to the cadence she had created. James and I held hands even tighter as we smiled together and felt the poem go deeply into our hearts and souls.

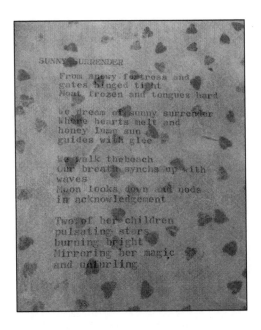

<u>SUNNY SURRENDER</u>

From snowy fortress and gates hinged tight

Moat frozen and tongues hard

We dream of sunny surrender where hearts melt

and honey lump sun guides with glee

We walk the beach

Our breath syncs up with waves

Moon looks down and nods in acknowledgement

Two of her children - pulsating stars burning bright

Mirroring her magic and unfurling

Getting back in the car with our poem to manifest a warmer life, we checked the map to continue heading toward the barn with the peace sign at the end of the earth. More winding roads led us through greener pastures as huge eucalyptus trees reminded our senses that clarity was around every bend.

Our car ended up at this little stretch of land in Bolinas, CA for a few hours as we combed the beach for shells and rocks. Along the way, we each placed a piece of our hair into the ocean as an inquiry to Great Spirit. If we were meant to plant ourselves in California, may it be so.

Checking the map for the clearest route back to our Airbnb, we opted for a direct path. Winding back through the hills of Marin, we passed a state park that our bodies whimsically remembered from a trip we had taken together many years back. Two months after James and I met, we went to California for a family wedding and found ourselves taking a nap on a picnic table at the same state park we were now driving past. We thought about another picnic table nap, but continued on as we mused about the synchronicity.

A few miles down the road, we stopped at a general store in a cute little town called Lagunitas and treated ourselves to a coffee malt in the rain. Continuing on, we spotted a sign that read *Spirit Rock Meditation Center* and we immediately pulled in.

Only a week prior, a friend had told us we should check out Spirit Rock. Somehow we hadn't written it down, but Great Spirit reminded us to turn our heads and pay attention.

Driving into Spirit Rock, we noticed a serenity as we neared what looked like a trailer surrounded by stone Buddha sculptures. As we tiptoed through the tulips - because that's what you're supposed to do at a meditation center - we became curious what this place was about. Nearing the front door of the community hall, we saw a flyer on the door that told us there was a couple's workshop happening that day. More tiptoes into the building, we removed our shoes and stuck our noses and hearts into the hall for a few minutes to breathe in the medicine of the Buddha and see what other couples were doing on Valentine's Day.

Walking out, my eye caught a flyer that shared an upcoming workshop in a few months with Jack Kornfield, the founder of Spirit Rock and one of my favorite authors many years prior. I remember reading one of Jack's earlier books, *After the Ecstasy, the Laundry*, when Java and I lived alone outside of Madison, WI. That book was a teacher for me after my divorce - when Java was a puppy and so was I.

Synchronicity?

As you might think, two tiptoeing Midwestern tulips might cause a bit of a stir at a somewhat silent retreat, so someone came out of the office to ask if they could help us. We told them we were considering a move to California and had interest in Jack Kornfield's workshop that was coming up in April of that year. The office person told us we could volunteer for Jack's workshop as a trade for coming at no cost.

Jaws dropped, as we looked at one another knowing full well we were going to plan another trip to this magical place in the Spring! We told them we'd be back to volunteer at Spirit Rock, and headed through the land of Buddha and Kwan Yin statues back to the spiritual parking lot.

Back in our car, we headed over a gorgeous green hill that dropped us into the edge of a small town with a fluttering heartbeat. We both needed to go to the bathroom, so we pulled into a market on the left side of the road to do our business. Walking out of our prospective bathrooms and into the parking lot, James and I looked at each other and both said simultaneously,

"We could live here!"

It was amazing that we both felt exactly the same thing at the same time, and we wondered where we were. It felt like some sort of vortex that was sucking us in, yet at the same time it felt peaceful and right. We decided to follow the thread and figure out where we were and why it was so intoxicating to our souls to be there.

Across the street we saw a coffee shop and headed that direction – seeing a sign along the way that said *Fairfax*. Okay, I guess we were in Fairfax.

As coffeeshops are so good at, this one hooked us up to the internet so we could research what town we were in, what we could find out about it, where we had been and where we might want to go next. Fairfax felt like the energy of Madison, WI where I had spent most of my life, and James said it felt familiar to him, too. Something about this little town resonated with our spirits, and the people in Fairfax seemed free, colorful and fun. It just plain felt great there.

After more research and doing some astrological woo woo, we found out that the planetary energy of Fairfax was astonishingly the same as the cities we each were born in – Madison, WI and Council Bluffs, IA. No wonder this funky small-town felt familiar to both of us. On some level, we had been there before.

After that day at the coffee shop in Fairfax, we both became curious. We became curious enough to get more curious, and curious enough to surrender to making a move toward the ocean. Together.

Chapter Nine

MOTHER OCEAN

"NOTHING
IS EVER
PERSONAL."
- MOTHER OCEAN

I felt and heard her long before I saw her. Her smell permeated every cell of my body and made me feel more alive than I ever had felt before. Like the rush that happens right before an orgasm, her power creates a surge of energy in everything she touches. And when she touches me, she *really* touches me.

Water matters to all living things. In some organisms, up to 90% of their body weight comes from water. Up to 60% of the human adult body is water, and men often need more water than women. According to H.H. Mitchell, Journal of Biological Chemistry 158, the brain and heart are composed of 73% water, and the lungs are about 83% water. The skin contains 64% water, muscles and kidneys are 79%, and even the bones are 31% water.

Electrifying, water is a conduit from here to there. She holds and contains yet flows and crashes. She carries and allows and never asks for anything in return. She is completely accepting and willing to allow and let go.

"Nothing is ever personal." She once told me. "The waves don't apologize to the shore and the shore doesn't judge the waves for being who they are. Yet why do you as humans judge and apologize for being who you are and how you behave? Nature works in harmony with itself and one another so why don't you?"

Good questions, Mother Ocean!

I could sit and watch her for hours - the up and down, in and out, rise and fall, full release, her retreat and crashing forward. Carrying with her a history and mystery, she drops the remnants of all she has held onto with seemingly haphazard intention. The shore becomes littered with stories of indescribable wisdom.

She pulls back and takes with her that which is ready to be released - sucking and slurping as she swallows what she needs completely. She leaves behind all that isn't necessary to maintain her composure – discarding what isn't helpful anymore, or just discarding because she can. I wonder if the ocean has a conscious spring-cleaning day like we humans tend to do. I highly doubt it.

When I go to the ocean I become the ocean. When the ocean comes to me she becomes me. It's like there is no separation between she and I. Her saltwater tears run through my spirit. I was once told by my ex-husband, the wild drummer, that we don't drum the drum but that the drum drums us. Well, the ocean oceans me.

"Grieve not," she told me, "for all that you hold onto is the cause of your suffering. Let go and there will be no grief. It's in the holding that you suffer. The wave doesn't ask permission to crash. She just crashes. Allow yourself to let go into the power, release and full ecstasy of oneness."

The best massage in the world might be amazingly wonderful for the body and mind, but nothing beats a barefoot walk on the beach for soothing the soul.

On many sunny and also blustery days, I walked barefoot on her beach and listened intently to Mother Ocean teach me how to live and how to die with reverence. She speaks directly to me and speaks directly through me.

On my most recent walk upon her shore, I noticed a peacefulness I hadn't had before. It was like I finally moved into a place of deep conversation that was simple and clear. Rather than wondering if what I was hearing and feeling was real or not, I just knew that it was. We were one that day, she and I.

Gathering my yellow and teal silk peace sign scarf up around my neck to shelter myself from her cool breeze, I felt the saltwater tears flow from my eyes down my already saltwater stained face. Like the grief that comes when we say goodbye to a beloved friend or loved one, my heart could feel the letting go.

"Don't look back." she said as I blew her one last kiss goodbye. "I will be here when you come back."

She has taught me love and passion and power and more gratitude than I knew I was able to feel. She has taught me to let go and not take things personally, and how to be in relationship with myself and others.

With my back to her, I meandered my way back to the car as the frogs began to sing.

And we sang together all the way down the path.

ON RELATIONSHIP
- THE PACIFIC OCEAN

In and out. Up and down.

Back and forth.

That's what we call relationship.

You suffer because you suffer.

You grieve because you hold on.

Joy is the only thing that exists,

but you haven't totally figured that one out yet.

Let go to the rhythm of life,

then nothing is a big deal. Nothing.

In and out. Up and down.

Back and forth.

Can you feel how easy that is?

Chapter Ten

ONE STEP CLOSER

"ONE DAY YOU FINALLY KNEW
WHAT YOU HAD TO DO, AND BEGAN..."
- FROM "THE JOURNEY"
BY MARY OLIVER

With the ocean as my goal, somehow I managed to get whatever really mattered from my entire two-bedroom house in St. Paul, MN into the inside of my Volkswagen Golf. Piece by piece, I let go of my history, my comfort, my story, my grief, the life I thought I wanted to live and the life I didn't want to live anymore. Finally, all that was left was a 4' x 3' x 3' pile of what seemed like it really mattered.

There's been a trend to downsize and minimize – to declutter our homes and our lives so that we are left with only the things that bring us joy. But what nobody tells us is that downsizing hurts like hell and that we have to get through that hell before the joy comes.

For over ten years, I had been living in my healing house and now I was letting go of all of the memories and the stuff that went along with the memories. It was kind of like ripping off a band aid really slowly on hairy skin. It's easier if someone else does it for you and you don't know it's coming. Ouch!

Keeping my heart on the prize the entire time, I knew what my soul most wanted: to be warm and to be near Mother Ocean. I unraveled and Craigslisted. I gave away and donated. I sold and held on. I cried little whimpers and I bawled buckets. I laughed and shut down. I got angry, laughed some more and finally, finally, finally I felt amazing.

The Beatles cassettes that were recorded the night John Lennon was shot were sold for pennies to a woman whose daughter was blind and loved the Beatles. I sold the Brownie camera I had since I was four to someone on eBay who was unbelievably excited to find a Brownie camera. I gifted special friends with a multitude of sacred objects – items that I knew would be cared for and appreciated until it was time for them to move on again.

I threw away my entire art portfolio from my days owning a graphic design studio, and tossed the tear stained memories that went along with seeing my ex-husband's handwriting on the artwork I had done for our steel drum band's final recording together. I tore one random page from each of my 18 journals – a keepsake of something or another – and asked my beloved, James, to please run out to the garbage truck that was passing by. He did it because I couldn't, and yet once the bag of journals was out the door, it just didn't even matter anymore.

There's a veil in letting go that is palpable and permeable. It reminds me of those beads that some of us had hanging in our closets in the 70s where you'd get tangled up in the beads when you'd try to get in or out of the closet. Sometimes the veil is easy to get through and other times it feels like we get caught up.

There were some objects that I let go of where I felt tangled up and others that were not a big deal at all. For the most part, it hurt to let go, and yet as the year began to unfold it became easier. I either had to haul it across the country or let it go.

Catharsis means we are acknowledging painful truths. The painful truth was that I had carried and collected for most of my life, and I thought all these material objects carried meaning themselves. In reality, it was the energy that I gave these objects that carried the meaning.

One of the greatest gifts I was given was from James. He told me that before I let go of anything that was hard to let go of – anything dear to me - just say goodbye and give it a kiss. With tears and resistance, I kissed and I let go, and I kissed and I let go. I bet there are still items at the thrift store in St. Paul, MN with my kisses on them. Kissing really does help to let go. So does hugging and saying *I love you*.

If there's one amazing nugget that I learned from downsizing my 956 square foot home to what fit into 12 square feet in my Volkswagen, it's this: Most of what we have a tight grip on doesn't matter in the long run at all.

It took one more trip to California, 10 months of downsizing, plus many grueling sessions with two therapists and a life coach to help me stay on track with my goal of living near the ocean. If you've ever had a dream, and had any fear, you know what I'm talking about. One of them has to win out. I chose the dream which meant I chose life.

As Spring came that year, I found myself back in California for a soul-searching journey alongside my beloved, James. We had packed our bags and decided this time to explore the area a bit more, and to make sure that we were making a conscious decision before leaping. We were also on a mission to release the last little bits of Java's cremains into the Pacific Ocean – back to the dolphins so they could take her home.

I honestly don't remember much about that trip other than volunteering at Spirit Rock Meditation Center with Jack Kornfield, a lot of sunshine, a very poignant time at the ocean and a short jaunt to Santa Cruz. I'm sure there was more to remember, but sometimes what really matters floats to the top or sinks to the bottom.

On the last day of our trip - with sacred objects and sacred cremains in tow - James and I headed down one of the many winding roads in Marin County. We knew we were heading toward the ocean – due West - but we didn't really know where we were going. I've learned that it's just as important to have a clear destination as it is to be open to spontaneity.

As we passed through green hill after green hill, and cow pasture after cow pasture, we came upon a group of parked cars near what looked like a trailhead. James rolled down the window and asked a passerby why all the cars were parked there. The person informed us we were at one of the most magical trailheads to what would soon become our favorite beach.

Strapping my shamanic drum to my back, with Java's last bone fragment wrapped gently inside my backpack, James and I headed down the wild orange poppy lined trail with a combination of joy and grief. It had taken me just over a year to gift Java's cremains to the people she loved, and those who loved her – thirty-two people in seven different states. Now, the last physical memory – a perfect vertebrae bone that had rested gently on my altar for just over a year - was about to return home.

Kehoe beach is one of the most magical beaches I've ever been to. It's not that the sand is particularly special, or the waves are this or that. It's just magical because it has a spiritual presence that's unlike most other beaches I've visited in my life so far. The waves at Kehoe definitely have a power and majesty, and the rock formations have crazy strong energy. It's fairly remote with a decent hike in and expansive in many ways, and you can throw a frisbee forever.

As James and I walked hand in hand along the beach I could feel my heart unraveling – knowing that I was about to let go of one thing that really mattered to me – the last tangible memory of Java's physical form. For 12-1/2 years I had held her body, bathed it, clipped her nails, brushed her teeth, cleaned her ears, lifted her up, led her out of harm's way, touched every little spot on her powerful brindle frame with love and care, and so much more. All that was left of her physical memory was one bone. One very, very special, beautiful bone.

With the sand, the ocean and James as my witnesses, I climbed my way to the top of a huge rock covered with blue and white barnacles. Powerful waves rushed up and licked my feet, as I felt the crunch of the crustaceans below me.

The heartbeat of Mother Earth pounded inside of me, while I drummed and wailed and drummed and wailed. I asked Great Spirit to please help me let go of the last little bits of what I was holding onto as I prayed passionately for Java to be taken home. Then, with all of the courage I could muster up, I tossed the last physical memory of my beloved animal companion deep into the mouth of Mother Ocean.

One last full belly exhale, I stood in sacred stillness with salty tears streaming down my cheeks and the taste and smell of the ocean on my tongue and in my nostrils. I felt more like myself than I had in a long time, and yet I could feel that a part of me was rebirthing into someone new.

Watching the waves suck the last little bits of Java's body out to sea, I felt my heart release one more step closer to victory, as each wave soothed the part of me that was hurting. I was almost home, and Java *was* home.

James made his way to the top of the rock to hold me closely as we both wept in silence. After however long it took, we climbed back down the rock together and began our trek toward what was next.

Strolling hand in hand down the shore and up a sandy bank, we hiked our way back down the poppy lined trail to our car and weaved our way back through the curves and cows.

Stopping at a roadside deli on the way back to civilization, I spotted a huge map of the coast that was painted on the side of the building. The map had all of the beaches listed along the coast and as my eyes moved up the shoreline to the beach we had just been to, my heart skipped a beat.

Kehoe Beach – Dogs Ok.

Great Spirit had definitely led us straight to the perfect spot where dogs were okay and Java's spirit could swim and run free forever. She would have loved that.

As Spring ended and Summer in Minnesota began, it brought with it a lot of fun and frivolity along with a plethora of trips to the thrift store. One sure way to make certain to get things out of your house is to fill a bag next to the door that bothers you enough to take it outside. After it bugs you enough, it goes directly in the front seat of the car so there's no room for any friends until the thrift store run. In addition to the thrift store bag by the door, I kept a running garbage bag going as well. And then there were the leftover piles of things I kept since I was a kid that I needed to photograph, get on eBay, try to sell, cry because nobody wanted them, try again, sell them or give them away.

What I learned through this letting go process is that I did it the way I needed to in order to really feel my heart. I remember the night I sat on the floor of my second bedroom and cried alone as I let go of old memories that nobody but me would really care about or understand.

You might wonder why I threw so much stuff away rather than hiring movers and keeping it all. Maybe you totally get it because you've downsized before, too. Or maybe you wonder how I handpicked certain people in my life to gift specific items or you wonder what I chose to keep that only took up 12 square feet of space?

What I can tell you is this: Downsizing is important. We die with our bodies, and that's it. All the stuff we leave behind really doesn't matter too much to other people after a while. Some of it we might hang onto because there's a memory or an energetic charge, but it's in the letting go that we get closer to being able to do the big letting go at the end of our lives. And all that stuff we leave behind is going to get thrown away, gifted, sold, kept or sent to the thrift store anyway. Why not start now?

I remember watching a deer walk through the woods one day as I thought to myself, *What an amazingly Zen being to live in this world with only a body – no car keys, no wallet, no clothes, no baggage.*

"12 SQUARE FEET OF STUFF"

As the fun and frivolity of Summer began to subside, my goal was coming closer and closer. Leaving for the ocean the beginning of December was starting to become more of a reality, as I had already said my goodbyes to Winter, then Spring and now Summer.

My house became emptier and I noticed that my heart became more spacious. I became more available to feel everything that maybe I hadn't allowed myself to feel, including the pain and agony of deeply letting go. I was letting go of an identity I had created that wasn't serving me anymore.

Walking out to my car on a crisp Fall day, about six weeks before our departure to the West Coast, I noticed a large white sign had blown my way from the church across the street. It had gotten wedged under the rear tires of my Volkswagen and read one simple phrase in bright red letter. I laughed out loud.

"ONE STEP CLOSER TO VICTORY."

Victory is like a triumph or conquest, so who was the enemy that I was defeating? Was there an enemy? I felt somewhat victorious, yet I was very aware that something was holding me back from fully feeling the victory.

Yep, the fear had crept back in, like fear tends to do. I feared that I would freeze to death and have to live in a place that didn't feed my soul. I feared that my house wouldn't sell, and then fearful that it wouldn't rent. I was afraid that I'd have to settle for what I didn't want, and fearful that I'd be alone. I feared that my relationship wouldn't last if I stayed in Minnesota and fearful that it wouldn't last if I left Minnesota.

I was afraid that James wouldn't actually come with me to the West Coast, and afraid that he would and that it would be hard. My fear was that my fear would last, and that my fear would create more fear. You get the picture. It was a fear festival.

We can make it hard, or we can make it easy. After worrying about way too much for way too long, I decided to choose easy. My house became rented, and James and I courageously kissed our Midwest pasts goodbye as we drove away from a frigid December day toward a much warmer future.

We were one step closer to victory, one step closer to ourselves and each other, and one step closer to living and breathing near Mother Ocean.

Chapter Eleven

LIGHTNING STRIKES

"EVERYTHING IS ALIVE!"
- REGGAE

Lightning came into this world like a great jolt of electricity who struck the ground with the utmost power and playfulness. A force of nature, he was strikingly beautiful and electrified everything with joy along his path.

His siblings Storm, Thunder and Rain slid through the portal of life alongside his tiny little brindle frame, entering into a world of togetherness and separation. With a bright white blaze stretching from his polka dotted snout to the top of his head, Lightning was ready to take on the world one stick at a time. His tongue was his superpower.

As many young domesticated animals do, Lightning said goodbye to his family, packed his bags and toddled off to a new family that would hopefully love and care for him. They did just that until they were done doing just that. That's what we humans do sometimes – we stop loving and caring and leave it for someone else to do.

We also forget to tell the animals what's happening, so chances are pretty good that this 4-5-week-old puppy had absolutely no idea what was happening to himself and his family members. Can you imagine being separated from your family without anyone telling you? We do this with the animals every day, and the more I become aware, the more painful it seems at times. We have a responsibility when we say yes to bringing a domesticated animal into our lives. It is our job to create a safe haven that is filled with comfort, joy, love, playfulness and impeccable care.

Lightning had some work to do before he came to us. He needed to change homes seven times before the age of six months and have two different names before we got to live in the same house. At the same time, James and I had some work to do to prepare for Lightning's arrival. Especially since we didn't know it was going to happen.

After Java died, James and I had talked about getting another dog. However, one year later turned into a little over three years and here we were, *Dogless in California.*

We enjoyed the independence of not having to care for another being, and yet we also noticed that we had become a little overly focused on ourselves and each other. Not that that's a bad thing, but it can also turn into hyper focus. It's healthy to create and support an energy outside of ourselves. We were ready to create.

Synchronicity is an amazing thing. If James hadn't walked down *that street* at *that time* and seen *that dog* and talked to *those people* who knows what might have happened. But he did all of those things because something made him turn his head that Fall day and a dog who looked similar to Java happened to be walking by to catch his heart.

Crossing the street, he struck up a conversation with the people about their Plott Hound – the same breed that Java had been. The people told him that their dog was competing in a Dock Dog competition that weekend at a Pet Fair in town and they invited James and I to come and watch.

James came home with an invitation, and on a sunny Saturday in our now state of California, we headed to the Pet Fair to watch a dog who looked like Java jump into the water. Because we were living in a rental that didn't allow dogs, we were completely safe from coming home unconsciously with a dog. In fact, it wasn't even on our radar, but we did know we couldn't get a dog until we owned our own home or had a rental that allowed dogs. Or so we thought.

As lightning strikes, so did Lightning. Driving into the parking lot of the Pet Fair, James and I spotted a tannish looking dog with a white blaze up its head from across the parking lot. At exactly the same time, we looked at each other and both said,

"Look at that DOG!"

So, we looked. *Strike one.*

Lightning was made of rubber, marshmallows, unconditional love and beautiful fur. His brindle coloring, not unlike Java's, tugged at my heartstrings and yet he was such a different brindle it didn't tug too hard. He was his own precious cargo.

"He's available!" said the foster Mom on the other end of the light blue leash with sailboats on it.

Name #2 for this pup was Mozart, or Mozzie as he was now called, and as we petted him all over his sturdy little body, we were slathered in a multitude of sloppy, wet kisses. His tongue, was *definitely* his superpower.

The foster told us to come and visit her in the adoption building at the Pet Fair, and we told her that although he was a wonderful dog, we weren't in the market. Um, yet.

Off we went, to watch the Plott Hound plop into the water at the Dock Dogs competition – the dog that looked like Java that James had seen a few days earlier. You can't go wrong watching dogs run down a runway and fly through the air to see who can jump the farthest. With a huge splash into the water below, the dogs are cheered on to swim back to the ramp, get out, shake off and do it all over again.

I don't remember the name of the brindle Plott Hound who got us to the Pet Fair that day to watch him compete, but I would like to publicly thank him for being a catalyst for what would become one of the greatest love affairs of all time.

True to our spontaneous form and love of dogs, James and I found ourselves just checking out the adoption building and finding our way to Lightning/Mozart. There he was – a lump of love lying on the floor of the arena with dogs, kids, people and ice cream cones walking past him. He was unflappable. And, he was still available. *Strike two.*

After more petting and more kisses, James and I looked at each other and said,

"If we *EVER* get another dog, let's get one like this one!"

The foster Mom told us that if anything changed in our living situation, and we wanted to take Mozzie, we should give her a call. We exchanged information and off we went with two fairly broken hearts.

If you've ever walked away from a dog who was amazing, you know how it feels. Living in a house that didn't allow dogs made it simple for us to walk away in some way, and also a challenge to know what we really wanted. And, it wasn't more that 10 minutes after we left the Pet Fair before we started to wonder if we could find a house that would allow a dog.

Getting back to our sweet little cabin in the redwoods, we imagined what it might be like to have a dog again. I wondered if I could possibly ever love another dog nearly as much as I had loved Java, and whether it would even be fair to get another dog. Java had raised the bar on my heart.

I felt myself thinking about Lightning/Mozart and noticed I just couldn't take my mind off of him. There was something really special about that young dog, and I could feel my heart making a different shape. As the Universe works, we can manifest exactly what we want and also exactly what we don't want.

The day after the Pet Fair ended, we received a surprising phone call from Mozzie's foster Mom to tell us that he had found a new home. I felt both a sense of relief and deep, deep grief. The relief was the fact that James and I didn't have to decide, and the grief spoke to my heart which was already loving him.

The heart doesn't lie. When we love, we can feel every cell in our body filled with lightness and positivity. It's like our spirit is running the show and our ego is taking the back seat. There's a grounded floating feeling when we choose to love. Love is a choice. So is letting go.

James and I let go of Mozart that day, and went on with our lives. We dreamed of the next dog that might come around, and wondered who it would be and when. The Pet Fair had allowed us to take a look at what we were willing to do to bring a dog into our lives, and what type of dog we would enjoy caring for.

"If we ever get a dog, we should name him Reggae!" James said to me enthusiastically as he consoled our grief with hope.

I smiled at his creativity and exuberance. Reggae. What a perfect name. Yes, we will name our next dog, Reggae.

Two days later, the phone rang again. It was Mozart's foster Mom calling to tell us that his adoption hadn't worked out and that he had been returned. It seemed that he was too big and boisterous for the Chihuahua and Pomeranian that he was placed with.

Would we like to take him? An emphatic YES came over my heart, but we couldn't have a dog in the cabin where we were living. Now what?

I am blessed to live with a brilliant and creative man. James spoke up immediately and said,

"Let's ask our landlord again and offer her more money for rent and a dog deposit. He's a really special dog, and I know he'll be okay here."

My heart skipped a hundred beats like a hummingbird's wings doing a dance of joy. The outpouring of love from James' heart showed me that he and I were on the same page about this dog. We both really wanted to have him in our lives and to give him a great home.

For whatever reason, Mozart had already been back and forth seven times between homes, shelters and fosters and he was only six months old. Something told me that Great Spirit was watching over all of us to create the perfect storm for Lightning to come crashing into our lives at just the right time.

Third time's a charm. With a simple text to our landlord, the deal was sealed. She was very willing to allow us to have Mozart in her cabin as long as we picked up after him and kept the house intact. No problem. *Strike three. You're in!*

Within minutes, we phoned Mozart's foster Mom and told her we wanted to have him as part of our family. Celebration abounded as we spun around like whirling dervishes the next 24 hours to get ready to bring an unexpected young dog into our lives. Our dear Reggae, was coming through the portal of our hearts and into our home.

My job was to drive across the San Francisco Bay to pick up our new family member the next day while James was at work. What a wonderful job!

There were a myriad of feelings swirling around me as I crossed the Richmond Bridge that day – water below and future ahead. With Bob Marley's Greatest Hits playing on my cd player, I felt myself connecting with Mozart telepathically before I saw him physically. I asked him if he was okay being named Reggae. I no more than got the question out of my head, when Java showed up.

"Do you *know* how lucky you are, Reggae!?" Java said to him.

Within an hour, Mozart became Reggae, and the back window of my Volkswagen Golf became his safe haven as he said goodbye one last time to his foster Mom. Traveling back across the Richmond bridge with a brindle marshmallow in the back of my car, I felt my heart begin to open to a new place that I didn't know existed. It was clear I had more space to love.

When we grieve the loss of someone we love – whether it's a human, animal or both – we can create space for someone new to fill in its place. Reggae was something new in our lives that was filling in the space from the grieving and loving that I had done with Java.

A bright white blaze of lightning shaped fur crawled up his head and an adorable polka dotted muzzle held space for huge white whiskers that would stop passersby with delight. Reggae became a force of love with a heart of gold and a spirit to match. A possible boxer mixed with pit bull, maybe lab and lots of marshmallows, Reggae was soft and squishy and solid as the redwoods. He also had the intelligence and loyalty that was going to make him an absolutely amazing grown up dog.

The first time we took Reggae to the ocean, he stopped dead in his tracks from about a hundred yards away. With eyes wide open as whale eyes, he his breath in awe at the playground that he saw before him.

Within moments, he ran straight up to the shoreline, did a huge play bow in front of his new friend, Mother Ocean, as if to say to her, *C'mon! Let's play!*

Then he ran straight into the water and hopped around like a grasshopper on a pogo stick like he was reunited with an old friend. In time, Reggae learned how to body surf, how to swim like a dolphin (often for hours and without care of concern) and he learned very easily how to come back to us when we called his name. It didn't take long until I learned that he was amazing.

Reggae spent a lot of time with James and I in a safe, comfortable and loving home, and he also had to work through some issues. Not unlike most of us, Reggae had come to us feeling uncertain, a little aloof, a little out of balance and not totally trusting the world around him. There were a couple of occasions where I heard a low growl coming from him, and I thought to myself, *I can't live with another challenging dog!*

The thought of letting him go crossed my mind, and my heart knew exactly what I needed to do.

Stepping up my game by adding more Tellington TTouch® Training in his daily routine, he began to trust that the world was a safe place and that we would keep him in our lives forever. He became more balanced on all levels and began to play more with his toys and interact more. He became more affectionate, and stopped using his mouth inappropriately when we got near his feet to wipe off the mud he had found along the way. His growls quickly became a slight lip lick when he wasn't feeling safe, and he stopped jumping up in the air like a kangaroo when he was ungrounded.

Reggae learned that the world we brought him into is a safe place, and that we would care for him, respect his needs, and provide not only his basic needs, but also a lot of love. He has taught me that everything is alive – the ocean, a puddle, a tennis ball, a stick, the trees, the wind, sunshine, the raindrops, the snow, the sand. You name it. It's all alive and it's all worth playing with. Reggae makes his *own* sunshine.

Today, Reggae and I are a registered therapy team for teenagers at a juvenile detention center. He teaches people to be gentle and to relax, and that stress can be released in healthy ways. He puts a smile on the faces of everyone he meets because nobody can resist that face. Reggae helps people feel safe, comfortable and loved, and helps them remember how to smile, laugh and play. He helps people remember that when marshmallows are mixed with a little reggae music, sprinkled with some Mozart and lightning, and a lot of love and safety are tossed in, great things can happen.

Reggae is reggae. He's chill, funny, loving and trustworthy with a great backbeat that you can easily dance to. Lightning struck and I have been electrified.

"YOU ARE SUCH A GREAT DOG!

IT FEELS LIKE

YOU'VE BEEN HERE BEFORE."

— SAGE

" I AM EVERYTHING THAT JAVA

WANTED TO BE."

— REGGAE

Chapter Twelve

SLOW DOWN
& PAY ATTENTION

"BE THANKFUL FOR EVERYTHING."
- ALICE SCHATTAUER

"Be thankful for everything." She said to me on one of our weekly calls.

I took me some time to slow down to the point of realizing I wanted a more intimate relationship with her. Sparkling blue eyes and hair as white as the fallen snow, Alice reminded me on many occasions that every day is a gift and we should appreciate all that comes our way.

We are blessed to run across people in our lives who teach us things that are useful. I remember when I was much younger, there was a man who lived across the street and he seemed old. He was nearing retirement, and every day when I came home from work he walked across the street to greet me as I was walking from the mailbox back to my house.

Bill was an art teacher, and so was I, so we had that in common. What we didn't have in common was speed. I wanted to get the mail and hurry up back inside the house and he wanted to chat. It took me a few weeks of agitation to finally realize that when I sat down to talk with him, time seemed to stop and the mail didn't matter anymore.

Day after day, Bill and I sat on the rock wall outside my house when I came home from work and we talked about life and whatever else seemed important that day. I grew to really appreciate the gift of slowing down, and I looked forward to our time together. Bill soon retired and our daily chats continued for only a few more weeks until he was found dead just inside his front door.

What I learned from Bill was to slow down, take time to connect, and don't wait to retire before you start having fun. I went to Bill's funeral and was both astounded and not surprised at what appeared to be hundreds of people who loved him dearly – all coming to pay their respects. I went to Bill's funeral alone, and didn't seem to fit in. I'm not sure I even knew his last name, but I had grown closer to him in a few short months than maybe some family members had in a lifetime. There were a few people who asked how I knew Bill, and my response was simple. Bill was my neighbor, and we sat on my rock wall every day and chatted about life.

We can hurry up, or we can take our time. When I'm in a hurry, I seldom feel like I'm grounded or enjoying myself. I'm not so sure anyone else is enjoying me either. When I'm rushing around, I become unaware of my breath, my life, my surroundings, how I'm speaking, where I'm placing things, what's happening in my body, my mind, how and who I'm being.

I often wonder why we hurry. Do we really think we're going to get things done that much faster or better? Do we really need to be first or best or to win? And what really *is* winning? Is it sitting on a rock wall to connect with a friend, or is it whoever gets the bigger number on the scoreboard? I sometimes laugh at myself thinking that at the end of my life I'll have like what, an extra twelve minutes from all the hurrying I did my entire life?

Like a symphony becomes a symphony because of the silence between the notes, we become more sacred and connected when we allow for the spaciousness within us. As a former tuba player, the rests between the notes in the sheet of music were vital just to be able to take a breath and play the next measure. Breath is life. Breath creates space. Space creates a symphony.

When I was in my early 20s, I used to lie on the bed and imagine that there was black construction paper on the inside of my head. I suppose I could've imagined white paper, but there was something about black that made it easier to let go of any thoughts and go into what I would later learn was deep theta or still point. What a pleasurable feeling it was to lie on a bed and learn how to think about nothing!

As a kid, I watched my Mom in the mornings – sitting at the kitchen table with her cigarette and coffee – just "staring at the wall" as she called it. That was her form of black construction paper. What I learned over time is how she modeled to me the importance of slowing down and paying attention. She told me how important it was to stare at the wall and I didn't understand until I got older. It seemed really, really boring, but as an adult I totally get it and love it.

Having cultivated a stillness practice for the past 30 some years, I've learned that when I begin to run around myself, it's time (or way past time!) to stop moving something. Maybe I need to stop moving my body, my mouth, my thoughts or all of the above.

Like that snowglobe that I imagined the Earth was when I was a kid, I'm also like a snowglobe. I am nature. So, when I get shaken up, it takes a dose of stillness to let the inner snowflakes settle. Finding balance between movement and stillness is an artform. The animals do it naturally when we allow them to, but we humans often need permission and discipline to both move our bodies and to hold them still.

Let's take another breath together...

I was on my way one day to get a haircut – driving like I normally do with most of my attention on what I was doing, and some of my attention on other things. The emphasis is on *most*. As I approached the exit ramp off the highway, I took a wide turn from one lane to the next, and two blocks later went through a yellow light that turned red somewhere while I was crossing the intersection. With flashing lights behind me, I pulled over and took an exhale. I knew I was going to be late for my haircut and I immediately let go of any attachment to outcome. Thank you, spiritual practice.

Police officers seem to take quite a few breaths before they get out of their car because it seemed like an eternity before she got to my window. With hands on her hips - just like in the movies - the dark haired, pony tailed officer sauntered up to my car in slow motion with her aviator sunglasses. I took another breath as she bent down to look in my window while I bent up to look into her sunglasses.

"Are you in a hurry?" She asked.

Shaking my head, I took another inhale and exhale, and felt the sun on my face and some nervousness in my body.

"No." I replied.

"Were you aware that you crossed lanes and went through a yellow light?" She asked.

"Yes. I'm sorry."

When we get pulled over by the cops, something happens. It's like we turn into five-year old kids who are getting scolded and have to sit on a chair for a time out. I've learned that being honest and being kind is all that really matters in life. When we make a mistake, we acknowledge what we did and we apologize.

The police officer took another breath, walked back to her car at the pace of a turtle and then ate lunch (or whatever they do that seems to take so long before they walk back to deliver the sentencing). Meanwhile, I held still and noticed my breath. I went to the place of black construction paper in my head and totally let go of the need to get a haircut in the near future.

Time sometimes feels like it stops or slows to a place of being suspended between time and space. Like a balloon that frees itself from a child's arm, we too can find ourselves floating into that blissful place without a clock. And, in order to run our lives, hold a job, be in relationships and drive a car, we need a combination of both chronos and kairos sense of time.

When we're impatiently tapping our foot like our life is ticking away, or we're focusing on the clock – waiting for something to start or end - we're in chronos. When we are in kairos, we become so deeply involved in something that time seems to stand still and we can forget about anything and everything.

Kairos is like a quiet lake that we swim in on a hot summer day, and chronos is like a flowing river that we can get swept up in. We experience both all the time in whatever we do, and if we're lucky enough, we can balance chronos and kairos without getting swept up and missing appointments.

Within some span of time, the police officer came back to my car. I was somewhere between the floating balloon and awareness. As I rolled down my window, she handed me back my driver's license and no citation then shared with me five simple words that would change my life forever.

"Slow down and pay attention." She said.

"Thank you." I replied slowly, with a smile and another exhale.

Starting my car, I noticed that life felt a little different as I drove off down the road with mindful intention. I wasn't in a hurry, and I felt completely peaceful and humbled.

And I still made it to my haircut appointment on time!

Chapter Thirteen

I LOVE YOU. GOODBYE.

"TAKE EACH DAY ONE AT A TIME.
THAT'S HOW THEY COME ANYWAY."
— KAREN LEWIS AKA MOM

She left long before she died. Her relationship with alcohol, cigarettes and pain medication was a steady companion for decades before I came into this world. And even though she came and went in many ways, the love that was woven between us grew exponentially throughout our 18,348 days together. She was my Mom, and I loved her for being just that.

There is nothing like our mothers, and mine was absolutely amazing. She and I wove a glorious quilt of love, laughter, compassion and peace that will forever be irreplaceable and unforgettable. She taught me to love every moment as if it was my last and to let go of worrying. She once said to me,

"We can go to bed worrying but we just wake up worried and tired."

She was right.

My Mom was one of the most generous, patient, wise, creative, fun-loving and funny-beyond-words human beings I've ever known. I got to be her daughter. She was also like many of us – a human being who suffered.

We can distract ourselves from our pain in so many different ways – drugs, alcohol, pills, Facebook, television, food, thoughts, busyness and so much more. The world is a candy store for distraction – bright lights, pretty things, stuff that sparkles and says,

"Hey, look at me! Look over here! C'mon! You know you wanna distract yourself!"

We distract ourselves because we suffer – mentally, physically, emotionally, spiritually and/or financially. We find ways to procrastinate, to suppress, to pretend, to push away. But, just as a pot that is not watched can boil over, so can we. We can also boil inside.

Depression is an emotion that I'm still trying to figure out. It's not an emotion I've spent much time exploring for myself, however, I have certainly had hours playing in the pool of depression on behalf of other people. I'm aware that depression feels like fog, tar and quicksand, and that it's easy to get sucked in and get caught up in it.

Just as I can do, my Mom found ways to distract herself from herself. She also found ways to come more deeply into herself. In her later years, she was able to talk openly about feeling depressed. I'm not sure if she felt depressed earlier in her life, but I was proud of her for acknowledging that she wasn't enjoying her life anymore. It took a lot of courage to admit that.

It seems more common to pretend rather than to be real. My Mom pretended at times and she was also very real – just like the rest of us who dance in the land of vulnerability. She told it like it was and at the same time she also knew how to smile and laugh easily. Sometimes, the smiles and laughter seemed like a distraction from the chronic stomach pain she had for years. A slew of doctors weren't able to figure out the source, but I think some of it was from losing our Dad suddenly and not grieving in a healthy way. My sister and I were most definitely the main source of her joy.

There's a sweet spot that shows up between life and death. That's where angels play – the place between the long exhale and the next big inhale where the energy is palpable, time goes away and there is no division between here and there.

I felt such a strong urgency to go visit my Mom a few weeks before she died. The same thing happened with my Dad 15 years earlier. It's like a gravitational pull when someone we love is moving toward a different realm. She came to me in a dream just two months prior as a body of light who rested herself fully on top of me, and I felt my entire being filled with the lightness of her light. Prior to that, she had come to me in my dreamtime a number of times the previous year – looking healthy and happy and having a whole lot of fun. I knew something was shifting.

There was an actual cord that once attached my body to my Mom's – an umbilical cord that was severed at birth and probably tossed into a garbage can, but remained in some form or another for our entire time together. And now that cord was unraveling and I could feel it Would I let it go? Could I? What I knew for sure was that I could feel the cord pulling me closer and closer and closer to my Mom. We can listen to the pull or we can ignore and distract. Both are choices, and both have consequences.

I chose to listen to the pull, and by the grace of God or whoever's grace it was, I made what would be my last trip to see my Mom still laughing and smiling. I think she knew she was slipping away. I think we all knew.

I had planned for months to find a flight to go see her since it was faster, easier and cheaper, but the cost of flights was outrageous and the Summer was fading away. As if a force was shoving me from behind, I couldn't get the trip out of my mind and heart. On a whim, something outside of myself told me to ask her if she'd like to see our dog, Reggae, again. She absolutely lit up at the idea, and so I decided that a dog friendly road trip was in the cards.

Off we went, just Reggae and I, on what seemed like the hottest drive from California to Arizona, to follow the nudge from Great Spirit. Why was I being pushed to go? I had seen my Mom so many times before, yet for whatever reason I couldn't wait any longer. When Spirit calls, we pick up the spiritual phone.

That trip was the first time that Reggae got to experience whipped cream and Starbucks®. I had no idea they had something made especially for dogs, but we did find that on a long road trip that most Starbucks stores were incredibly open to allowing Reggae and I to enter so I could use the restroom. Since I wanted to offer reciprocity for using the restroom, I made sure to buy something in return. The first stop, I ordered a decaf latte with coconut milk for me, and then the barista asked if Reggae wanted a Puppuccino. Whatever it was, he sure wanted it because the drool coming off of his floppy jowls was visible from across the counter. From then on, employees from every Starbucks we visited along the way came around the counter to see Reggae and his drippy lips, and to offer him his very own cup of whipped cream. He *is* a looker, and he now knows the word *Starbucks®*, too.

My Mom was in a lot of pain that last visit – holding her stomach more, removing herself from social activities more, sleeping more, sitting on the patio with her cigarette and glass of wine more. I remembered it felt like work to try to really be with her, and it was incredible heart work to realize I would not be with her forever. I took the time to listen, to touch her, to hold her, to love her, to really be with her. I took the time to try to understand her anger and frustration more, and to find that sweet spot that she and I came to every single time we were together. I took the time to tell her that I would hold her hand not only in her life, but also in her death. And most of all, I took the time to love her no matter what.

My Mom seemed to experience an incredible amount of joy from engaging with Reggae during our time together on that trip. Animals have a way of being 100% accepting and totally present, and helping the rest of us see how amazing life can be when we slow down and pay attention. They are such amazing teachers. It felt like my Mom and Reggae both knew something was shifting because their relationship seemed like it had a secret bond. Their connection was heartwarming, and I remembered feeling so grateful that I had listened to the calling to bring Reggae along on the trip.

Lying in bed with her, I held my Mom's hand while we pretended to watch the news. I felt the strength and power in her veins from raising two girls mostly on her own, and the familiarity of her long, painted fingernails that gently caressed my hair from the time I was a child. Hand in hand, we sat in peaceful silence.

When people and animals are letting go, they tend to pull away. My Mom seemed more distant on this visit and yet I did all I could to keep my connection in whatever way I was able. I watched for days as she offered Reggae the mixed nuts she didn't want as much as the pecans and cashews that went in her own mouth. I watched as she looked straight into his soul - stroking him gently on the side of his head and telling him what a beautiful dog he was.

I watched with painful curiosity as I noticed her withering body still filled with a powerful spirit made of iron and hummingbirds, and I wondered how the mystery would unfold. As the cord became thinner, I watched my Mom letting go and I had no other healthy choice but to let go along with her.

The night before I was planning to leave to drive back home to California, my Mom, sister and I were having dinner together. Reggae was trying to join in by begging at my Mom's side for anything that she might be willing to offer him. My Mom had done a wonderful job of teaching both Java and Reggae how to beg at the table, and then they'd come home and do the same and she thought it was funny. I can laugh now, but at the time I didn't think it was funny. That night, I asked her if she would please stop feeding him table scraps since his tummy was responding with undigested almonds and corn on the cob from her generosity the day before.

She clearly wasn't happy with the boundary I had set, and proceeded to poke some little verbal jabs at me during dinner. This type of poking energy had never been a part of my relationship with my Mom, so I noticed it and did my best to not take it personally. Deep inside, I felt curious and a scalding pain in my heart to hear her making fun of me for setting a boundary. I could feel that some sort of ending was nearing, and I wondered if it would end unpleasantly.

After I left my Mom's house that last night and returned to my Airbnb, I took time to swim in the pool under a starry night sky with the moon as my witness. Surrounded in a womb of warm water, I asked Great Spirit to please release my Mom from all of her pain in whatever way was in her highest good. As the moon looked back with a nod, the stars gave a wink while tears of grief and gratitude fell swiftly from my soul into the womb of the Great Mother.

I slept better that night than I had in a long time. Somehow I had been able to manage a full release of expectations and holding onto what I wanted. What I had wanted was for my Mom to feel better and play with me again. I missed the Mom I wanted her to be, and I was letting go of who and where she really was.

We never know when someone is going to die. That's the mystery. If we can actually live into the not knowing in every single breath we are blessed. Every breath is sacred. Every single breath. James and I will often leave one another by saying,

"I love you. Goodbye."

When we remember to remember, we remember.

I had a choice that night. Did I want to hold the upset in my heart and allow the upset to be what might be our last time together or did I want to transform it into something that felt a lot better? Although I was having unpleasant feelings from the poking festival, I dug deep and chose the high road of love instead of fear. In my moonlit grief, I relaxed easily and quickly into a place of love and compassion and decided I would return to my Mom's house the next morning. I wanted to hug her, tell her I loved her and to say goodbye from a place of love and kindness.

I came to her door the next morning with a smile and a hug, and we looked into each other with a knowing that the cord was stretching. We sat for a while and distracted ourselves with more mixed nuts and idle chatter about driving home and other stuff that didn't really seem to matter. We were stalling for the painful *I love you. Goodbye.* part.

Somehow I had let go of the need for Reggae to have better digestion, and somehow she had let go of the need to feed him mixed nuts. It all worked out, and in my speaking up the night before and setting boundaries, there had also been a changing of the guard.

After a classic Midwest goodbye that lasts forever, we finally made it to the doorway of her apartment for one last hug. She looked deep into my eyes and soul with what looked like excruciating emotional pain mixed with a depth of love and devotion.

Her soul spoke directly to mine, as she said, "I'm sorry I'm not the same fun Mom I used to be."

Shoving her bright red walker out of the way, she wrapped her skinny, little strong-as-steel arms gently around my waist and snuggled into me.

"I don't need you to be anyone other than who you are, Mom. I love you so much." I replied, as we held each other even closer while the world went away.

"I love you, too, honey. I'm really glad you came." She whispered quietly into my ear with the sound of a lump in her throat.

"Me, too, Mom. Thank you so much for letting us come."

Reaching down, she patted Reggae on the head and told him she loved him. As I walked away, I could feel our umbilical cord ripping apart. Every time I had visited my Mom over the years had felt different than this time, and now it felt far more sacred.

As she had done for so many years, my Mom followed me out the door and watched me walk to my car from her second-floor balcony. Standing next to her red bistro set with a pot of flowers in the middle, she waved an exuberant goodbye with a smile as wide as the world. I waved back with the smile she had given me at birth, and then I drove off in tears.

My Mom died unexpectedly nineteen days later.

Chapter Fourteen

EVERYTHING
IS WONDERFUL

"YOU ARE MY SUNSHINE.
MY ONLY SUNSHINE.
YOU MAKE ME HAPPY.
WHEN SKIES ARE GREY."
— JIMMIE DAVIS
AND CHARLES MITCHELL

French toast is amazing. I can totally understand why she picked it as her favorite and how they knew. Whenever there was French Toast, the workers brought it to her because she went on and on about how much she loved it. I love it, too.

Always with lots of butter, lots of syrup and a side of crispy bacon, my Mom was a connoisseur of Americana. If the bacon wasn't crispy, she sent it back. She did the same thing with Burger King fries – waited for the fresh, hot crispy ones instead of settling for cold and soggy. My Mom was hilarious.

She knew how to ask for what she wanted and she knew how to eat. With a frame the size of a third grader, it was astonishing how much food she could pack away. She loved hamburgers, hot fudge sundaes with pecans, lemon meringue pie, carrot cake and a really good cup of hot, black coffee. She also loved my sister and I even more than she loved French Toast. It's good to have more than one passion.

The day my Mom collapsed on the patio was a Saturday. She had just eaten her first bite of French Toast that had been graciously delivered by the staff at Independent Living. Something must've happened to make her fall out of her chair, and something must've happened to make her last meal at home be French Toast. I was training dogs and people through a study at UC Davis in California when I heard the text come in from my sister that our Mother had fallen and the ambulance was on its way.

It appeared that an angel who just happened to stop by to say hello had found our Mom lying on her back on the floor of her patio. At least she had fallen in the place she loved the most doing what she loved the most. Dressed in a glitzy tank top and bike shorts, her 82# frame was drenched in her own sweat while she looked up at the clear blue sky – most likely pondering her life and her death.

She had been lying in the hot Arizona sun for 5-1/2 hours - completely lucid and unable to get up. I'm not sure why she didn't yell for help, but my best guess is that she was done, and she didn't want any help.

She went to the emergency room that day with pain all over her body from the fall. It appeared that she had fallen out of her chair and had landed on her back – most likely hitting the back of her head on the cement floor. She was treated for dehydration and given pain medication for the pain, but the pain wasn't subsiding and the doctors weren't listening. X-rays showed no broken bones, and since she was able to state her name, birthdate and who the president was they sent her home for my sister to care for her for the night to writhe in pain. It was totally out of my sister's job description and skillset to care for her, and I felt helpless being so far away.

There was a letting go that started to take place in me about a decade before when I wasn't able to see her as often. I felt helpless because I was at a distance, even though we still talked almost every day.

With my sister on the ground and living near our Mom, she had taken the lead for over a decade for a multitude of hospital visits and Walgreens® runs.

Up all night, my sister and Mom tried to find a way to become comfortable while the pain and frustration were beyond tolerable for both of them. After a midnight run to Walmart® for diapers, and a few frustrated phone calls to me, my sister finally called a nurse from Assisted Living to help. They were at least able to get her somewhat settled for a few hours before the dawn broke.

When the sun came up, my Mom and sister had what would begin the end of their karmic healing process together. For most of her life, my sister had cared for our Mom at the expense of caring for herself. Now, on this morning, there was one more opportunity to shift the quality of the relationship between the two of them.

With all the might she could muster up, my sister told her that she would call another ambulance, but she wasn't going to ride with her this time. She told her that she needed to care for herself and would be staying home, and that she would come to the hospital to see her later.

There was probably some friction, but within a few minutes a gaggle of hunky EMT's came to carry her out and she had something else to think about.

As things can go with siblings, there was a changing of the guard when my sister began to let go of her role as caregiver and asked me to take over. Doing so from California was a bit of a challenge and yet I felt my power rise up within me – knowing that I would do whatever I could to make conscious choices, and to support my sister in letting go of the need to keep an unhealthy role.

My Mom and sister came to a place of peace within their relationship that day, as they both let go of the codependency that had been tying them together. I was now the one on call to talk with doctors and nurses, and to gather information in order to make conscious decisions.

Throughout my shift as the main point person, I continued to ask for a head scan since she had fallen in what appeared to be backwards out of a chair onto cement. She didn't have symptoms of a head injury, yet, they were keeping her for observation. Then, they sent her to a rehab facility to rehabilitate.

The doctors continued to deny a head scan – stating that she wasn't showing symptoms, but I could tell there were symptoms showing themselves. Our Mother was made of steel and rainbows – colorful and fun, she ruled with an iron fist, so, when the doctors asked her a question, she answered it. Yet after a few days I noticed she was sleeping more and wasn't tracking as well.

The first full day into rehab I was having a hard time reaching the nurses. Nobody was calling back and my sister was taking a healthy break from decades of codependency. I felt frustrated and alone and uncertain whether I needed to jump on a plane to do my job as her healthcare advocate or hold still and have faith. I prayed and I held still.

That night, my Mom came to me in my dreamtime. We would find out later that she also came to my sister in her dreamtime at the same time that night. A lucid dream around 3:30am, I could hear my Mom's voice as clear as a bell as if she were speaking through me. It was early on a Wednesday morning, and at that time she was still recovering at the rehab center from the fall she had at home five days earlier.

This is what she said to me:

"GOD IS CHOSEN

IN THE SUNSHINE.

EVERYTHING IS WONDERFUL.

REST IN PEACE."

- MOM

Little did I know, the words she gifted me during my dreamtime would be some of the last ones I would receive from her. Rolling over in bed, I turned to James to tell him about the visit from my Mom during the night, and he said,

"I want to write a song with your Mom's words. They are really beautiful."

After waking fully, I phoned the rehab center again and still no answer. I tried again and again, and still no answer. Finally, around Noon, I called a third time and my sister answered. I was surprised to hear her voice since she had been taking a much-needed break from caregiver fatigue.

"What are you doing there?" I asked curiously.

"I found her phone cord at home and decided to bring it over." She said.

Love works in mysterious ways. With my Mom in the background - one nurse on each side of her helping her to supposedly rehabilitate - I asked my sister to tell our Mom that I loved her.

"She knows." My sister said.

"Please tell her anyway." I replied.

"Sage loves you." She said on my behalf.

"I love you, too, honey." Her voice echoed across the room and resounded deeply in my heart.

I could hear and feel the pain in her voice and I felt the sadness in my heart. I wanted to hear the joy I had heard so many times before, and at the same time, I was elated at the power of synchronicity. My sister just happened to be there at the same time that I happened to call. If that hadn't happened, I wouldn't have had those poignant words as our last.

James and I headed out on a trail with Reggae for a beautiful off leash hike, and meandered through some woods and up a mountain and back. Nature is my nurture. It can mend anything. No matter what's going on in my life, if I can get out into Mother Nature for any length of time, I can drop down into that magical place between here and there – that place where angels play.

When I got home, I had a message on my phone from the rehab center. The nurse had phoned 20 minutes earlier to tell me that my Mom had come out of an occupational therapy session with stroke and seizure symptoms and was unresponsive. My heart sank and I knew the umbilical cord between us was becoming stretched to completion.

Fear kicked in, and I immediately went back through my brain and heart to retrieve the last thing my Mom and I said to one another just a few hours earlier. The three words – I love you - rang like a bell at a boxing match – loud, clear, concise and with power. When our hearts are in alignment with the thoughts we have and the words we speak, the bell is louder and clearer. That day was the last time I heard my Mom's voice.

As I took a deep breath and phoned the nurse back, I began to pack a backpack at the same time. I knew my Mom was dying and I knew I needed to get on a plane, and get on a plane fast. The nurse told me that my Mom had come out of the shower with the occupational therapist, and that they had only left her for a minute. Well, in that minute, my Mom's brain exploded to the point of a fatal stroke.

The nurse sounded frantic and apologetic, and I will forever be curious about what really happened. In her franticness, she mentioned that they had doubled her medication, and then she said,

"I don't know what happened."
My inner red flag was flaring and my heart was letting go. Phoning my sister and waking her from a nap, I told her the news and told her which emergency room to go to. Ironically, the nurse had told me the name of the wrong hospital, so at first I couldn't find my Mom, and I had to call around to find her. That was hard.

Once my sister got to her side at the hospital, it became even more real. God bless FaceTime for allowing me to see what was really happening in real time, and God bless my sister for being able to go to our Mother's side as fast as she did.

Removing the gold and diamonds for safe keeping from her listless body, my sister informed me that our Mom was getting med flighted to an intensive care neuro unit across town. A myriad of thoughts raced through my head with feelings to match flying erratically through my heart. And then I had a moment of whimsy and I grinned. A helicopter ride? My Mom would've *loved* that!

Things were feeling really intense, and I remember placing my left hand across my heart and automatically pushing the skin in a 1-1/4 circle – a Tellington TTouch Heart Hug that I had learned and used for many years to self soothe. At the same time as I was doing the Heart Hugs on my own body, my right hand was booking a flight and my eyes were watching my beloved Mother on FaceTime being strapped to a gurney, unresponsive, and getting ready for her last ride in the sky. I told her I was on my way and that if she needed to let go before I got there that it was okay. James and I sang one of her favorite songs, Sanctuary, and we told her how much we loved her. Then I wept right along with my big sister.

With James and Reggae at my side on the couch, I looked up from my computer and saw what appeared to be at least a dozen hummingbirds flying all over our tiny little patio. It was definitely a connection to my Mom letting go of her beautiful spirit, and it felt like an incredible gift. I have yet to see more than two hummingbirds at the same time since.

My Mom carried hummingbird medicine and she carried elk and crane medicine, too. She was pure joy with a smile and laugh that could clear a room. As I watched the fleet of hummingbirds buzzing around our patio, and watched my Mom on FaceTime begin her journey of being airlifted, I pressed PAY NOW on my computer screen and purchased a one-way flight that was leaving San Francisco in just under three hours.

Grabbing my already packed backpack, James, Reggae and I got in the car to usher me to the airport. As we headed through the hills of Marin, and across the Golden Gate Bridge, James looked over and pointed out the window past my serious and somber face. Covering the entire sky was a glorious orange and pink sunset filled with joy and delight. He smiled as he snapped a photo of what would be the final sunset of my Mom's life and my life with her.

My sister and I make a great team. We always have. She was holding vigil at the hospital, and letting friends and family say their final words via telephone, while I was navigating how to get to the airport on time, so I could hopefully get to my Mom before she died.

"IT TAKES

TOO MUCH ENERGY

TO GET MAD."

— MOM

James dropped me off at the San Francisco airport with a big kiss and a hug, and we waved each other goodbye with tears in our eyes and love in our hearts. As I walked into the airport and looked at the kiosk, I realized my plane was delayed. Chalk it up to one more round of spiritual practice in letting go of outcome. I took an exhale, texted my sister and called the hospital to talk with the doctors.

Our Mom gave us the wisdom, "When in doubt, don't." and our Dad told us, "If it feels good, do it." Although they seem like conflicting phrases, they're actually saying the same thing in different ways.

When we hold still until there is certainty and clarity we become solid like a tree and that feels much better than the fearful and anxious energy of running in circles. Even when we say no, we might still feel some sadness, but if we're in alignment it still feels good on a soul level. Both bits of wisdom have guided me my entire life.

Without doubt and with a sense of peace, I made a conscious decision for the doctors to cease any medication for blood pressure, and to allow her to die on her own before I got there if she needed to. The doctors reminded me that due to her condition, her blood pressure could easily escalate to a fatal level which would result in a heart attack or another stroke. I took a breath and trusted that whatever was in her highest good would prevail, and I released another piece of the cord that connected us.

I let go of my need to see her one more time, and I let go of attachment. I was letting go of my Mom, and that was really hard. I also knew that if she died before I got there that it was still just as important to be there for my sister. It was my sister's birthday in a few hours, which was not necessarily the best day for our Mother to choose to die.

Phoning my sister at the hospital, we shared some tears and a few laughs, and then I felt a sharp pain on the left side of my head. This was the same side that my Mom had just had a stroke, and I was aware enough to let it go.

Although I had been connected in the womb from an umbilical cord, I knew I didn't need to take on the physical manifestation that was happening with my Mom.

It was 10pm before I boarded the plane, and what was before me was completely uncertain. Looking down at my boarding pass, I noticed a coupon for a free drink once aboard the plane. How ironic was that? For years my Mom drank a glass of wine on her patio before bed. I wondered if it was another little wink and I chuckled since I had never seen a drink coupon on a plane before. I asked the flight attendant for a Ginger Ale and then changed my mind to water. The flight attendant, not knowing what was happening in my life, was unkind because I had changed my mind.

"You SAID you wanted ginger ale!" She told me from a voice of shame.

"Yes." I replied. "I changed my mind."

When we're trapped in an airplane, there's not much we can do. We can move the tray up and down, the seat back and forth, futz with what's in our carry on, go to the bathroom, talk to our seat buddy or hold still. I often wonder what everyone's story is on a plane. We seldom really get to know the person who's sitting less than an inch away. That night, I wondered if anyone could tell that my Mom was dying. I wondered what was happening with the people around me and if anyone else's Mom was dying.

After futzing for a bit, and realizing there was no way of knowing whether my Mom was alive or not, I let go even further. I smiled at the thought of her in a helicopter, and now me in an airplane. For some reason it was comforting to know we were both in the air on her last day. I thought of my poor sister sitting alone at the side of our Mother's bed just a few hours before her birthday would chime in at midnight, and I felt myself feeling compassion.

Plugging in my headset, I took a sip of water and dove into a shamanic journeying cd and surrendered to what was. Drums beating wildly and the sweet sounds of nature filled my body as my spirit floated into non-ordinary reality for the duration of the plane ride. I was fully at peace when the plane landed just after midnight, and as I turned on my phone, a text came in from my sister.

"She's still here." She said.

"Happy birthday, Steph." I wrote back.

I thought that taxis were *always* at airports. Boy, was I wrong. I've since learned that at 12:30am the Phoenix airport doesn't always have taxis. The taxi line man told me that he could get a taxi for me in a half hour or so, and I told him my Mom was dying. Somehow he didn't acknowledge what I said, and kept talking. And then an angel drove up.

It was a private angel taxi I guess - a car with dark windows that had beams of light shining through from the inside. I stepped off the curb as the window rolled down.

"My Mom is dying. Can you get me to Banner University?" I said with a huge lump in my throat and fearlessness in my bones.

"Hop in." he said.

Off we went. Me in an unmarked angel taxi with a complete stranger who felt like God. I was only 8 minutes from the hospital and my sister told me she would meet me downstairs. My heart pounded with anticipation. Although I had completely surrendered to whatever was in the highest good while I was on the airplane, once I was on the ground it was a different story. I was struck with the desire to see, smell, feel and hear my Mom still alive.

The taxi driver and I exchanged names and he told me he was from West Africa. He asked me about my Mom, and kept me talking the entire time to keep me from getting stuck with the stories in my head. He pointed up ahead and showed me the lights of the hospital and assured me that we were almost there. Then he told me he would pray for our family. God bless unmarked angel taxis and the drivers of light inside.

Driving up to the curb at the hospital, I saw my sister sitting outside in the dark on a bench by herself. It was now her birthday and our Mother was dying. She looked as vulnerable as I felt. The angel taxi driver gifted me a free ride, and as I got out of the taxi I looked straight through him and thanked him from every part of myself.

"You are an angel." I said.

He smiled as his eyes sparkled back, and I turned around and hugged my beloved sister.

Holding hands, my sister, Stephanie, and I walked through the hospital doors, past a wall hanging with hummingbirds, down a long hallway, and onto what felt like the longest elevator ride of my life. When the elevator doors opened, I could feel my Mom as I walked hand in hand with my sister into her room. She was still there. God bless whoever I need to bless.

Walking into the room holding my sister's hand reminded me that our family was getting smaller. With our father dying 15 years prior, we were soon to be down to just the two of us. Letting go of Steph's hand, I walked over to our Mom, brushed her silky soft salt and pepper hair and kissed the warm forehead that I knew so well.

"Mom, I'm here." I said, as the respirator filled in the silence in between.

Let's take another breath together...

If you've ever been in charge, you know that with that comes great responsibility. My sister had told the doctors that I was clergy, and they had left the respirator intact until I arrived to decide what the next step was. Surprisingly, her blood pressure had stabilized during my entire plane ride and her vitals were actually quite good.

Steph and I both knew our Mom wouldn't want a respirator, so eight minutes into my time in the room I asked the nurses to take it out. We knew that removing support meant she would die, but we didn't know when.

The nurses came in and pulled the curtain, while my sister and I looked at each other like two little girls who were losing their Mom. As the nurses finished up, the curtain was pulled open to reveal a much more peaceful Mom. She was able to relax more fully, breathe more easily and went into a deeper place of peace.

I walked over to her right side and sat at the edge of her bedside - placing my hand underneath hers. I had held my Mom's hand my entire life - just something we did every time we were together, and now here I was, feeling my Mom's limp hand lying completely still on top of mine. When I drove with her in the car, I held her hand. When I laid with her on her bed to watch the news, I held her hand. When I was feeling frightened, angry, sad or happy, I held her hand. And now, there was nothing else I could do except to just be, and hold her hand. Or maybe she was holding mine.

Seconds turned into minutes, and minutes turned into the middle of the night. For what would be hours, my sister and I sat on either side of her, holding her hands, and singing, telling stories and being silent. We shared stories of the always full cookie jar, and the "I've had it up to here!" threats, and the wooden spoon hitting the door to let us know we were supposed to be quiet and go to sleep, and the challenges, the gifts, the countless laughs and the depth of what it was like to have her as our Mother.

My sister left the bedside at some point, and went to a recliner to recline and try to rest. When she left her side, there was a deeper shift. The death rattle started to come, and at one point she began to move her legs almost frantically like she was a little kid riding a bicycle down a hill - which was pretty amazing considering the stroke had affected her entire right side and there had been no movement.

Go, Mom! Go!

I prayed deeply to Great Spirit and connected with loved ones from the other side - asking six men who had crossed over to please help our Mom across the threshold from here to there with love and care. Pall bearers from the light, I saw them gather one by one in an angelic formation that was filled with bright white light. I saw my Father, her Father, my ex-husband, my sister's ex-husband, my Mom's boss and a dear friend of mine. I could feel the energy starting to build like a campfire on a crisp Fall night.

I sang *You Are My Sunshine* and *Sanctuary* as many times as possible and I took in every sensation that the middle of the night and death call forth. I released her completely and told her it was okay to go, and I breathed in and I breathed out. I breathed with her, into her and her into me, and I felt myself becoming one with all of the sacred silence that was in the room.

Without moving a muscle for hours, I kept my Mom's hand on top of mine - feeling its familiar warmth and the love and honor that was attached to it for my 50 plus years. As the minutes passed more deeply, I started to notice a shift. The energy that was coming from her hand to mine started to move and I felt it in the palm of my hand like a thread that was dancing playfully on my palm. It was moving in a figure eight pattern - her palm on top of my palm - and I could feel the energy inside of her moving around. Her legs started to move again, and there was a cough that roused my sister.

"It's time." I said to Steph.

As Stephanie walked over next to me, there was a healing that took place for all of us as my sister and I started to chant,

"Go, Mom! Go! Go, Mom! Go!"

The energy in my Mom's hand started to move more freely, and the weight of her hand began to rest more fully in mine. They say the spirit weighs 11 grams, and I believe it. With each exhale, the energy dissipated and her hand became heavier and heavier and heavier, until the energy stopped moving.

I held my sister's right hand in one hand, and our Mother's right hand in the other. We were linked together like a chain of women who would forever be bonded from the life that was given to us. I sang softly and slowly and the monitors began to slow along with my song. Her breathing slowed even more, until one last final ecstatic exhale as her hand fell fully into mine. She was done.

There's a moment at death where time stands completely still. It's outside of any concept of space and time. And, there's a moment when we let go of our mothers where the umbilical cord gets severed and the excruciating pain of letting go of everything feels like a part of us is getting ripped out. For the last time ever, I let go of my Mother's hand, turned to my sister, and we held each other and wept.

THEN THERE WERE TWO.

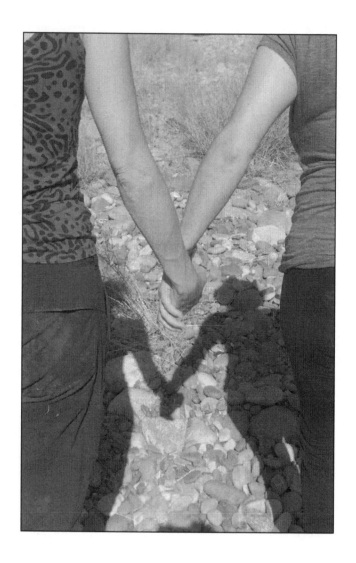

EVERYTHING IS WONDERFUL

BY JAMES SCHATTAUER
& KAREN LEWIS – 9/20/2017

She saw Jesus in a flower.

She saw Moses at the mall

She had wisdom like a Buddha.

A bigger smile than she was small

And one hand was always waving

While the other held her pain

And somehow she kept on smiling

As she made us laugh again

God is chosen in the sunshine

Everything is wonderful

God is chosen in the sunshine

Rest in peace

Is the glass half full or empty?

Do the stars fill up the night?

We can choose to sit in darkness

Or find a way to see the light

God is chosen in the sunshine.

Everything is wonderful

God is chosen in the sunshine.

Rest in peace

She has gone into the mystery

We will follow one by one

Sometimes I hear her whispering

As the night becomes the dawn

God is chosen in the sunshine

Everything is wonderful

God is chosen in the sunshine

Rest in peace

God is chosen in the sunshine

Rest in peace

Rest in peace

Chapter Fifteen

HOT PINK
DRAGONFLIES

"LET GO."

— THE AMAZON JUNGLE

It is said that the Amazon calls people to heal, to be healed or to die. For years I have been called to the jungle of Peru, yet I wasn't sure why. One of my beloved teachers of plant spirit medicine had been traveling to the Amazon for over two decades to apprentice with her teacher, and I was curious enough to want to go.

There's something elusive about wanting. When we want something to be a certain way, it can be just out of our reach. Wanting can be a bit like whining. I want this, or I want that, or I don't want this, or I don't want that.

For many years I wanted my teacher to invite me to go to the jungle on one of her many excursions and I couldn't understand why after 15 years it hadn't happened. After a few years of wanting and wishing, I stopped whining and held still. Grasping is not very sexy.

Turning 50 was a milestone for me. I made a conscious commitment to step more deeply into my personal power and to go after what I wanted. Yes, I still had desire, but it came from a place of power rather than whining. What I wanted was to see a blue whale and then I wanted to go to the Amazon. I saw the blue whale the day I turned 50. Now, for the jungle.

Calling my teacher/mentor, who had become a dear friend, I told her I planned to gift myself a trip for my 50th birthday. At this point, she was spending most of her time living in the Amazon, so I thought I could at least come for a visit. Little did I know what was in store.

As a good teacher does, I was nudged to grow. She told me that I was welcome to come and why not create a group to lead on an Amazon adventure. As a good student, I immediately said yes and jumped in with all of my heart while my knees were shaking below.

The word shaman means he or she who knows and who sees with the heart. We are either born into this work or called to it. In May of 2000 I was called by Great Spirit to open my heart, and now as a shamanic practitioner I was being called to the jungle.

As the months rolled by, the circle started to form and heading to the Amazon became a reality. I had my arms poked for all sorts of vaccinations, followed by homeopathic meds to offset the symptoms. I had my passport in tow and all of my matching and not so matching colorful Columbia® clothes.

The idea of leading a trip felt exciting and also scary. I had no idea where I was going, had never been to the Amazon before and had no idea what to expect or not expect.

Overcoming fear seems to be a pastime for leaders. When I'm feeling fearful, I can move through it much more quickly if I hold still and allow myself to feel it. I also move through it when I say "Yes" and trust that I'll figure it out along the way.

When I went through my coach's training, there was an exercise we had to do that I'll never forget. Each one of us was blindfolded (The Client) on one side of the hotel conference room, and we had a guide (The Coach) on the other side of the room who was going to give us verbal directions how to cross the room blindfolded.

The room was booby trapped with tables and plants and all sorts of obstacles that we had to work our way around from a place of being blindfolded. The name of the game was that whoever got to the other side of the room first, won. I didn't know what we won, but I wanted to win.

The blindfold went on each of the "Clients" on our side of the room, and we were told the rules. It went like this: The Coach/guide could have three 10 second time outs where they could walk across the room to The Client to give them more direction. I was blessed to have the most creative Coach ever. I think she wanted to win, too.

When the start bell went off, I started flailing my arms to knock anything (and anyone) out of my path as I moved my body into complete darkness in front of me. I felt determined, and I remember beaming from ear to ear and giggling. I couldn't see a thing yet I felt everything. Then a miracle happened.

Within the first five seconds of the start bell, my Coach ran from the other side of the room for her first 10 second time out and came to my side. She told me that she had a quiet voice and that I'd never hear her above all the other coaches who were yelling and cheering for their blindfolded "Clients" to make it across the room at the same time. As I flailed alongside her, she told me she was going to walk right next to me the entire way and tell me what to do, and that she was going to use up all three of her time outs right away to stay next to me. Not one other coach thought of this and it was absolutely brilliant.

So here I was, totally blindfolded, giggling and smiling, with my coach coaching me to go around this, and step over that, and to watch out for the table, and run forward etc. There were more gremlins popping up all over the place in the form of our instructors for the training. Their job was to help us stay safe, comfortable and stuck and to prevent us from moving forward in any way possible. That's what's called a saboteur in action – that voice that tells us we suck so why try anyway. Well, it was fuel for me, and I felt like a rocket engine.

I remember vividly feeling one of the instructor gremlins tugging on my clothes – trying to prevent me from moving forward across the room and telling me I would never be able to do it. I remember laughing. All the while, my Coach was right next to me - cheering me on and telling me what to do and where to go. We won with flying colors that day. The prize for winning was waiting and watching another 30 seconds for the other teams to get across the room, and the feeling of absolute oneness with my true spirit.

When I took off my blindfold I was shocked to see how many obstacles had been created in the room in front of me. The instructors told me later that they couldn't keep up – that I kept plowing ahead and they kept trying to find more tables, lamps, chairs and plants to put in my way to prevent me from succeeding. The saboteurs hadn't gotten the best of me. What had gotten the best of me was determination mixed with creativity and curiosity.

What I learned that day is that I can do anything as long as I have someone by my side and on my team who believes in me. I also learned that fear is short lived and that if you flail your arms wildly while you're laughing then it's not as scary. I also found out that sometimes when we flail, we hit people like the instructor I evidently whapped that day while I was winning.

I wasn't sure whether the jungle was calling me to be healed, to heal or to die. In actuality, I don't think I heard about those options until after I landed in Iquitos – the buzzingly loud river city on the Amazon. It's quite possible that if I had heard that those were my options I would have stayed home where I was safe, stuck and comfortable.

Before I left for the jungle, life felt really uncertain. James and I had somehow shifted to feeling like we were on different paths and wanting different things in some ways, and yet we were both wanting to find a way out of California. There was definitely some creative tension. After my Mom died, I was clear I wanted to find a place to live that was closer to my sister. James and I both wanted to reduce expenses and leave the aftermath of the fires in the North Bay. Where we weren't seeing eye to eye was where we were headed – together or separate. I wanted to check out Prescott, Arizona.
He didn't.

Tossing in the pale green t-shirt that my Mom wore the last day of her life, I boarded a plane and let go. I let go of expectation. I let go of desire. I let go of control. I let go of fear. I hadn't let go yet of the grief of my Mom's death, and I was determined to ask the jungle to help me let go. The Amazon is the lungs of the earth, and the lungs are about grief. What better place to let go of what I had been holding onto – including my Mom's t-shirt that I had slept in every night since the day she had died. Okay, I washed it a few times.

Off I went on a day and nightlong adventure in the air to contemplate and meditate about my life and what was next. I would be unable to communicate with anyone other than the plants and animals and the people I was with for the next 12 days, and that felt new and a bit challenging. Without cell service. I was relying on telepathy.

Flying solo can be really fun. There's anonymity and autonomy that's palpable. It's the strangest thing to be one place on one day and then someplace super far away on another day. Then there's that part about sleeping, or trying to sleep, next to a complete stranger on an overnight flight.

Nearing Lima, I was struck by the mountaintops jutting out over the top of the clouds. I could feel the mountain energy as our plane began to descend as if they were peeking above the clouds to see who was on the plane. A short layover and I was on my way to Iquitos with the luxury of a window seat.

I had heard that the Amazon was powerful, yet I had no frame of reference until that first flight from Lima to Iquitos. Looking out the window, I saw a murky brown snake of water winding its way through a dense jungle that I couldn't comprehend. For over 50 years I have flown in planes and never seen such density in nature.

Tears fell like crocodile sized raindrops as I felt the gratitude for the animals and plants who were still able to have such a home. As I looked out the window at the winding brown snake of water below, I could feel the sound of the Amazon River coursing through my heart like a powerful bass drum beating the solid and powerful heartbeat of Mother Earth. The River has a sound of her own, and she was showing it to me and through me. I felt grateful and humbled, and could feel her humility and intention infusing itself into me.

As the plane continued on, so did the jungle. Denser than any head of broccoli I've ever seen or eaten, the jungle went on for what seemed like forever, and my tears coincided. What we have done to our space on this planet is challenging for me to accept. We have cut her, sliced her, moved her, exploded her, stolen from her – all for the sake of what serves us best as humans. To see our dear Mother in such density and power is still beyond words. If you ever get a chance to have a window seat in the jungle, grab it.

Landing at the airport in Iquitos I felt a combination of exhaustion and exhilaration. My mentor and friend, Connie, met me just outside the baggage with a huge smile and hug and off we went in the hotel van together. Two peas in a pod. Two shamanas on a bus.

Within the first 24 hours, the circle began to fill with eager eyes and hearts who were arriving at the hotel, and my throat began to arrive with soreness. I could tell I was getting sick, and I felt concerned and really bummed. By the time the last people landed into our circle, I had a full-blown sore throat and felt myself feeling angry, scared and very disappointed.

How was I going to lead a group of people into a spiritual adventure with a sore throat? What if it got worse, or what if I made everyone else sick? Now what? I felt completely out of my comfort zone and was beyond vulnerable. And then the cold set it and it got a lot worse. Or maybe, I was getting better?

More snot than I ever could have imagined began to flow from my nasal passages for what would be an entire week. I got to experience embarrassment, vulnerability, amusement, regret, anger, resentment, delight and finally gratitude, love and peace. There's nothing like the Amazon jungle to help move the heart from where it's been to where it needs to be. There are leaves the size of couch pads, hot pink dragonflies, orange fireflies, caterpillars dressed like American flags, sounds that get astonishingly louder at night and the energy of being electrified by a million plants all at once. The energy that exists in the jungle is beyond powerful, and here I was, right in the middle of the depth of her lungs, having a full-blown snot festival.

On day 5 of the trip, I lost my voice. Waking up with barely a whisper left inside of me, I had a choice. I could head to breakfast feeling embarrassed and ashamed, or I could step fully into myself. Writing a note on a humid sheet of journal paper, I let the circle know that I was not going to be speaking for the day, and to feel free to join me in my forced silent retreat. It's incredible what can happen when we shut our mouths. There's so much more we can hear, feel, taste, smell and see, and our hearts and minds have the space to expand when we can access the silence and stillness inside ourselves. There's also the discomfort of the space that's created when silence enters a room.

As I quieted myself, and offered the same invitation to the group, most of the group deepened. Some were challenged, others were not, and some didn't notice anything different. What I noticed in myself was that I could still lead without a voice that could be heard.

Pink dolphins, piranhas, the mighty Amazon River, the sounds of the jungle, rainbow boas, tarantulas, sweat, mud and bigness. She was speaking to me in every step that I took and every beat of my heart. Back at home I had no idea what was happening so I kept surrendering to what was in the highest good for everyone, and trusted that Great Spirit had a plan that was unfolding perfectly.

My mentor, friend and colleague, Connie, reminded me that if anything catastrophic happened at home while I was in the Amazon, it would still have happened when I got out. She was teaching me to continue to let go, and to trust in the rhythm of nature. The words *getting out* sounded like I was locked up somewhere, but in reality I was freer than I had ever been. I felt free from distraction and concern, and completely immersed in the lungs of the Great Mother.

Breathing in, I took in life. Breathing out, I let go more fully. With each day that passed, I let go more and more – let go to the lightness that existed in every cell in my body, and let go to the lightness that exists in the veil between holding on and letting go.

There is a rainbow of light between here and there where suspension of time and space becomes like a hammock for the spirit. And as I let go more even more, the plants, animals, stars and Great Spirit began to talk through me more clearly.

We always have access to the rainbow of light – that place between the worlds where angels play, and everything is communicating in its own way all the time. When we quiet ourselves enough to listen, we can become what it is we are listening to.

THE SPIRIT OF THE AMAZON

- SAGE LEWIS

Down her veins

Passion. Power. Energy

Full of power

Calling to me

Cicadas play a symphony

Full of power

Electrocuted by a million plants all at once

Cicadas play a symphony

I see you. I feel you. I love you. I am you.

Electrocuted by a million plants all at once

Calling to me

I see you. I feel you. I love you. I am you.

Full of power

Calling to me

Electrocuted by a million plants all at once

Full of power

Down her veins

Passion. Power. Energy.

Something substantial was unfolding within me, as I felt my heart relaxing and opening like a lotus flower with each blow of my nose that week. I moved from being fearful prior to the trip, to being humbled and in my full power from a place of love and grace. I relaxed into who I was and let go of expectations of who I was supposed to be.

Spirit was moving through me as hot pink dragonflies flitted around by day and orange fireflies lit up the night. The smell of moisture in the air filled my senses from the dew drops of leaves the size of trash can lids. Deepening each day, I could feel the healing take place within myself and also within the circle that I was leading. We were all having our own personal experience and unfolding just as we were supposed to.

I had graciously been asked by Connie to lead our closing circle the last night, and I humbly accepted. There was a shift happening and I was being called forth from apprentice to teacher. We gathered inside the spirit hut at the end of a long walkway that jutted its way through the night sounds and smells of the jungle.

A circular room with wood floors and high ceilings, we had a front row seat to the sounds of the cicada symphony and orange fireflies as the cool and wet breezes came through the screened in windows that took up half of the room.

Sitting around the candlelit altar, our circle began to silence as I began to lead the circle in a sacred blessing. With the shamanic torch being passed through the lineage, I chose to invite my mentor, teacher, dear friend and colleague, Connie, to join me in smudging and fanning each person with Palo Santo and the palm leaf fan she had gifted me earlier in the week.

We shared the gift of an indigenous song she had taught me many years before when I had received a healing from her during my apprenticeship. Coming to a new place in our hearts, a deeper healing was taking place as the ceremony continued. There was a knowing that was felt between us as we glanced into each other's eyes and souls that night – a deepening that required a deeper letting go for each one of us.

In the sacredness of ceremony and darkness, I asked our deeply spirited eco guide for the week, Victor, if he would please close the circle by blessing each of us with his special little bell that he had received from a local shaman. The sound of a million angels washed over each one of us as he shook his little bell gently through the mystery of the sacred air.

Coming to a close, we sat in silence – some in tears and others in curiosity and awe at the profundity of what the jungle experience had done to our hearts. For some of us, it might be days, weeks, months or even years before we could fully understand what had shifted in our hearts.

We all walked in silence back through the jungle to our cabin rooms that night, and I could feel something deep had shifted within me. Connie came to me as I approached my room, and placing her hand on my shoulder I turned to her with a smile as she spoke.

"That was the *best* closing circle I have been to." She said as we hugged each other a sweet shamana goodnight.

One thing that all happy people have in common is gratitude. For over 15 years I had been working with Connie in one way or another as an apprentice of the heart. She had been a guide to me in so many different ways and now there was a tipping point. What would be next, I wondered? No matter what, I was grateful.

I fell into a deep slumber that night with one pillow over my head to try to drown out the cicada explosion and one huge smile on my face and peace in my heart. Around 3am, I awoke with a pounding headache – pounding louder and more intense than the drumbeat of the Amazon River.

I was in that place of not knowing what was happening and totally knowing what was happening. Before bed, I had taken a cold pill that was offered by one of the other participants in the circle – thinking that as a last resort, maybe I could get some relief from my cold. I was hopeful to get one great night of sleep before we headed back to the river city of Iquitos the next day, and in hindsight, it was not a good idea.

As someone who seldom puts anything synthetic in my body, I found out the hard way that cold medicine mixed with malaria pills makes a bad cocktail. Getting up to find some water to try to ease the pounding, my stomach contents ejected out of my body and across the room.

Projectile vomiting is actually quite fascinating – talk about letting go of control! I was somewhere between shocked and amused, and as I cleaned up after myself, I knew I was in trouble. Drinking a sip of water, I slipped my weary body back into bed and felt my fear creep in bigtime. How was I going to lead the circle the next day and how was I even going to get on the boat? Was I dying? Was I going to stay in the jungle forever?

As someone who has had more than one near death experience, this was definitely another test. When the sun began to rise, I began to fall. Connie came to my door to ask why I wasn't coming to breakfast, and I told her I was really, really sick.

As many great teachers do, she pushed me deeper into my healing process and told me I had a group to lead, and then she asked how I was going to do it. I flailed inside from a place of anger to fear to worry to sadness and back through each again as I pondered what was next. I wasn't sure I was going to make it out of the jungle alive, and I thought of James and Reggae at home and how I may never see them again.

I am a warrior at heart – a woman who has seen and felt a lot of extreme experiences in my lifetime. And yet, now I was feeling something big that was ending and it felt like it was my life. As my heart pounded ferociously inside me, I laid in my bed, held still and faced my death. I asked Connie if she would please help gather the circle so they could get ready to pack up to head out, and to have the circle gather belongings to gift to the villagers.

Again, as a good teacher does, she pushed me more. Sometimes our spiritual practices are so uncomfortable that I like to call them spiritual cactuses. Connie said she would gather the circle together, and then she told me she'd leave a huge bin in my room for the circle to bring their belongings to me. We were gifting to the Yagua villagers whatever we were ready to let go of. I was clear I didn't want anyone in my room watching projectile vomiting, sweating, crying, writhing, and yet that was all part of my healing. So, one by one, each person from the circle entered my room, told me they hoped I would feel better, offered some prayers and healing and put some personal gifts for the villagers into the bin.

As the clock continued to move toward leaving time, I continued to struggle. I told Connie that I wasn't sure I was going to be able to get on the boat, and she told me I had to. God bless a person who pushes us to learn and grow because if we didn't have one or many, we'd all lie in a bed in the jungle and feel sorry for ourselves and never get home.

With the bin for the Yagua filling up with shoes, socks, clothes and books, I asked myself what it was that I was ready to let go of. I felt like I had already let go of so much, and now it was time for the material stuff. Head still pounding like thunder inside my skull, I hauled my sorry ass out of bed and made myself vertical. With no more projectile vomiting, I felt like I might make it to the other side of the room to put my items into the bin. Looking at my suitcase, I tossed in my favorite hot pink Columbia shirt, the Teva sandals I had worn the entire trip and my binoculars.

And then, I remembered my intention for the trip – to grieve the death of my mother in whatever way I needed to in order to heal in my highest good. Looking down at the pale green t-shirt on my body that read "Arizona – The Grand Canyon State - Established 1912", I began to cry. The shirt my Mom had worn on the last day of her life, and the one I had been wearing to sleep in for six months, was ready to heal the heart that was wearing it and possibly also the heart who would receive it. Taking off the sweaty shirt that had been my security blanket, I folded it neatly, and laid it on top of everyone else's stuff. I was grieving my mother in the lungs of Mother Earth, and now I was complete.

As I righted myself for an extended period, I realized I could walk, and I could talk, and that I wasn't going to die. I still wasn't sure how I was going to make it on a boat, up the Amazon River, back to the hotel in Iquitos for the night, and a 24-hour plane ride home, but one step at a time.

As angels do, one more appeared and told me to drink a Coca-Cola® with pure cane sugar to help with dehydration.

I grew up on white bread, Coca Cola, Kentucky Fried Chicken® and Pringles®. And now as a vegan in the jungle, I was returning to my roots. As the bubbles of Coke entered my system, I felt my Mom and Dad coming in from the other side to surround me with love and frivolity. Another angel handed me a piece of plain white toast, and as I took one small bite and then the next, I noticed it tasted like heaven on a plate and that I might actually be able to get on a boat and get home. Head still pounding but not as badly after my Coke ceremony, I boarded the boat and stroked my ears vigorously with the Ear TTouch to keep myself from throwing up.

It worked, and I made it back to the hotel with enough energy to go to my room and lie down while everyone else went to a market to find some last little souvenirs before boarding their plane. I will forever be indebted to the angel of Coke because I believe it saved my life.

I felt humbled and alone, a little embarrassed and a lot in process. I wasn't really sure what had happened to me that week. I could tell it might take some time for me to make sense of it all. Hugging the circle members as they boarded the van to the airport, we all knew we had experienced a sacred week together that nobody else would truly understand.

Heading back to my room for the night, I began to hand wash my clothes that smelled to high heaven, and hung them on every hangable spot to dry. You might think you know what clothes smell like that have been in the jungle in plastic bags for a week, but multiple by two and then add some.

I slept like an angel that night, and thanked my parents for coming to me at the time when I needed help the most, and for the angels who helped me to get out of the jungle. When I awoke, my headache was almost gone, and I was beginning to feel able to greet the day. Opening the hotel refrigerator that was filled with stuff you could add to your room tab, I cracked up. Here I was, in a hotel in Iquitos, Peru, surrounded by the lungs of Mother Earth, staring at a can of Pringles® and a Coca-Cola®.

I swear to God, I have no idea how my parents found their way into my refrigerator that day, but that's what I had for breakfast.

That, and a huge smile on my face.

Chapter Sixteen

DRAGONFLY COTTAGE

"NOTHING IS BROKEN.
EVERYTHING IS ON THE JOURNEY TO
THE BLESSED RETURN."
— THE DRAGONFLY

I returned from the Amazon with a new heart to a new heart. James greeted me with clarity that he wanted to head to Central Arizona on a family trip to check out the area for possible relocation. Amazing what can happen when we let go and let Great Spirit!

With a desire to move closer to my sister without the heat and air quality in the Phoenix area, we looked North to Prescott – an area we knew nothing about but were about to learn. I had a dear friend who lived there while he was caring for his elderly parents, so I thought it might be nice to move somewhere where I had a close friend and James had someone to watch a game with, hike with and hang out with, too.

Four days before we left California for our adventure, I got a random inner nudge to contact a connection via email. Founding pioneer Animal Communication Specialist, Penelope Smith, had endorsed my JAVA book many years before, and I knew she had lived in Prescott, AZ at one point, as well as close to where we had been living in California, so I reached out. I emailed her on a Sunday and told her we were leaving California on Wednesday, would be in Prescott, AZ on Thursday and that we had some curiosity about relocation.

I asked if she would like to get together for a cup of coffee and also asked if she had a referral for a holistic veterinarian. Then, I let go of any expectation or agenda.

Whoosh!

Up to this point James and I had only done research online for the area, but what we saw we really loved. There were 93 dog friendly trails in the 1 million-acre Prescott National Forest and we could have lunch at the Grand Canyon or Sedona on a day trip if we wanted. The cost of living was more like we were familiar with in the Midwest, and the land of the Yavapai (People of the Sun) seemed to be calling us closer.

On Monday night, I opened my laptop, and there was an email response from Penelope. As I read her words, my jaw dropped and my eyes opened wider. At this point in my life you'd think that I would just keep expecting miracles, but I guess I hadn't found that place of confidence yet.

Penelope shared her gratitude for reconnection, and that surprisingly, her renter at her house, Dragonfly Cottage, in the Prescott National Forest was leaving in the next 24 hours. She told me that she was going to sell the house and asked if we'd like to see it while we were in town. She told me she'd be in Prescott on Thursday, and so would we. How perfect!

Walking over to James with my laptop and heart wide open, I smiled and shared the email with him. James has carried dragonfly medicine as a totem for as long as I've known him. He had an experience many years ago of communicating with a dragonfly one day when it landed on his bald head at the St. Croix River.

From that he created an entire series called the Dragonfly Dialogues. Not only was there a house for sale in the Prescott National Forest, it had come to us through a magical connection with Java and it was already named Dragonfly Cottage. Serendipity was raining from the heavens.

James and I hadn't considered purchasing a home at that point, but we had a few rental houses to look at when we got into Prescott, so why not add another to the mix? With an emphatic yes, we told Penelope we'd be in town by Noon on Thursday and asked if we could meet her at Dragonfly Cottage at 2pm that day. Yes, we could.

Magic is really something. It has a life of its own and the energy expands into more magic. When we're in that place of expansion, words can't really describe what's happening. It's more of a visceral feeling.

So, with two jaws dropped, one tail wagging and three hearts wide open, James, Reggae and I hopped in my VW Golf on that auspicious Wednesday for our adventure to Arizona. Stopping at many Starbucks® along the way for Puppuccino's for Reggae, and staying overnight in the cement town of Needles – which happens to have an amazing dog park - we woke up Thursday morning to finish our trek into Prescott. We had the wonderful idea of sharing our visit with my sister, Stephanie, and an old coaching buddy and friend, Timothy, who had recently relocated to Prescott. We decided to grab an Airbnb in downtown Prescott for the weekend, and make it a family and friend festival.

Somewhere between there and here, with my feet up on the dashboard of the passenger side and James at the steering wheel, James popped out the idea that maybe we could buy a house. Yes, maybe we could!

Lollygagging our way through Flagstaff and then on toward Prescott, my phone rang. It was my mentor, colleague and friend, Linda Tellington-Jones who is the founder and director of Tellington TTouch® Training - the animal work that I've taught for close to two decades. She asked me where I was in the world, and how the house hunting was going.

When I shared that we were on our way to Prescott, she squealed with delight – telling me she had taught at the college there many years before and that it was one of her all-time favorite places. She asked me to let her know what we thought of the area, and I shared with her that we were planning to look at Penelope's house in a few hours and she giggled with delight. With smiles in our hearts, we hung up the phone and continued our trek through the Granite Dells – a glorious outcropping of boulders with voices larger and wiser than their existence.

We had two hours to spare before taking a look at Dragonfly Cottage, so we headed for the heartbeat of the town and found a parking spot around the Courthouse Square. Getting out of the car to stretch our legs and hearts, James, Reggae and I headed for a picnic spot while running into one dog lover after another.

The energy was filled with joy and exuberance, and we were already loving what we were feeling. One picnic down and visiting with some locals, we headed to my friend Timothy's house for a short visit along the way and then found ourselves entering the Prescott National Forest for our 2:00 meeting with Penelope at Dragonfly Cottage.

Ironically, my sister had worked with Penelope many years prior for an animal communication session with her dog, Molly, so she wanted to meet Penelope at Dragonfly Cottage as well. The more the merrier!

There's something really special about forests. I can feel the trees standing tall at attention – patiently awaiting the wind, the rain, someone to maybe notice them or not. I often wonder how many plants, trees and rocks have been touched or untouched by human hands. When I move through a forest, my goal is to acknowledge the forest and all of its family members.

A deep silence washed over us like a warm Summer breeze as we began our trek into the forest. Noticing a large family of boulders on the left side of the road, I heard them speak to me to come and play. Continuing on, we rounded a bend to see a mountain standing strongly before us in the distance – beckoning us to connect more deeply with the strength and beauty. Taking another deep breath, I felt the majestic mountain enter me as James and I held hands more tightly, smiled and shook our heads in amazement.

As we entered Ponderosa Park – a small community in the Prescott National Forest that was established in 1884 – a sense of wonderment came over us. Around another bend and up a very steep hill, the sweet smell of the pines and juniper filled our nostrils as Reggae stuck his head out the window to fill his nose, too. Our minds wondered what Dragonfly Cottage might look and feel like, and we chose to stay open to anything from a run-down Minnesota Northwoods cabin shack to anything that was other than that.

I love the GPS person who says,

"You have arrived."

That's exactly what happened. Rounding one last bend, we turned our car into Dragonfly Cottage to see a beautiful cottage in the woods, and my sister's car just pulling in. Penelope was standing on the front porch of her house with a humongous smile and a peacock blue streak in her hair.

We had arrived.

Walking up with huge smiles and wags mirroring Penelope's, we exchanged hugs as we walked past the Dragonfly Cottage sign in front of the dog gate leading to the fully fenced yard. My sister and I caught a glance that only sisters know, which was the "Are you kidding me? This is perfect!" glance. As we walked into the front yard, James and I looked at one another with amazement and excitement as our dog, Reggae, jumped through the perfectly sized doggie door that seemed like it had been placed there just for him.

James and I made it about 2 steps into the house before chuckling in our hearts with glee and shock. Yes, we had definitely arrived. Dragonfly Cottage was filled with turquoise, pistachio and yellow walls with white wainscoting trim, high ceilings in both bedrooms, open space with room to dance, a ton of light and a black, white and yellow kitchen that looked a jaguar. There was nature looking out of every single window, including the tiny little one in the bathroom that was close enough to touch a Ponderosa pine. A mountain view from the dining room caught our eye as we looked into the living room and spotted a gorgeous fireplace with a huge hearth and heart.

As James and I moved in unison throughout the house, we kept shaking our heads in amazement while Penelope let us know that she could repaint the inside of the house if we wanted. What she hadn't known was that our wedding ceremony colors were turquoise and lime green, and that we loved everything exactly how it was. Not to mention that all of our belongings and artwork would match perfectly. We loved the colors, the nature, the energy, absolutely everything!

Dragonfly medicine is about the winds of change. The dragonfly is one very special insect who flies not only forward and backwards, but also sideways. Able to move in many directions, dragonflies live between the realms of water and air – the place of emotions and intellect. They remind us to shed our light fearlessly and to be adaptable and resilient.

After touring the inside of Dragonfly Cottage, we walked outside as Penelope told us she was going to be selling and not renting anymore. We weren't sure what was next for us, but we knew we loved the house and we knew we were ready to take a leap. We asked her what her listing price was going to be, and she responded that she didn't know yet, but that she would put us in touch with her real estate agent. She encouraged us to take some time to think about it, and I smiled and giggled as I told her we'd be right back.

Around the corner of the house we went - looking at each other's wide smiles and beaming hearts. James and I held hands as we turned our heads to see the fire circle in the back yard surrounded by log seating. We talked about how we could buy the house, how we could afford a down payment, and felt the leap taking hold inside our spirits. It just kept getting better and better.

"We're interested." We said, with confidence and delight. "Let us know the price when you figure it out."

When magic happens, pay attention. Not only a day earlier, James had mentioned that maybe we could buy a house, and now here we were, standing in front of Dragonfly Cottage with Penelope Smith talking about buying her house in Prescott, Arizona – a small, funky cowboy town we had never been to yet it had lassoed us in like a magnet on steroids.

We left Dragonfly Cottage that day with an intention to purchase it, but not sure how we could do it, how much it would cost, or when we could move. After a night of dreaming, my sister encouraged James and I to go to the bank to get preapproved for a loan while we were in town. I love that I have a sister who knows how to leap and knows how to push other people to do the same.

Taking a big leap of faith, we called Penelope's real estate agent and got the name of a mortgage broker, and we went for it. While my sister, Stephanie, walked Reggae around the parking lot for an hour and a half, James and I sat with a broker and told her our life story. We were two entrepreneurs who were leaving California, coming to Arizona and were taking our work with us. We were certainly not an ideal profile for a loan, but bless the magic that's available when we let go and keep our eye on the prize.

We left the bank that morning with a preapproval letter for what we knew deep in our gut was our top dollar for purchasing a home. We both felt vulnerable with what we could afford, and we also didn't have a price yet from Penelope so we felt some curiosity and uncertainty. It was kind of like handing over some hand-picked flowers to someone you care about on May Day and hoping they are able to receive them fully into their heart.

With my Mom dying earlier that year and leaving me some of her hard-earned money, I felt a bit more secure about using my retirement for part of the down payment if we needed to. If my Mom hadn't died, I never would have had the money for a home, and I wouldn't have considered living near my sister. It was definitely a test of fearlessness for both James and I, but in our hearts, we knew that Prescott was going to be home. *Where* our home was going to be was still yet to be revealed, but we trusted the process.

It was Friday, March 23 and it was Reggae's 3rd birthday, so we headed to downtown Prescott to a cute little pet store to let him pick out a present for himself. Magic can even happen to dogs. After walking up and down the aisles of the pet store and not finding anything he really loved, Reggae dove head first into a basket of used toys and picked out a huge purple toy that you can shove treats into. The toy was covered with tons of dog hair and slobber and someone else's half-eaten treats, and it was perfect. He was so smitten with it that the store owner allowed us to have it for a donation to the local Humane Society, and off he walked with a wag in his step and a birthday present in his mouth.

After that, we headed to Timothy's house for a birthday party for Reggae and then decided to drive around the area to see if any other properties jumped out at us. We were waiting for a price for Dragonfly Cottage from Penelope's real estate agent and we were in that zone of complete surrender.

Clarity creates certainty, and by this time we knew we were ready to make a move. James and I have a really wonderful way of getting on the same page for super important things. After having taken a leap to move to California a few years earlier, somehow this felt easier. We knew the house would come somewhere and somehow, so we decided to jump in by starting with a post office box.

Just as we had done in Fairfax, California, we were now heading to the UPS store in Prescott, Arizona to buy ourselves an address and trusting the house would follow. The PO Box was a really small house, but it did have a key and it had certainty. Just as we pulled into to the UPS store, having just made the commitment to move to Prescott, the phone rang.

On the line was Penelope's real estate agent sharing with us the financial details of selling Dragonfly Cottage. She gave us the asking price of the house, and we immediately felt our hearts sink. What we could afford was far less than what Penelope was asking for Dragonfly Cottage, and the difference between our preapproval amount and Penelope's asking price was about the cost of two new cars. James looked at me and told me we should keep looking for other housing options, and I told him we needed to hold still. And hold still we did.

With some back and forth the next few hours, the agent let us know that Penelope would like to meditate for the night on our offer. Just the fact that she was willing to meditate on it rather than immediately saying no, was a huge gift of generosity. We felt humbled and very, very vulnerable, and also deeply touched by Penelope's consciousness. There was not much else for us to do besides trust and let go that night, so we decided to have a pizza party with Timothy and Steph, and to give our notice at our apartment in California. We set a moving date of April 20, and took a big exhale. When we let go, magic happens.

So, on a crisp March night in the Courthouse Square of Prescott, Arizona, James and I lifted our hands up to the sky like we were holding a chalice of opportunity and grace, and we gave it up to Great Spirit. We knew that whatever was in the highest good for everyone would prevail. And then we headed back to our Airbnb, ate some amazing pizza, and fell sound asleep with the key to our new post office box on the nightstand next to us.

They say that spirits are the most alive between 2 and 4 in the morning. Whoever they are, I believe them. Around 2:30am, I startled myself awake from a night vision. In the vision, I saw myself walking into the entryway of Dragonfly Cottage toward a large turquoise shadowbox that was cut out from the wall at the end of the foyer. Inside the shadowbox, I envisioned a huge 3-D mixed media dragonfly that was made from found objects.

217

There was a sense or knowing that it was a piece of artwork that James and I had already created together, and that it already existed in the house. In that moment, it was clear that Dragonfly Cottage would be our home.

Waking up the next morning, I rolled over to tell James about my vision and he smiled a smile of deep knowing. He and I have always had a really amazing spiritual connection and I feel incredibly blessed. As I got up and headed to the kitchen, my sister came around the corner, and almost at the same time, we said to one another,

"It's done."

My sister and I had both had the same sense that the transaction had been completed on a spiritual and energetic level, and now for the tangible level.

We spent time that day just going about our day – walking around Watson Lake, and driving past the Juvenile Detention Center with a glimmer of knowing that Reggae and I would be a Therapy Team there some day.

Stephanie helped both James and I keep our shoulders back with a hilarious "shoulders back" dance that we did the entire day and into the night. We waited and wondered what the result would be from Penelope's meditation the night before, and we let go even further into the abyss.

Would Dragonfly Cottage become *our* Dragonfly Cottage? Would we be back in an apartment on a busy highway like we had been in California? What was in the highest good for everyone? Monkey mind became Zen mind became monkey mind became trust and faith.

At the end of our last night in Prescott, the phone rang. It was Penelope's real estate agent, and James and I looked at each other like two little kids bubbling up in anticipation. We snuggled up more closely on the Airbnb couch, took a deep breath together, held our chalice of openness up toward the sky, and said hello to the possibility on the other end of the line. The agent spoke to us with sweetness in her voice, as James and I held hands more tightly than we ever have before.

"Penelope really likes both of you, and she wants you to have Dragonfly Cottage. She has accepted your offer." She said with peace and love in her heart.

James and I held each other even more tightly and wept huge tears of gratitude at the immense generosity that had just been gifted to us. With shoulders back, we celebrated with cheers of joy and raised our chalice to the sky with gratitude and grace.

We had arrived.

Welcome to Dragonfly Cottage.

Chapter Seventeen

THE PILGRIMAGE

"HOOLIJINX!"

— WOMEN FROM THE CLASS OF 1958

I heard about it on Facebook after my Mom died. One of her classmates from Washington High School Class of 1958 in Brainerd, MN contacted me to send her condolences. She told me that there was going to be a 60th class reunion in the Fall and she asked me to send her a photo of my Mom for the board that would be displayed for deceased classmates.

When a seed is planted, it either takes root or not. In order for it to take root, it needs the right environment – good soil, plenty of sunshine, water and love. I thought about the possibility of crashing my Mom's class reunion and then thought it was a crazy idea. Back and forth I went until I finally landed on what would be a magical solo pilgrimage to Northern Minnesota.

A true Minnesotan, my Mother loved wild rice, ice skating, roller skating, being at the lake, popcorn and Paul Bunyan. As a kid, we spent a lot of time at my grandparent's lake house in Baxter, and I remember my Mom talking fondly her whole life about growing up in Brainerd.

On one specific occasion many years ago, I had taken my Mom into a shamanic journey to discover her Power Animal. She was often curious about the spiritual work that I shared in the world and she wanted to try a journey on her own. Lying down on the couch at my house one day, she shut her eyes tightly as I began to drum her spirit into connecting with her power animal.

As the drumbeat began to take me deep into a Theta state, my body could feel that my client/Mom was not going into the spirit realm anytime soon. Looking over, I saw her pop up off the couch like a jack in the box with just one eye open, as she exclaimed,

"When's the video gonna start?!"

What a GREAT analogy for a shamanic journey!

"Press the PLAY button, Mom." I said, and off she went.

For the next half hour, she found herself journeying to one of her favorite spots in nature, the Mississippi Headwaters at Lake Itasca near Brainerd. As she called forth her Power Animal, an elk came to her side, and she merged with him/her. Riding off together, my Mom had what would be the first of a handful of shamanic journeys with me. S

he came out of that journey that day realizing she had an animal friend who was always with her, and that her power spot in nature was the place she had spent many summers with her family and especially her father – the Headwaters of the Mighty Mississippi.

She shared stories with me about walking across the rocks with her father, and it always touched me deeply to think of her as a little girl playing with her Dad at the Mississippi River.

When she left to drive back to her home in Madison, WI that weekend, I reminded her that her elk could ride shotgun in the front seat of her car. She carried elk medicine for many years, which is the medicine of endurance and patience.

As I filled out the form for my Mom's class reunion dinner, I grinned at the choices for food. No wonder she ate the way she did! As a vegan, I knew I was going to have to change my diet for a night, or eat beforehand. Fresh walleye, chicken or prime rib were the top options and then there was a vegetable something or other smothered in cheese. I chose the latter, requested vegan if possible, licked the envelope goodbye and sent it to the post office.

I come from a line of entrepreneurs. Originally from Sweden, my great grandfather, Victor Peterson, got off the boat and headed to Anoka, Minnesota to start a greenhouse. He met my great grandmother in a hotel in Anoka, and ended up moving his family to Brainerd soon after.

He continued to run a greenhouse in Brainerd and then opened up a gas station. His son, Carl, my grandfather, grew up playing music and ended up conducting the Men's Glee Choir at First Lutheran and owned Time Jewelry in downtown Brainerd.

I knew that my family was fairly well known, having been very connected with First Lutheran and being local business owners, so I got my sleuth out and began what would become an incredible spiritual adventure. I love the definition *holy expedition* for a pilgrimage. That's exactly what it felt like.

In my Mom's place, I was going to be attending her 60th high school class reunion, diving into her past and also diving into the history of our family as they had lived and died in Brainerd. Nobody wanted to go along with me, so the pilgrimage became a solo journey that would forever change the shape of my heart, and also many others.

As a good sleuth does, I got online and starting to research and share my research. I found a Facebook page for Brainerd history and started to post that I was Karen (Lewis) Peterson's daughter and that I was coming for her class reunion. People who knew my Mom's family started to come out of the woodwork – sharing sweet stories of connections with my grandparents, great grandparents, my Mom, my Dad, my aunt and uncle and even a woman who was there the night my Mom went into labor with me. She knew me before I knew me!

I received Facebook messages from a multitude of my Mom's high school friends, and it was a pilgrimage parade already beginning to take shape. This felt like my first conscious pilgrimage even though I've had many other holy expeditions in my life. With a different energy behind it, I continued to plan my solo journey into the depths of my heart and the depths of the Northwoods of Minnesota.

As part of my journey, I had a t-shirt made with a photo of my Mom from high school. She looked to be about 16 and she was sitting on the ground barefoot wearing someone else's leather jacket in front of a really cool 1950s car. Across the photo on the shirt, I added a phrase in lime green – the color she wore on her last day on the planet. This saying has helped me to live my life more fully - something my Mom shared with me on many occasions.

"Take it a day at a time. That's how they come anyway." She used to say.

I was more than ready to face my Mom's death and also her life.

"A MEETING WITH DEATH IS AN INVITATION TO TAKE LIFE SERIOUSLY."
– THOMAS MOORE

My plan was to head to Brainerd as soon as my plane landed rather than visiting friends first, and I knew I needed a cabin in the Northwoods to call home for a few days. I knew I wanted to find the Mississippi Headwaters and I knew I wanted to go to Lake Itasca and to find the duck hunting cabin where my grandfather died when I was two. I knew I wanted to go to the church where my Mom was confirmed and my grandfather led the choir, and I knew I wanted to find my grandfather's jewelry store and my great grandfather's gas station. I knew I wanted to be open to spontaneity, to grow and learn, to explore, to release and share.

As the trip took more shape, so did my connections with people who knew my mother. I started to become well known on the Brainerd History page and I started to connect with some of my Mom's friends and even a junior high school suitor. At one point, I connected with my Mom on the other side and told her that I was going to Brainerd for her reunion and asked her blessing. Had she been alive, I think she would've thought I was nuts, but from the afterlife, I felt her sly grin and a thumb's up.

She told me to find Doodles and Dee Dee and go to the soda fountain. That's all she said to me, but I tucked it away and wondered how it would all unfold. I remembered her talking about Doodles when I was a kid because who can't remember a fun name like Doodles! Dee Dee seemed to go along with Doodles, and I knew my Mom had worked at a soda fountain with a candy counter, but I just didn't know which one.

While I was organizing my trip and making connections on Facebook, a woman named Gert reached out to me in a private message. She told me that she and my Mom had been close friends and that her daughter was my Mom's god daughter. I remembered her daughter's name and had a slight memory of her coming to our house when I was a kid, so we had a sweet little back and forth through Facebook Messenger.

We both wanted to meet one another while I was in town, and she told me that she and a bunch of Washington High School buddies gathered Monday through Friday at 8am at the McDonald's in town. I told her I'd be there.

Another woman named Bonny reached out and shared that she had lived next to my grandparents on the lake, and that it would be fun to meet when I was in town. Little by little, I was making dates to gather with people my Mom knew growing up that I had met before I was born or soon after. God bless Minnesotans for being hearty and wanting to always meet for coffee.

With the trip sketched out and just around the corner, I had a plan. My first Brainerd stop was to visit my old friend, Paul Bunyan, and then move on to whatever else popped up. I had found a little cabin on a lake randomly on Airbnb, and I would be meeting with Gert and the gang at McDonald's my first morning in town.

Then, I was headed to have an adventure with some of my Mom's friends who lived next to her at the lake house, head to the class reunion dinner at a supper club, go to First Lutheran church, go to the reunion picnic, and then head to the Headwaters at Lake Itasca for a few solo days to recharge, contemplate and hopefully walk and breathe on the same path my grandfather had walked on the last day of his life.

I've heard that a warrior has four qualities – patience, timing, discipline and self-control. I felt like a warrior of the heart – ready to take action from a place of groundedness and a willingness to face whatever came my way. Forging ahead with a really great plan, and willing to navigate the spontaneity that showed up, I was ready to expect miracles while the Washington High School Class of 1958 was getting excited to receive me.

I remember going to Brainerd as a kid, and playing at the lake house in Baxter. In fact, my very first memory as a human on the planet was at the lake house when I was just over two years old. It was October and my grandpa was down at the beach to offer boat rides. I remember my sister, Stephanie, getting in the canoe, and off they went while I stood on the beach with a broken heart from being left behind.

Turning around, with hot two-year-old tears running down my chubby cheeks, I began to run up the hill, which I would later find out was a very slight incline. Running as fast as my little tender feet could go, I felt prickers embedding themselves in the bottoms of my feet.

I cried.
It hurt.
I cried.
It hurt.

When I finally reached the picnic table - which felt like way too long of a time - my Mom, grandmother and aunt were there with tweezers and Kleenex® to help ease my physical and emotional pain.

One by one, they pulled the prickers from my new little feet, and wiped the crocodile sized tears from my eyes. They reassured me that grandpa would be coming right back to give me a ride, too, and that Stephanie would also come back. At two years old, I didn't believe any of it. I only believed the pain that I felt in my heart and in my body, and the gratitude and safety of the three female pillars in my family helping me to get my warrior suit back on. I have no idea whether I ever took a boat ride with my grandpa that day or not. I'm sure I did, but my memory was about the pain, not the joy.

My grandpa Carl died suddenly at age 58 only ten days after that trip. I still remember his voice, his heart, his lap and his soft skin, and have always had an ache in my heart because I didn't really get to know him. Now was a chance to learn more.

He was at the duck hunting cabin on the day he died and it was the Fall of 1969. As an avid duck hunter, my grandpa decided to pool some money together about 20 years earlier with an old buddy from elementary school days named Chuck. They had a rustic cabin built on Gill Lake near Lake Itasca, and did what duck hunters do in the Northwoods – drink whiskey and shoot ducks.

The only story I ever heard was that my grandpa had dropped dead at the cabin and his friend, Chuck, was with him. Almost fifty years had passed since then, and I was curious enough to add this to my pilgrimage. Our family hadn't said much, and I wasn't getting a lot of support to go digging. In fact, I was told it wasn't possible to even find the cabin anymore.

When I'm told that something isn't possible, it's almost like adding fuel to the fire, and I become even more determined. Adding this curiosity of my grandfather's sudden death to my Minnesota adventure list, I was inspired to learn more and to honor his passing in whatever way I could while I was in the area.

Facebook is an incredible tool for finding people. Since I had the name of the guy who was with my grandfather at the time he died, I looked to see if his name showed up when I did a search. With not much digging, I found his son and nephew very quickly – both of whom were still connected with my grandfather's duck hunting cabin near Lake Itasca. Bingo! I had cracked the code, and was willing to deepen my holy expedition – even if it meant hiking through who knows what to get to the cabin.

I love how guys work. When I contacted these men, both of them were totally open to sharing with me, and both of them told me I'd have no trouble finding the place. They also told me that they didn't know what kind of state the cabin was in, but that I was welcome to go through the front window and look around inside because they always left it unlocked. Since there was no address for the cabin, we worked through Facebook Messenger and Google Earth to find a speck of a cabin near Gill Lake.

I was told I might want to contact the farmer who owns the land, may have to jump a fence if a crow stole the key again, and I'd have to hike through a field with cows, past a deer stand, jump another fence and walk in however far it really was – possibly through a marsh. I was totally up for the adventure, and added it to the itinerary for the last full day of my pilgrimage.

The first day on the ground in Minnesota, off I went with my yoga mat in tow, a journal and my hiking boots. I had brought my Mom's long orange and yellow watercolor looking tank dress to wear for the class reunion dinner – a dress which somehow fit both my Mom and I even though she was half my size – and a pearl and diamond necklace my grandpa had given my Mom for her 16th birthday. It had come from his jewelry store in Brainers, and she had given to me for Valentine's Day a few decades earlier. My medicine bag was filled with sacred herbs to honor my grandfather's passing and I brought along one of my Mom's photo albums from high school to see what would happen from that. Brainerd, here I come!

Driving from the airport to Northern Minnesota, I started to see why my Mom loved trees and water so much. It was Fall, and the tall pines were swaying gently in the breeze while the trees were just beginning to think about changing colors.

As I pulled up to the cabin on the lake, I smiled at how perfect it was. It was one of the last cabins available on Airbnb for that weekend, and I had done great. The living room looked out to Rice Lake, and was surrounded by beautiful areas to walk and fun lake homes to see. Unpacking all of my pilgrimage stuff, I noticed a sensation in my heart that felt new. I felt like I was carrying my Mom inside of me, and I felt a little naughty and nervous about crashing her reunion.

Surrounded by pine paneling, I sat on the way too soft bed and opened my Mom's high school photo album. I noticed that the first few pages were filled with photos of my joyful, young Mom in intimate embraces with a very good-looking young man who shall remain nameless to protect the innocent. It was obviously a fun time for her or she wouldn't have put so many pictures of the two of them in her album *and* kept it all those years. We'll call him Exhibit B for the sake of keeping things squeaky clean. Before I went to bed that night, I confirmed with Gert, an old friend of my Mom's, that I would meet she and her gang at the McDonald's in town. She was ready and so was I.

Waking up the next morning to the sight of the sunrise over the lake, I did some yoga poses in the living room, took a shower, ate some sautéed beet greens and tempeh, and put on the t-shirt with my Mom's photo on it. In the photo on the shirt, before I cropped it, she's sitting next to the handsome young man in the photo album, Exhibit B, wearing his leather jacket in front of his car. Tuck that away for later.

Heading out the door to McDonald's to meet Gert, I grabbed the photo album with the plethora of Exhibit B photos and set it on the front seat of the car next to me. Winding through the roads along the lake, I looked at some of the houses, and smiled at the thought of my Mom getting to grow up around so much water. No wonder she loved to sit by the pool and give whale rides! If you've never had a whale ride, you should ask my Mom to come to you in your dreams and give you one. There's nothing like them!

As kids, we had a pool in the backyard which meant lots of summer fun. My Mom used to jump into the pool to give my sister and I, and all of our friends, a magical, mystical whale ride. Holding her breath, a kid would get on her back and wrap their legs around her skinny little slippery waist. She'd push off from the wall, and with just our head sticking out of the water so we could breathe, we would drift across the pool on her back and giggle as we pretended we were riding a whale. It's quite possible that that's why I love whales so much. Either that, or that I *was* one once. Or both.

On the way to McDonald's to meet Gert, I looked out of the corner of my eye and noticed the side of a building that seemed familiar. Digging through my memory, I remembered that my great grandfather had a photo taken of him in front of his gas station and there was a building in the background. Pulling over into a State Farm parking lot, I found the photo of my great grandfather and matched it up to the same building that I was now looking at across the street.

I looked back at the photo, and back to where I was standing, and realized that the State Farm parking lot used to be my great grandfather's gas station, and the photo was taken in the same spot I just happened to stop my car. Me being me, I walked into State Farm, told everyone the story about my great grandfather, and we took photos and gave hugs. Pretty cool to be standing in the same spot as my great grandfather probably 80 years later.

Off I went, with a smile on my face, and curiosity in my heart. Pulling into McDonald's I felt nervous. I had no clue who Gert was or who else might be there, but I took in a breath and I went for it. Grabbing the photo album from the front seat of the car, I walked in and looked around. Spotting a bunch of guys with white hair and cups of coffee sitting around a table, I told them I was looking for Gert and they pointed across the room. There she was, a dear friend of my Mom's, all glitzy and full of joy with the same little feisty frame. Of *course* they had been friends.

We gave each other a hug and she remarked how much I looked like my Mom before introducing me to her friend, Joni, who wanted to come along to meet me. Sitting down with the first McDonald's pancakes and coffee I'd eaten in decades (which tasted amazing by the way) I pushed the photo album across the table to Gert. I turned to Joni to introduce myself, and as angels play, magic started to happen. She told me that my grandparents were her godparents and were also in her parent's wedding, and then shared with me photos of my grandparents from the 1930s and a charm bracelet from my grandfather's jewelry store.

Joni told me that each year on her birthday, all the way through college, my grandparents had given her a charm for her bracelet. She then went on to tell me stories of my grandparents I had never heard, and told me what lovely people they were. Then she told me how much I looked like my Grandma Fern.

Gert began to breeze through the photo album with her well painted fingernails, and stopped immediately at the photos of Exhibit B. Pointing him out, she told me that he and my Mom had gone steady for some time. Another picture of Exhibit B and another and another.

"Last I knew he and his wife were living on Rice Lake just across from me." She said.

"Um. I'm at a cabin on Rice Lake." I responded with hesitation, curiosity and a bit of shock in my voice.

Small world? Coincidence? Divine intervention? Exhibit B was still alive and living somewhere on Rice Lake across from Gert, and so was I for the next few days. This meant I was staying somewhere near Exhibit B. Gert looked at me with a sideways grin and told me to leave it alone. No problem, Gert. I didn't need to dig for Exhibit B.

As the coffee turned into another cup of coffee and more stories, I could feel myself melting into my Mom inside me. It was as if she was sitting in McDonald's across from Gert and she was 15. At one point, Gert looked up and asked me when I had changed my name and why. She had known me since I was a kid, and I told her that I had wanted to change my name for a really long time but nothing ever seemed to stick.

Then one day, I was inside of a creative visualization during my coach's training and we were supposed to access our Future Self. When mine showed up at the door in my vision, she was about 60 years old, with longer, wavy, almost white hair, a white blouse and jeans and a demeanor that was super peaceful and grounded.

Inviting me in, my Future Self sat across from me at a table and I asked her some questions about how I could become more peaceful and more grounded, and how she got to where she was. And then I asked her what her name was and she said, Sage. Like the New Year's Eve ball dropping at Time Square, Sage dropped deeply into my heart. When I came out of that visualization journey, I changed my name immediately. A few years later, I changed my first and middle name legally.

Gert looked at me intently after I shared my story and said,

"I've always wanted to change my name from Gert and I never did. Everyone calls me Doodles."

I immediately burst into tears, got up to get a napkin to dry my eyes and told Doodles I'd be right back to tell her why I was crying. Sitting back down, I told she and her friend, Joni, the story of how I had connected with my Mom in the afterlife a couple of weeks before coming to Brainerd and how she had told me to make sure I found Doodles and Dee Dee. Here I was, sitting across from Gert who went by Doodles. Oh, and then I found out that Doodles has a sister named Dee. Nice work, Mom!

Doodles invited me to her house later that day for a cup of coffee and a deeper visit, and true to the Surrender Experiment, I said yes. That was my goal for the pilgrimage – to say yes to whatever came my way. As we sat on her couch and shared stories of my Mom, we grew closer to one another in our hearts. And, her house was indeed directly across the lake from where I was staying, which put me somewhere near where Exhibit B lived. Of course it did.

I spent some time later that day walking through downtown Brainerd, and had a fantastic time at the Historical Society finding old photos of my grandfather when he was a child in school, and spent time enjoying the roller skating exhibit at the Museum from the 1950s – my Mom's era. My Mom absolutely loved to roller skate and ice skate, and she taught us to love roller skating, too.

The Palladium was the "in place" to hang out in her years. In the exhibit at the museum they had an original red corduroy Palladium skating jacket with a police whistle hanging around the neck of it, and next to it, a pair of white skates with red and white yarn pom pons on the toes. The police whistle had been used by the owner of the Palladium like a bell or signal to change to the next thing that roller skaters change to. Maybe a whistle was a way to get young kids to stop fooling around!

It was all becoming clear to me. My Mom loved her youth, and brought so much of it into her adulthood. For her entire life, my Mom wore red – just like the pom pons on the toes of the skates, and the Palladium jacket. And, when we were kids, she used a police whistle to get us to come in from outside when we were playing down the hill with the neighbor kids. When she died, my Mom's police whistle was the *only* material object that my sister and I had any tension over. My sister got the whistle, and I bought a new one from the same company.

I started to search for the drugstore where my Mom worked when she was a kid, and with enough digging, I found that it was now a bar. It had the same soda fountain look to it, and of course, it was right next to a store called Purple Fern, which was obviously a wink from my Grandma Fern. More magic, and more smiles as I walked through the soda fountain/bar energy and told the somewhat amused people at the bar that my Mom worked there in the 50s.

Walking down Laurel street to find a place to eat, I stopped directly across from where I thought my grandfather's jewelry store used to be. Before me, larger than life, was an organic restaurant with vegan options called "Sage on Laurel." Grabbing a seat outside, I ate my veggie burger facing the storefront that my grandfather owned for decades and smiled some more at the serendipity.

As the sun began to set, I took a contemplative walk along the Mississippi River and read more about the Ojibwe and history of the Brainerd area before calling it a very good night. Back to my lake cabin, I mused at the incredible magic of the day and wondered what the next day would have in store. Waking up early again, a few yoga poses and some sautéed veggies later, I decided to head out for a short walk near my cabin before running into the cute little city of Baxter to meet with some old neighbors of my Mom's from the days when she lived at the lake house.

As I walked through the neighborhood near my cabin on Rice Lake, the smell of the pines reminded me how much I love deep nature. I noticed myself wondering where Exhibit B lived as I meandered along the winding roads that lined the lake. I wondered whether Exhibit B might still remember my Mom, and I promised myself, and Doodles, that I wouldn't pry.

Heading into Baxter, I stopped to buy some flowers for the women who were going to drive me around Brainerd for the day and show me things they knew I'd love to see. Cheryl and Janice were cousins, and grew up down the street from my Mom when she lived at the lake house. Our adventures took us to my Mom's junior high, where I delighted in watching these two wonderful women remember which teacher had been in which room, and which ones they liked and didn't like. Not only was I taking my Mom with me down memory lane, I was bringing her friends along with me.

We stopped at my grandfather's jewelry store, and I remembered seeing the same flooring when I was two. They told me stories about how kind and generous my grandparents were, and the story of seeing the police at the lake house the day my grandfather died at the cabin.

Janice told me the story of being at my Mom and Dad's house the night my Mom went into labor with me, and how my Mom didn't seem to be in much of a hurry to get to the hospital, but wanted to finish making spaghetti first. To this day, I still enjoy really good spaghetti and I don't like being rushed for anything.

After a super fun day together, Janice, Cheryl and I said our goodbyes, and I headed back to the cabin to shower and change clothes for the class reunion dinner. Putting on the orange and yellow watercolor looking tank dress my Mom had given me from her closet, I clasped the pearl and diamond necklace around my neck – a gift from her father when she turned 16. The necklace had come from his jewelry store, Time Jewelry, in Brainerd, and felt like I was wearing my entire ancestral lineage in one gold chain. I was wearing a secret – a dress my Mom had worn, and a necklace that had been hers for decades and mine for decades now, too.

As I neared the supper club, I started to get nervous and wondered how I would be received. Driving up, I noticed the marquee: "Welcome Washington High School Class of 1958!" What on *earth* was I doing? I thought of my parent's advice: "When in doubt, don't", and "If it feels good, do it.". Taking a deep breath as I parked the car, I knew in my heart I was in the right place. I smiled deeply inside when I realized that this same supper club was the only restaurant my Mom and I had visited years ago when we went on a trip together to Brainerd. That was another huge angel wink from the other side.

Walking in with the smile my parents had given me, I was greeted with joy.

"You must be Karen Peterson's daughter!" said the woman at the registration table with delight as she came around to give me a hug.

One by one, people walked up to me to share their delight about knowing my Mom and their condolences for her death. People were telling me that she was the life of the party, one classy lady, or one of a kind. Over and over I kept hearing how wonderful my Mom was, and I was beaming inside as brightly as the diamonds and gold that were hanging sweetly around my neck.

Walking over to a table to get a seat, I noticed a group of women who were gathered together and laughing hysterically. One seat was still available, and I felt vulnerable. Taking in another deep breath, I channeled my Mom and asked if the only seat left at the table was taken. Each woman looked over at me one at a time with a look like, "who the heck are YOU?" and without hesitation, I gave a big smile and said,

"I'm Karen Peterson's daughter!"

They all cracked up at the same time, and motioned for me to sit down with them.

"Your Mom was a part of our group. She was one of us. And man, do you look like her!" Said the platinum blonde ring leader with the leopard print top.

We connected immediately and took photos of the gang like I had been hanging out with them since high school. Then, they proceeded to show me their secret "Hoolijinx" handshake, which I can't share with you because it's a secret and I'm now part of their group.

After a wonderful meal and heartfelt and hilarious conversation, the emcee and football quarterback from back in the day approached me and asked if I'd like to speak at the class reunion picnic the following day. Not a week prior, James had said to me,

"If they ask you to speak, just say yes."

So, I said an emphatic "yes" while my heart pounded, my knees rattled and my face smiled.

It's quite an experiment to say yes and surrender to that simple little word that moves us off of our comfort zone. I knew what not going to Brainerd looked like and I knew what not speaking at my Mom's class reunion looked like. When we say yes, we say yes to life.

After another great night of sleep, I awoke to get ready to go to the church where my grandfather had been choir director and my entire family took communion. Growing up with nature as my guide, I had a Jewish father and Lutheran mother who converted to Judaism.

We celebrated everything under the sun, including the sun. And here I was, finding myself in the midst of Northern Minnesota Lutheran land filled with great hearts, sugar cookies and plenty of strong, black coffee.

I walked into the church, found the Fellowship Room and sat down at a table. With wide eyes before me, I introduced myself and explained that I was on a pilgrimage to retrace my ancestry. Just doing that takes courage because it means we could be judged or rejected. I was handed a cookie and a cup of coffee with lightning speed, and the elder at the table told me that when she was a young kid she delivered the newspaper to my Grandpa Carl at his store, Time Jewelry. Another woman spoke up and invited me over for coffee, telling me she heard I was coming and wanted to connect more. Angels were flying around me, and magic became second hand.

One yes after another, I finally found myself at the reunion picnic wearing my Mom's leather jacket photo on my chest and a huge smile on my face. More awkwardness became ease as the same people from the night before came to hug me and tell me they were glad I was there. Me, too.

After a short program, I was asked to come up to the front of the room and speak. The emcee had shared with the group that I was the first family member they had ever had come to a reunion, and that I might be a trendsetter. And now, what to say?

Speaking from the heart, as my parents taught me to do since I was a kid, I shared with everyone how touched I was to be received so fully at her reunion.

I shared how much my Mom loved growing up in Brainerd, and how she told me to take one day at a time because that's how they come anyway. I told them that if my Mom were here, she would tell everyone to smile no matter what, and to always eat dessert first. A few tears fell out of my heart as I looked out toward my Mom's high school classmates while they wiped the tears from their smiling faces.

I did it! I did it! I spoke at my Mom's 60th high school class reunion, and now, it was time for more food. Before the food though, there needed to be a prayer. Sitting right in front of me was an angel disguised as a bald-headed man in a light blue shirt.

For years I had been trying to remember the prayer my Mom said at the dinner table, and I had finally given up. Growing up with Jewish and Lutheran customs, we had both a Hebrew prayer, which I remembered, and then my Mom shared one from her upbringing which I had forgotten and couldn't dredge up. The bald-headed angel in the light blue shirt took a deep breath as the room silenced.

The smell of sloppy joes was felt in the excitement as people rustled in their chairs as he unknowingly led the prayer from my Mom that I had said every day as a kid. Right before me, in a small pole building in the middle of Brainerd, MN, my prayers were answered.

"WE THANK THE LORD, FOR THIS OUR FOOD, FOR LIFE AND HEALTH AND EVERY GOOD. AMEN."

As a vegan, I was about to find out what it meant to have a catered lunch from the local hangout from 1958. Everything was yellow except for the barbeque. I'm not kidding. Grateful that I had eaten something before I got there, and touched so incredibly deeply by the heart and generosity of everyone in the room, I filled my plate with non-vegan lemon meringue pie (my Mom's favorite), some non-vegan potato salad (my Mom's favorite) and some vegan potato chips (my Mom's favorite).

One of her classmates came by and gave me another piece of lemon meringue pie in honor of my Mom and said with a smile,

"Eat it first, like Karen!"

I graciously accepted, added it to the meal of yellow in front of me, then regifted it after the reunion to someone who was very delighted to receive it. There was only so much non-vegan yellow food my stomach could hold, and yet I was unbelievably touched. Having a sloppy joe *did* cross my mind.

At the end of the picnic, all tables and chairs were whisked away by hearty Minnesota men in their late 70s, and then they were ready for their 60th reunion class photo. I smiled ear to ear as I watched my Mom's remaining classmates fool around like high school kids while the photographer was getting ready. I could see each of them in their letter jackets and poodle skirts sixty years earlier as they wrestled for who stood in back and who sat in front. At the last moment, just as the photographer was getting ready to say cheese, I skidded into the front of the group and laid down in front of my Mom's classmates like a trophy.

"That's EXACTLY what Karen would have done!" a woman exclaimed with delight as she wrapped her arms and heart around mine.

With smiles as big as Paul Bunyan, and bellies full of lemon pie and sloppy joe's, the Washington High School Class of 1958 photo was snapped into Brainerd history. My Mom and I had gotten prime real estate in the front row with her classmates surrounding us with bright beams of love and light.

I left the picnic that afternoon with a heart that had found more space to love, and started to head back to my cabin on Rice Lake. I was full of joy and full of grief all at the same time. Tears came swiftly as I realized the power of stepping into my ancestor's footsteps and retracing the world they had lived in.

Knowing I was leaving early the next morning to look for my grandfather's duck hunting cabin near Lake Itasca, I decided to head out for an easy walk in the neighborhood rather than driving to find another place to hike. A gorgeous sunny afternoon, I looked down at the photo of my Mom on my chest – barefoot with a leather jacket in front of a really cool car - and I smiled as I zipped up my jacket.

Off we went, my Mom and I, winding our way through the narrow cabin lined roads until Great Spirit told me to head through a yard and toward the lake. Finding myself in the back of someone's vacant yard, I sat at the edge of Rice Lake and prayed a prayer of gratitude while I sat in stillness.

The breeze coming off the lake reminded me once again why my Mom had loved the North so much, and why she had loved water. Off in the distance, a hawk began to squawk, and I listened as if it was calling me toward it. I paid attention, and the hawk kept calling as I followed it through some trees, down one street and then down another.

I was somewhere between this world and the next when I looked up and saw the last name of Exhibit B boldy emblazoned next to the garage door that I was passing by. I mean, it was *huge* and totally obvious, and it knocked my socks off. Who has their last name etched the size of a yardstick on the side of their garage? I guess Exhibit B does.

With my heart pounding like the school girl my Mom had been, I took in a deep breath as I looked over and saw who I thought might be Exhibit B. He was sitting peacefully on the sidewalk in front of his house and was painting some steps with white paint.

My head starting to spin while the bass drum in my heart drowned out most of my thoughts except, *Should I stop or keep going?* Everything felt like it started to move in slow motion, as I turned my head away from staring at Exhibit B and walked past the house about 25 yards. I stopped, took another breath, and asked my Mom

"What am I supposed to do NOW!?"

"Raise a little hell!" I heard her say, and I turned around to find out where angels play.

Walking up to the edge of the yard, I noticed Exhibit B looking up toward me with his pure white hair, big smile and sweaty face from painting in the sun. As I walked toward him with my Mom's high school photo zipped underneath my jacket, I gathered my courage and spoke directly to him.

"I'm Karen Peterson's daughter, and I'm in town for her class reunion. She passed away last year, and your photo was all over an album that I found. I just saw your name on the garage, and I'm staying at a cabin around the corner...." I said nervously, as I watched the look on his face move from curiosity, to knowing, to sadness to peace.

A few words were exchanged, as he told me he had a bunch of photos of my Mom in his house, and then shared with me how he remembered eating chicken off the grill at my grandfather's house when he was a kid.

"The chicken wasn't even cooked, but I wanted to be a gentleman so I ate it. I haven't been able to eat chicken since." He said with a big laugh and a smile.

I unzipped my jacket and showed him the photo of my Mom on my t-shirt – the one where she was wearing *his* leather jacket and standing in front of *his* car. He looked up at me with eyes of wonder, and asked me if my Mom had every told me that they had met for dinner many years back. It was obvious they had had a very deep heart connection for many years.

I think it was more magic than either of us could really take in fully, and we did what we could, exchanged our gratitude and parted ways.

As I began to pack up to head out the next morning, I opened my toiletries bag and pulled out a tiny little cardboard box that contained one of my Mom's necklaces. It had been wrapped up since I took it from her jewelry box two weeks after she died, and I was delighted to find one of her grey hairs had woven its way into the chain. Unweaving the sacred Mom hair from the necklace, I placed the hair gently into my medicine bag and put the necklace around my neck.

On my way out of town, I had one stop at Hardees left on my Brainerd pilgrimage to hug Doodles and the gang. Hardees was the Plan B because their favorite McDonald's had just closed for remodeling. After a few days of Doodles, even *I* was bummed that our McDonald's was closed! With coupons in hand, Doodles treated me to a free honey biscuit and a cup of hot, black coffee. My Mom's high school neighbor, Bonny, from the White Sand Lake days in Baxter, joined us for more laughter and stories, and we all hugged one another like we had known each other forever. Then, I hit the road in my rental car for what was next on this journey called life.

My holy expedition continued with a beautiful little cabin stay on Lake Itasca so I could see, hear, feel and smell my Mom's favorite place in nature - the Headwaters of the Mississippi. I was excited for my final adventure to not only the Headwaters, but also my Grandpa Carl's duck cabin to honor his life and his death. I was ready to embrace whatever mystery would be laid before me.

The Headwaters of the Mississippi are a powerful and unbelievably peaceful source of sacredness. I can understand why my Mom went there as her special place in nature in her shamanic journey to retrieve her power animal, the elk, and I can understand why my grandfather took her there as a child to walk across the water like Jesus.

As Great Spirit works, everything was perfect. The sun was beginning to set, as I grasped my medicine bag with my right hand and held it purposefully against my heart. The loons were looning far off in the distance, and the reflection of the cattails were dancing playfully on the water. There was an angelic golden glow to the light of day, and the clouds had a sense of reverence against the cool blue sky of dusk.

Taking off my shoes, I walked toward the actual place my Mom had entered in her shamanic journey years before, and a tear fell down my cheek. Phoning my sister, I connected with her on FaceTime, as I sat down on a wooden beam that bridged the shores of the Headwaters. My feet dangled playfully from the beam while my toes dipped sporadically into the coolness of the water below. My sister, Stephanie, and I looked into each other's hearts, as I reached into my medicine bag with utmost care. Unwrapping a small piece of tissue, I pulled out the one remaining grey hair that had once lived on our Mother's head, and we watched it float down the river in silence.

After a few moments, I got up and Stephanie and I "FaceTime walked together" down the beam and onto the shore. Holding the phone up above my waist so she could see, my sister and I rolled up our pants and walked across the freezing cold Headwaters together. We were letting go of one more piece of the woman who had birthed each of us into being who we were, while we deepened our relationship with one another and Great Spirit even further.

My Northwoods cabin came complete with two mouse traps placed evenly on the mantle, and I noticed I had conflicted feelings. My first thought was, *Eeek! Mice!!* and my second thought was, *Manifest what you DO want, and don't kill anyone.* Putting the mouse traps in the kitchen cupboard, I had a great night's sleep - trusting that nobody would be crawling on me while I slept.

I awoke to the sweet sound of birdsongs in the pines, and opted for a gorgeous hike along Lake Itasca to retrieve some wild rice pancakes the next morning. Afterwards, I headed to the gift shop to see what was for sale. Noticing a map of Lake Itasca at the entryway, I stopped in my tracks as I saw the outline of the lake in the shape of an elk. The exhibit went on to share that the Ojibwe people had originally named the lake *Omashkoozo-zaaga'igan* which translated to Elk Lake and later became Lake Itasca.

Here I was, revisiting the sacred garden where my Mom entered into her first shamanic journey to retrieve her first power animal, the elk, and the actual lake was shaped like an elk.

Was my Mom a shamana of some sort? Quite possibly.

I started to become aware that I was in some sort of altered state most of the time those last few days. The trees began to speak more loudly, and the energy of the Ojibwe were pounding their drumbeats inside of my heart as I felt their wooden canoes coursing down the river to harvest wild rice.

I could see, feel, smell and taste the world around me and within me as nature became me and I became nature.

My last afternoon of ancestral pilgrimage was the adventure to my Grandpa Carl's cabin. I had no idea if it was possible, and I had every intention of making it possible. When there's a will there's a way, and when there's a farmer who lets you traipse all over their property to get there, even more miracles can happen.

I had promised my family that if I didn't have a phone signal, I wouldn't go to the cabin, but when I got to the farmer's place, and he gave me the green light, it didn't matter whether I had a clear signal on my phone or not. I had a clear signal with Great Spirit, and I was heading in.

At the edge of the road was a huge red gate staring me in the heart. Like I was searching for the key to the Emerald City, I looked in the hole in the side of the gate as directed. The guys who gave me direction had told me that the key may or may not be in the hole in the gate because a crow steals it on a regular basis. Somewhere in Northern Minnesota there's a really clever crow with a whole bunch of keys to that gate.

Taking in a deep breath, I walked through a forest of white pines until I reached the clearing I had been told I would reach. A sharp left after the clearing, I headed toward the next clue I was given which was the deer stand. Taking a right at the deer stand, I jumped another big cattle gate, and began my journey down a path that would forever change my heart.

When we walk in our ancestor's footsteps, we can feel them moving along with us. My Grandpa Carl was an avid duck hunter and he died doing what he loved. Walking in his footsteps fifty years later, I was reminded that we should all be so lucky to share our last breath doing something we really love.

As the sun beat down, the crisp, fall breeze cooled the air around me. Surrounded by the sights, sounds and smells of nature, I was completely immersed. My body became fully aware that this was the last walk my grandfather had to the cabin and here I was walking the same path. It felt like I was wearing waders and sloshing in the marsh.

Even though I was me I still felt like I was him. Reaching down, I pulled some purple and yellow wildflowers into my hand, and began to hum as a warm tear fell down my cheek. I walked and I walked and I walked for what felt like 45 minutes, until finally I spotted it off in the distance.

Like a band of angels who were glowing and singing, I had literally come to the end of the path and was standing in front of the cabin that my grandfather had built with his elementary school buddy, Chuck, some 80 years earlier. My hairs stood up as I felt the spirit wind blow through me and saw the front door open and close with an invitation from the breeze.

I remembered seeing the photo of my grandfather standing in front of the cabin door, and as I approached the porch, I could feel him moving around me. Peering in the window - the one that Chuck Jr. told me I could wiggle open to go inside - I felt waves of fear and curiosity all bundled up together.

The cabin felt like my grandfather was still there, and as I looked into the tiny unlocked window I saw some really old furniture and artwork that looked like they'd been there since day one. I wondered if any women had ever been to the duck cabin as I began to fenagle the window open.

Noticing that the window only opened about 14" I stopped and reassessed the situation. There was a water heater shoved up next to a refrigerator right in front of the window, and I mused at how in the heck at 5'10" tall I was going to get through a 14" gap and then slide through a 6" space.

Crumpling myself up like a pretzel, thanks to many years of yoga classes, I had a fleeting thought of the water heater falling over, the window breaking and me being stuck in this position until the police arrived. Common sense took over after I snapped a few photos of the inside of the cabin before wriggling my way back carefully out of the window without breaking and entering.

I was elated to have gotten at least *part* of my body into the same cabin that my grandfather had had his body in for so many years. It also felt a bit creepy, too, because I could feel the ghosts that were still on the property. Maybe it was just my grandfather still there or maybe others have come and stayed as well.

Out on the porch, I lit some sacred tobacco that I received in Peru, and blew the smoke in the seven directions. Calling in Great Spirit, my ancestors, teachers and guides, I asked for my grandfather's spirit to be fully released from anything that had been holding him back, and to allow him to be free forever.

I then gathered an old abandoned duck decoy from the shore, and placed it on top of an upside-down fishing boat that looked like it had been there since my grandpa. Gathering up the purple and yellow wildflowers I had found along the path on the hike in, I placed them with intention next to the decoy and set the remaining tobacco nearby.

Digging in my right-hand pocket, I placed two stones I had received from the Headwaters of the Mississippi onto the family altar I was creating. It was a way I could honor my ancestors who had crossed over and were now sharing space and time in the afterlife together. I sat on the porch for some time and just listened to the sounds and smells around and within me, as the breezes came off of Gill Lake and found their way more fully into my soul.

After I felt complete, I started my conscious trek back toward the car, and imagined what it may have been like that October day in 1969 when my grandfather died. What was it like for the EMT's to carry my Grandpa Carl's body out of a rustic cabin on a stretcher, down a really long and winding path, through a field with cattle and sheep, over a couple of cattle gates and out to the gravel road?

Walking each step with sacred intention, I sang the same song, Sanctuary, that I had sung when Java died – over and over and over – until I finally found myself back at the car after 45 minutes with a sore throat from singing. I got in my car and wondered if there had been a phone at the cabin in 1969, and I wondered what it must have been like for his lifelong buddy, Chuck, to be with my grandfather's body until the EMT's arrived. I wondered whether my grandfather died alone or with his friend, and whether he was frightened, happy, peaceful or unaware. Most of all, I just wondered what really happened, so I called Chuck Jr. while I sat in my rental car on the gravel road outside the red gate where the crow steals keys.

It turned out my grandfather had been out duck hunting early in the morning that day with his lifelong friend, Chuck, and he said he needed to head back to the cabin because he didn't feel well. A few hours later, Chuck, headed up from the duck hunting blind for breakfast and found my grandfather's body on the way to the cabin. My Grandpa Carl had collapsed and died from a fatal heart attack on the trail he had traversed for decades while he was doing what he loved most. I found out there wasn't phone service at the cabin in 1969, and that Chuck actually carried my grandfather's body out himself – down the mile-long path, over the silver cattle gate, past the deer stand, through the clearing, past the forest of white pines, and over the last red gate to his car at the gravel road.

We should all have a friend so dear to us that they are willing to carry us home. After I found out the details of the last day of my grandpa's life, I thanked Chuck's son and nephew on behalf of our entire family. I'm not sure anyone ever really knew the medal of honor my grandpa's friend deserved for his bold and heroic act of kindness. Walking the same path some fifty years later, I realized it was an incredible hero's journey.

I've always felt like my grandfather's spirit stayed on the trail the day he died, and a part of me went with him in not knowing what the truth was. Now he was free. When we die, our spirit can either float off freely or stay stuck in this world. Just like with death, life is no different. When we are stuck, we can stay stuck or we can do the work to find freedom. We have choices.

My parents offered me choices when I was a kid. It taught me an incredible life lesson that there is no real right or wrong, but rather choices and consequences. If we choose Rice Krispies®, we can't have Corn Flakes®. Once in a while, though, we get to choose Froot Loops®.

Driving my rental car down the same gravel road my grandfather's body had taken, I heard the sound of the tires vibrating on the road beneath me as the dust of my ancestry swirled around. I was reminded of the immense courage it takes to move through life with a heart wide open. The taste of holy tobacco, sweet lemon pie and hot, black coffee danced in my mouth while the wispy white clouds winked joyfully at me from up above.

I was complete.

Epilogue

WHERE ANGELS PLAY

"WHEN WE ARE FULLY ALIGNED,
WE ARE FULLY ALIGNED
WITH MOTHER NATURE."
— GREAT SPIRIT

There's a place between the worlds where angels play. It's that place where goosebumps remind us that there's something more to this world that what we can see and hear. Throughout my life, I have been playing with angels in all sorts of forms. From the days as a young child looking up at the stars with wonderment, to the powerful drumbeat in my heart that reminds me that Great Spirit is in everything, I am an angel just as much as you are, and you and you.

When Java died, there was a part of her that began to live more fully. The cover photo of this book was taken after James and I buried the last of Java's cremains on a 250-acre plot of land in Wisconsin where she had run free for many summers. Right after her burial ceremony, we planted daisies on her behalf and then walked through the prairie to see the sunbeam shooting out of the sky to rest at my feet. God speaks to us in so many different ways and it's our work to pay attention.

When James was in Minnesota recording my Mom's song, *Everything is Wonderful*, I was at home in Arizona on a cloudy, cold day installing a surprise hot tub at our house with some money my Mom had left me when she died. The phone rang, and as he played the final cut for me, the clouds parted for the first time they had all day.

A huge beam of sunshine blasted me in the back of my head while I sat on the couch and listened, just as the lyric "God is chosen in the sunshine" came through the phone. The sun filled the entire house for about 60 seconds as tears catapulted out of my heart and down my face. When the song moved into the lyric "She has gone into the mystery," the clouds covered up the sun again for the entire rest of the day.

After my mother in law, Alice, had her stroke, I saw an image of her deceased husband, Carl, standing at the left side of her bed wearing black dress clothes and a white collar from his days as a Lutheran pastor. He looked younger and stronger, and was holding her hand with vibrancy and peacefulness. He told me very clearly to make sure that Pastor Mike had been contacted because she needed to connect with him before she died. I shared this with my husband, James, and he made sure to complete the connection.

The morning I finished editing this book, I took our dog, Reggae, for a solo hike on a beautiful trail near own home in the Prescott National Forest. Nearing the top of a climb, I looked up at the bright blue sky to notice a red tail hawk soaring from East to West directly in front of me. Watching it land gracefully in a Ponderosa Pine, I could feel the smile on my face and also in my heart.

When Java died, she told me she would return in the form of a red tail hawk or a monarch butterfly, and that she would only show up in ways that would make my head and heart spin. I very seldom see red tail hawks in Arizona, and the visit of one the morning I finished editing this very book was definitely a blessing that came directly from Java.

You can slide down the banister at the same school where your ancestors walked the halls, eat a meal in the same seat as someone who shares your DNA, and speak to the trees, the rocks, the moon and the stars. Everyone is listening all the time, and it's our work to remember to listen more deeply, too.

There are stories after stories about the places where angels play. Ask yourself tonight when you go to bed if there is an angel in your life who would like to come and play. Then slow down, pay attention and wait for the magic to happen.

I double dog dare you!

WHERE ANGELS PLAY
- SAGE LEWIS

Velvet voices

Sounds of love

Sacred silence

Dark of night

Listen deeply

Spacious wonder

Heartbeats slow

While angels hover

Breath of life

In space of death

Veils thin

Where angels play

ABOUT THE AUTHOR

"NEVER FORGET WHO YOU ARE."
— GREAT SPIRIT

Sage Lewis is the Creature Teacher with Dancing Porcupine and is an Advanced Tellington TTouch® Practitioner for Companion Animals & People, Certified Life Coach, Shamanic Practitioner, Animal Communicator, Intuitive/Medium, Wedding and Funeral Officiant, Animal Hospice Consultant, Author and Fun Person.

Sage's passion is guiding all creatures to live a fulfilling life, and to move through life's transitions with peace and grace. She is the author of *JAVA: The True Story* and *Where Angels Play: Life, Death & the Magic Beyond*.

Sage lives in the Prescott National Forest in Prescott, AZ with her wonderfully creative husband, James, and their hilariously brilliant dog, Reggae.

To become happier, healthier and better behaved, contact Sage:

www.DancingPorcupine.com

SAGE LEWIS 6/28/67 - ?